# ILTS
## Social Science: History (114) Exam
# SECRETS

## Study Guide
### Your Key to Exam Success

ILTS Test Review for the
Illinois Licensure Testing System

Dear Future Exam Success Story:

Congratulations on your purchase of our study guide. Our goal in writing our study guide was to cover the content on the test, as well as provide insight into typical test taking mistakes and how to overcome them.

Standardized tests are a key component of being successful, which only increases the importance of doing well in the high-pressure high-stakes environment of test day. How well you do on this test will have a significant impact on your future, and we have the research and practical advice to help you execute on test day.

The product you're reading now is designed to exploit weaknesses in the test itself, and help you avoid the most common errors test takers frequently make.

## How to use this study guide

We don't want to waste your time. Our study guide is fast-paced and fluff-free. We suggest going through it a number of times, as repetition is an important part of learning new information and concepts.

First, read through the study guide completely to get a feel for the content and organization. Read the general success strategies first, and then proceed to the content sections. Each tip has been carefully selected for its effectiveness.

Second, read through the study guide again, and take notes in the margins and highlight those sections where you may have a particular weakness.

Finally, bring the manual with you on test day and study it before the exam begins.

## Your success is our success

We would be delighted to hear about your success. Send us an email and tell us your story. Thanks for your business and we wish you continued success.

Sincerely,

Mometrix Test Preparation Team

**Need more help? Check out our flashcards at:** http://MometrixFlashcards.com/ILTS

# TABLE OF CONTENTS

# Top 20 Test Taking Tips

1. Carefully follow all the test registration procedures
2. Know the test directions, duration, topics, question types, how many questions
3. Setup a flexible study schedule at least 3-4 weeks before test day
4. Study during the time of day you are most alert, relaxed, and stress free
5. Maximize your learning style; visual learner use visual study aids, auditory learner use auditory study aids
6. Focus on your weakest knowledge base
7. Find a study partner to review with and help clarify questions
8. Practice, practice, practice
9. Get a good night's sleep; don't try to cram the night before the test
10. Eat a well balanced meal
11. Know the exact physical location of the testing site; drive the route to the site prior to test day
12. Bring a set of ear plugs; the testing center could be noisy
13. Wear comfortable, loose fitting, layered clothing to the testing center; prepare for it to be either cold or hot during the test
14. Bring at least 2 current forms of ID to the testing center
15. Arrive to the test early; be prepared to wait and be patient
16. Eliminate the obviously wrong answer choices, then guess the first remaining choice
17. Pace yourself; don't rush, but keep working and move on if you get stuck
18. Maintain a positive attitude even if the test is going poorly
19. Keep your first answer unless you are positive it is wrong
20. Check your work, don't make a careless mistake

# Social Science Foundations

### Interpreting Maps

The **map legend** is an area that provides interpretation information such as the key, the scale, and how to interpret the map. The **key** is the area that defines symbols, abbreviations, and color schemes used on the map. Any feature identified on the map should be defined in the key. The **scale** is a feature of the map legend that tells how distance on the map relates to distance on the ground. It can either be presented mathematically in a ratio or visually with a line segment. For example, it could say that one inch on the map equals one foot on the ground, or it could show a line segment and tell how much distance on the map the line symbolizes. **Latitude** and **longitude** are often shown on maps to relate their area to the world. Latitude shows how far a location is north or south from the earth's equator, and longitude shows how far a location is east or west from the earth's prime meridian. Latitude runs from 90 N (North Pole) – 0 (equator) – 90 S (South Pole), and longitude runs 180 E (international date line) – 0 (prime meridian) – 180 W (international date line).

### Popular Map Projections

- **Globe**: Earth's features are shown on a sphere. No distortion of distances, directions, or areas occurs.
- **Mercator**: projects Earth's features onto a cylinder wrapped around a globe. Generates a rectangular map that is not distorted at the equator but is greatly distorted near the poles. Lines of latitude and longitude form a square grid.
- **Robinson**: projects Earth's features onto an oval-looking map. Areas near the poles are truer to size than in the Mercator. Some distortion affects every point.
- **Orthographic**: Earth's features are shown on a circle, which is tangent to the globe at any point chosen by the mapmaker. Generates a circular, 3D-appearing map similar to how Earth is seen from space.
- **Conic maps**: A family of maps drawn by projecting the globe's features onto a cone set onto the globe. Some distortion affects most points.
- **Polar maps**: A circle onto which the land around the poles has been projected. Provides much less distortion of Antarctica and the land around the North Pole than other map types.

### Cartographic Distortion and its Influence on Map Projections

Cartographic distortion is the distortion caused by projecting a three-dimensional structure, in this case the surface of the earth, onto the two-dimensional surface of a map. Numerous map projections have been developed to minimize distortion, but the only way to eliminate distortion completely is to render the earth in three dimensions. Most map projections have minimal distortion in some location, usually the center, and the distortion becomes greater close to the edges of the map. Some map projections try to compromise and distribute the distortion more evenly across the map. Different categories of maps preserve, or do not distort, different features. Maps that preserve directions accurately are **azimuthal**, and maps that preserve shapes properly are **conformal**. Area-preserving maps are called **equal-area maps**, and maps that preserve distance are called **distance-preserving**. Maps that preserve the shortest routes are **gnomonic projections**.

## Comparing Maps of the Same Place from Different Time Periods

Maps of the same place from different time periods can often be initially aligned by **geographic features**. Political and land-use boundaries are most likely to change between time periods, whereas locations of waterways and geologic features such as mountains are relatively constant. Once geographic features have been used to align maps, they can be compared side-by-side to examine the changing locations of human settlement, smaller waterways, etc. This kind of map interpretation, at the smallest scale, provides information about how small groups of humans **interact with their environment**. For example, such analysis might show that major cities began around ports, and then moved inland as modes of transportation, like railroads and cars, became more common. Lands that were initially used for agriculture might become incorporated into a nearby city as the population grows. This kind of map analysis can also show the evolution of the **socio-economics** of an area, providing information about the relative importance of economic activities (manufacturing, agriculture or trade) and even the commuting behavior of workers.

## Natural, Political, and Cultural Features on Maps

Map legends will provide information about the types of natural, political, or cultural features on a map. Some maps show only one of these three features. **Natural features** such as waterways, wetlands, beaches, deserts, mountains, highlands and plains can be compared between regions by type, number, distribution, or any other physical characteristic. **Political features** such as state and county divisions or roads and railroads can be compared numerically, but examining their geographic distribution may be more informative. This provides information on settlement density and population. In addition, road and railroad density may show regions of intense urbanization, agricultural regions, or industrial centers. **Cultural features** may include roads and railroads, but might also include historic areas, museums, archaeological digs, early settlements and even campgrounds. Comparing and contrasting the number, distribution, and types of these features may provide information on the history of an area, the duration of settlement of an area, or the current use of the area (for example, many museums are found in current-day cultural centers).

## Comparing Maps with Datasets or Texts

Maps can provide a great deal of information about an area by showing specific locations where certain types of settlement, land use, or population growth occurred. **Datasets** and **texts** can provide more specific information about events that can be hypothesized from maps. This specific information may provide dates of significant events (for example, the date of a fire that gutted a downtown region, forcing suburban development) or important numerical data (e.g., population growth by year). Written datasets and texts enable map interpretation to become concrete and allow observed trends to be linked with specific causes ("Real estate prices rose in 2004, causing middle-class citizens to move northwest of the city"). Without specific information from additional sources, inferences drawn from maps cannot be put in **context** and interpreted in more than a vague way.

## Evaluating Graphic Formats

The type of information being conveyed guides the choice of **format**. Textual information and numeric information must be displayed with different techniques. Text-only information may be most easily summarized in a diagram or a timeline. If text includes numeric information, it may be converted into a chart that shows the size of groups, connects ideas in a table or graphic, or shows information in a hybridized format. Ideas or opinions can be effectively conveyed in political cartoons. Numeric information is often most helpfully presented in tables or graphs. When information will be referred to and looked up again and again, tables are often most helpful for the reader. When the trends in the numeric information are more important than the numbers themselves, graphs are often the best choice. Information that is linked to the land and has a spatial component is best conveyed using maps.

## Using Electronic Resources and Periodicals for Reference

Electronic resources are often the quickest, most convenient way to get background information on a topic. One of the particular strengths of **electronic resources** is that they can also provide primary-source multimedia video, audio, or other visual information on a topic that would not be accessible in print. Information available on the Internet is not often carefully screened for accuracy or for bias, so choosing the **source** of electronic information is often very important. Electronic encyclopedias can provide excellent overview information, but publicly edited resources like Wikipedia are open to error, rapid change, incompleteness, or bias. Students should be made aware of the different types and reliabilities of electronic resources, and they should be taught how to distinguish between them. Electronic resources can often be too detailed and overwhelm students with irrelevant information. **Periodicals** provide current information on social science events, but they too must be screened for bias. Some amount of identifiable bias can actually be an important source of information, because it indicates prevailing culture and standards. Periodicals generally have tighter editorial standards than electronic resources, so completeness and overt errors are not usually as problematic. Periodicals can also provide primary-source information with interviews and photographs.

## Using Encyclopedias, Bibliographies, or Almanacs for Social Science Research

Encyclopedias are ideal for getting background information on a topic. They provide an overview of the topic, and link it to other concepts that can provide additional keywords, information, or subjects. They can help students narrow their topic by showing the sub-topics within the overall topic, and by relating it to other topics. **Encyclopedias** are often more useful than the Internet because they provide a clearly organized, concise overview of material. **Bibliographies** are bound collections of references to periodicals and books, organized by topic. Students can begin researching more efficiently after they identify a topic, look it up in a bibliography, and look up the references listed there. This provides a branching network of information a student can follow. A pitfall of bibliographies is that when in textbooks or other journal articles, the references in them are chosen to support the author's point of view, and so may be limited in scope. **Almanacs** are volumes of facts published annually. They provide numerical information on just about every topic, and are organized by subject or geographic region. They are often helpful for supporting arguments made using other resources, and do not provide any interpretation of their own.

## Primary and Secondary Resources

Primary resources provide information about an event from the perspective of people who were present at the event. They might be letters, autobiographies, interviews, speeches, artworks, or anything created by people with first-hand experience. **Primary resources** are valuable because they provide not only facts about the event, but also information about the surrounding circumstances; for example, a letter might provide commentary about how a political speech was received. The Internet is a source of primary information, but care must be taken to evaluate the perspective of the website providing that information. Websites hosted by individuals or special-interest organizations are more likely to be biased than those hosted by public organizations, governments, educational institutions, or news associations.

**Secondary resources** provide information about an event, but were not written at the time the event occurred. They draw information from primary sources. Because secondary sources were written later, they have the added advantage of historical perspective, multiple points of view, or resultant outcomes. Newsmagazines that write about an event even a week after it occurred count as secondary sources. Secondary sources tend to analyze events more effectively or thoroughly than primary sources.

## Formulating Research Questions or Hypotheses

Formulating research questions or hypotheses is the process of finding questions to answer that have not yet been asked. The first step in the process is reading **background information**. Knowing about a general topic and reading about how other people have addressed it helps identify areas that are well understood. Areas that are not as well understood may either be lightly addressed in the available literature, or distinctly identified as a topic that is not well understood and deserves further study. Research questions or hypotheses may address such an unknown aspect, or they may focus on drawing parallels between similar, well-researched topics that have not been connected before. Students usually need practice in developing research questions that are of the appropriate scope so that they will find enough information to answer the question, yet not so much that they become overwhelmed. Hypotheses tend to be more specific than research questions.

## Collecting Information, Organizing and Reporting Results

The first step of writing a research paper involves narrowing down on a **topic**. The student should first read background information to identify areas that are interesting or need further study and that the student does not have a strong opinion about. The research question should be identified, and the student should refer to general sources that can point to more specific information. When he begins to take notes, his information must be **organized** with a clear system to identify the source. Any information from outside sources must be acknowledged with **footnotes** or a **bibliography**. To gain more specific information about his topic, the student can then research bibliographies of the general sources to narrow down on information pertinent to his topic. He should draft a thesis statement that summarizes the main point of the research. This should lead to a working **outline** that incorporates all the ideas needed to support the main point in a logical order. A rough draft should incorporate the results of the research in the outlined order, with all citations clearly inserted. The paper should then be edited for clarity, style, flow, and content.

## Analyzing Artifacts

Artifacts, or everyday objects used by previous cultures, are useful for understanding life in those cultures. Students should first discover, or be provided with, a **description** of the item. This description should tell during what period the **artifact** was used and what culture used it. From that description and/or from examination of the artifact, students should be able to discuss what the artifact is, what it is made of, its potential uses, and the people who likely used it. They should then be able to draw **conclusions** from all these pieces of evidence about life in that culture. For example, analysis of coins from an early American archaeological site might show that settlers brought coins with them, or that some classes of residents were wealthy, or that trade occurred with many different nations. The interpretation will vary depending on the circumstances surrounding the artifact. Students should consider these circumstances when drawing conclusions.

## Identifying Main Ideas in a Document

Main ideas in a paragraph are often found in the **topic sentence**, which is usually the first or second sentence in the paragraph. Every following sentence in the paragraph should relate to that initial information. Sometimes, the first or second sentence doesn't obviously set up the main idea. When that happens, each sentence in the paragraph should be read carefully to find the **common theme** between them all. This common theme is the main idea of the paragraph. Main ideas in an entire document can be found by analyzing the structure of the document. Frequently, the document begins with an introductory paragraph or abstract that will summarize the main ideas. Each paragraph often discusses one of the main ideas and contributes to the overall goal of the document. Some documents are divided up into chapters or sections, each of which discusses a main idea. The way that main ideas are described in a document (either in sentences, paragraphs, or chapters) depends on the length of the document.

## Organizing Information Chronologically and Analyzing the Sequence of Events

To organize information chronologically, each piece of information must be associated with a time or a date. Events are ordered according to the time or date at which they happened. In social sciences, chronological organization is the most straightforward way to arrange information, because it relies on a uniform, fixed scale – the passage of time. Information can also be organized based on any of the "who, what, when, where, why?" principles.

**Analyzing the sequence of chronological events** involves not only examining the event itself, but the preceding and following events. This can put the event in question into perspective, showing how a certain thing might have happened based on preceding history. One large disadvantage of chronological organization is that it may not highlight important events clearly relative to less important events. Determining the relative importance of events depends more strongly on interpreting their relationships to neighboring events.

## Recognizing Cause-and-Effect Relationships, and Comparing Similarities and Differences

Cause-and-effect relationships are simply linkages between an event that happened (the **effect**) because of some other event (the **cause**). Effects are always chronologically ordered after causes. Effects can be found by asking why something happened, or looking for information following words like so, consequently, since, because, therefore, this led to, as a result, and thus. Causes can be found by asking what happened. **Comparing similarities and differences** involves mentally setting two concepts next to each other and then listing the ways they are the same and the ways they are different. The level of comparison varies by student level; for example, younger students may compare the physical characteristics of two animals while older students compare the themes of a book. Similarity/difference comparisons can be done by listing written descriptions in a point-by-point approach, or they can be done in several graphic ways. Venn diagrams are commonly used to organize information, showing non-overlapping clouds filled with information about the different characteristics of A and B, and the overlapping area shows ways in which A and B are the same. Idea maps using arrows and bubbles can also be developed to show these differences.

## Distinguishing Between Fact and Opinion

Students easily recognize that **facts** are true statements that everyone agrees on, such as an object's name or a statement about a historical event. Students also recognize that **opinions** vary about matters of taste, such as preferences in food or music, that rely on people's interpretation of facts. Simple examples are easy to spot. **Fact-based passages** include certainty-grounded words like is, did, or saw. On the other hand, **passages containing opinions** often include words that indicate possibility rather than certainty, such as would, should or believe. First-person verbs also indicate opinions, showing that one person is talking about his experience. Less clear are examples found in higher-level texts. For example, primary-source accounts of a Civil War battle might include facts ("X battle was fought today") and also opinions ("Union soldiers are not as brave as Confederate soldiers") that are not clearly written as such ("I believe Union soldiers..."). At the same time as students learn to interpret sources critically (Was the battle account written by a Southerner?), they should practice sifting fact from these types of opinion. Other examples where fact and opinion blend together are self-authored internet websites.

## Determining the Adequacy, Relevance, and Consistency of Information

Before information is sought, a list of **guiding questions** should be developed to help determine whether information found is adequate, relevant, and consistent. These questions should be based on the **research goals**, which should be laid out in an outline or concept map. For example, a student writing a report on Navajo social structure might begin with questions concerning the general lifestyle and location of Navajos, and follow with questions about how Navajo society was organized. While researching his questions, he will come up with pieces of information. This information can be compared to his research questions to determine whether it is **relevant** to his report. Information from several sources should be compared to determine whether information is **consistent**. Information that is **adequate** helps answer specific questions that are part of the research goals. Inadequate information for this particular student might be a statement such as "Navajos had a strong societal structure," because the student is probably seeking more specific information.

## Drawing Conclusions and Making Generalizations About a Topic

Students reading about a topic will encounter different facts and opinions that contribute to their overall impression of the material. The student can critically examine the material by thinking about what facts have been included, how they have been presented, what they show, what they relate to outside the written material, and what the author's conclusion is. Students may agree or disagree with the author's conclusion, based on the student's interpretation of the facts the author presented. When working on a research project, a student's research questions will help him gather details that will enable him to **draw a conclusion** about the research material.

**Generalizations** are blanket statements that apply to a wide number of examples. They are similar to conclusions, but do not have to summarize the information as completely as conclusions. Generalizations in reading material may be flagged by words such as all, most, none, many, several, sometimes, often, never, overall, or in general. Generalizations are often followed by supporting information consisting of a list of facts. Generalizations can refer to facts or the author's opinions, and they provide a valuable summary of the text overall.

## Interpreting Charts and Tables

Charts used in social science are a visual representation of data. They combine graphic and textual elements to convey information in a concise format. Often, **charts** divide the space up in blocks, which are filled with text and/or pictures to convey a point. Charts are often organized in tabular form, where blocks below a heading all have information in common. Charts also divide information into conceptual, non-numeric groups (for example, "favorite color"), which are then plotted against a numerical axis (e.g., "number of students"). Charts should be labeled in such a way that a reader can locate a point on the chart and then consult the surrounding axes or table headings to understand how it compares to other points. **Tables** are a type of chart that divides textual information into rows and columns. Each row and column represents a characteristic of the information. For example, a table might be used to convey demographic information. The first column would provide "year," and the second would provide "population." Reading across the rows, one could see that in the year 1966, the population of Middletown was 53,847. Tracking the columns would show how frequently the population was counted.

## Interpreting Graphs and Diagrams

Graphs are similar to charts, except that they graphically show numeric information on both axes. For example, a **graph** might show population through the years, with years on the X-axis and population on the Y-axis. One advantage of graphs is that population during the time in between censuses can be estimated by locating that point on the graph. Each axis should be labeled to allow the information to be interpreted correctly, and the graph should have an informative title. **Diagrams** are usually drawings that show the progression of events. The drawings can be fairly schematic, as in a flow chart, or they can be quite detailed, as in a depiction of scenes from a battle. Diagrams usually have arrows connecting the events or boxes shown. Each event or box should be labeled to show what it represents. Diagrams are interpreted by following the progression along the arrows through all events.

## Using Timelines in Social Science

Timelines are used to show the relationships between people, places, and events. They are ordered chronologically, and usually are shown left-to-right or top-to-bottom. Each event on the **timeline** is associated with a date, which determines its location on the timeline. On electronic resources, timelines often contain hyperlinks associated with each event. Clicking on the event's hyperlink will open a page with more information about the event. **Cause-and-effect relationships** can be observed on timelines, which often show a key event and then resulting events following in close succession. These can be helpful for showing the order of events in time or the relationships between similar events. They help make the passage of time a concrete concept, and show that large periods pass between some events, and other events cluster very closely.

## Using Political Cartoons in Social Science Studies

Political cartoons are drawings that memorably convey an opinion. These opinions may be supportive or critical, and may summarize a series of events or pose a fictional situation that summarizes an attitude. **Political cartoons** are therefore secondary sources of information that provide social and cultural context about events. Political cartoons may have captions that help describe the action or put it in context. They may also have dialogue, labels, or other recognizable cultural symbols. For example, Uncle Sam frequently appears in political cartoons to represent the United States Government. Political cartoons frequently employ caricature to call attention to a situation or a person. The nature of the caricature helps show the cartoonist's attitude toward the issue being portrayed. Every element of the cartoon is included to support the artist's point, and should be considered in the cartoon's interpretation. When interpreting political cartoons, students should examine what issue is being discussed, what elements the artist chose to support his or her point, and what the message is. Considering who might agree or disagree with the cartoon is also helpful in determining the message of the cartoon.

## Political Science and Its Ties to Other Major Disciplines

Political science focuses on studying different governments and how they compare to each other, general political theory, ways political theory is put into action, how nations and governments interact with each other, and a general study of governmental structure and function. Other elements of **political science** include the study of elections, governmental administration at various levels, development and action of political parties, and how values such as freedom, power, justice and equality are expressed in different political cultures. Political science also encompasses elements of other disciplines, including:
- **History**—how historical events have shaped political thought and process
- **Sociology**—the effects of various stages of social development on the growth and development of government and politics
- **Anthropology**—the effects of governmental process on the culture of an individual group and its relationships with other groups
- **Economics**—how government policies regulate distribution of products and how they can control and/or influence the economy in general

## General Political Theory

Based on general political theory, the four major purposes of any given government are:
- **Ensuring national security**—the government protects against international, domestic and terrorist attacks and also ensures ongoing security through negotiating and establishing relationships with other governments.
- **Providing public services**—the government should "promote the general welfare," as stated in the Preamble to the US Constitution, by providing whatever is needed to its citizens.
- **Ensuring social order**—the government supplies means of settling conflicts among citizens as well as making laws to govern the nation, state, or city.
- **Making decisions regarding the economy**—laws help form the economic policy of the country, regarding both domestic and international trade and related issues. The government also has the ability to distribute goods and wealth to some extent among its citizens.

## Main Theories Regarding the Origin of the State

There are four main theories regarding the origin of the state:
- **Evolutionary**—the state evolved from the family, with the head of state the equivalent of the family's patriarch or matriarch.
- **Force**—one person or group of people brought everyone in an area under their control, forming the first government.
- **Divine Right**—certain people were chosen by the prevailing deity to be the rulers of the nation, which is itself created by the deity or deities.

- **Social Contract**—there is no natural order. The people allow themselves to be governed to maintain social order, while the state in turn promises to protect the people they govern. If the government fails to protect its people, the people have the right to seek new leaders.

## Influences of Philosophers on Political Study

Ancient Greek philosophers **Aristotle** and **Plato** believed political science would lead to order in political matters, and that this scientifically organized order would create stable, just societies.

**Thomas Aquinas** adapted the ideas of Aristotle to a Christian perspective. His ideas stated that individuals should have certain rights, but also certain duties, and that these rights and duties should determine the type and extent of government rule. In stating that laws should limit the role of government, he laid the groundwork for ideas that would eventually become modern constitutionalism.

**Niccolò Machiavelli**, author of *The Prince*, was a proponent of politics based on power. He is often considered the founder of modern political science.

**Thomas Hobbes**, author of *Leviathan* (1651), believed that individual's lives were focused solely on a quest for power, and that the state must work to control this urge. Hobbes felt that people were completely unable to live harmoniously without the intervention of a powerful, undivided government.

## Contributions of John Locke, Montesquieu, and Rousseau to Political Science

**John Locke** published *Two Treatises of Government* in 1689. This work argued against the ideas of Thomas Hobbes. He put forth the theory of *tabula rasa*—that people are born with minds like blank slates. Individual minds are molded by experience, not innate knowledge or intuition. He also believed that all men should be independent and equal. Many of Locke's ideas found their way into the Constitution of the United States.

The two French philosophers, **Montesquieu** and **Rousseau**, heavily influenced the French Revolution (1789-1799). They believed government policies and ideas should change to alleviate existing problems, an idea referred to as "liberalism." Rousseau in particular directly influenced the Revolution with writings such as *The Social Contract* (1762) and *Declaration of the Rights of Man and of the Citizen* (1789). Other ideas Rousseau and Montesquieu espoused included:
- Individual freedom and community welfare are of equal importance
- Man's innate goodness leads to natural harmony
- Reason develops with the rise of civilized society
- Individual citizens carry certain obligations to the existing government

## Political Ideologies of David Hume, Jeremy Bentham, John Stuart Mill, Johann Gottlieb Fichte, and Friedrich Hegel

**David Hume** and **Jeremy Bentham** believed politics should have as its main goal maintaining "the greatest happiness for the greatest number." Hume also believed in empiricism, or that ideas should not be believed until the proof has been observed. He was a natural skeptic and always sought out the truth of matters rather than believing what he was told.

**John Stuart Mill**, a British philosopher as well as an economist, believed in progressive policies such as women's suffrage, emancipation, and the development of labor unions and farming cooperatives.

**Johann Fichte** and **Georg Hegel**, German philosophers in the late eighteenth and early nineteenth centuries, supported a form of liberalism grounded largely in socialism and a sense of nationalism.

## Main Political Orientations

The four main political orientations are:
- **Liberal**—liberals believe that government should work to increase equality, even at the expense of some freedoms. Government should assist those in need. Focus on enforced social justice and free basic services for everyone.
- **Conservative**—a conservative believes that government should be limited in most cases. The government should allow its citizens to help one another and solve their own problems rather than enforcing solutions. Business should not be overregulated, allowing a free market.
- **Moderate**—this ideology incorporates some liberal and some conservative values, generally falling somewhere between in overall belief.
- **Libertarian**—libertarians believe that the government's role should be limited to protecting the life and liberty of citizens. Government should not be involved in any citizen's life unless that citizen is encroaching upon the rights of another.

## Major Principles of Government as Outlined in the United States Constitution

The six major principles of government as outlined in the United States Constitution are:
- **Federalism**—the power of the government does not belong entirely to the national government, but is divided between federal and state governments.
- **Popular sovereignty**—the government is determined by the people, and gains its authority and power from the people.
- **Separation of powers**—the government is divided into three branches, executive, legislative, and judicial, with each branch having its own set of powers.
- **Judicial review**—courts at all levels of government can declare laws invalid if they contradict the constitutions of individual states, or the US Constitution, with the Supreme Court serving as the final judicial authority on decisions of this kind.
- **Checks and balances**—no single branch can act without input from another, and each branch has the power to "check" any other, as well as balance other branches' powers.
- **Limited government**—governmental powers are limited and certain individual rights are defined as inviolable by the government.

## Types of Powers Delegated to the National Government by the US Constitution

The structure of the US government divides power between national and state governments. Powers delegated to the federal government by the Constitution are:
- **Expressed powers**—powers directly defined in the Constitution, including power to declare war, regulate commerce, make money, and collect taxes

- **Implied powers**—powers the national government must have in order to carry out the expressed powers
- **Inherent powers**—powers inherent to any government, not expressly defined in the Constitution

Some of these powers, such as collection and levying of taxes, are also granted to the individual state governments.

## Primary Positions of Federalism and Development Through the Years in the US

The way federalism should be practiced has been the subject of debate since writing of the Constitution. There were—and still are—two main factions regarding this issue:
- **States' rights**—those favoring the states' rights position feel that the state governments should take the lead in performing local actions to manage various problems.
- **Nationalist**—those favoring a nationalist position feel the national government should take the lead to deal with those same matters.

The flexibility of the Constitution has allowed the US government to shift and adapt as the needs of the country have changed. Power has often shifted from the state governments to the national government and back again, and both levels of government have developed various ways to influence each other.

## Effects of Federalism on Policy-Making and the Balance of Politics in the US

Federalism has three major effects on **public policy** in the US:
- Determining whether the local, state, or national government originates policy
- Affecting how policies are made
- Ensuring policy-making functions under a set of limitations

Federalism also influences the **political balance of power** in the US by:
- making it difficult, if not impossible, for a single political party to seize total power
- ensuring that individuals can participate in the political system at various levels
- making it possible for individuals working within the system to be able to affect policy at some level, whether local or more widespread

## Three Branches of the US Federal Government

The following are the three branches of the US Federal government and the individuals that belong to each branch:
- **Legislative Branch**—this consists of the two Houses of Congress: the House of Representatives and the Senate. All members of the Legislative Branch are elected officials.
- **Executive Branch**—this branch is made up of the President, Vice President, presidential advisors, and other various cabinet members. Advisors and cabinet are appointed by the President, but must be approved by Congress.
- **Judicial Branch**—the federal court system, headed by the Supreme Court.

Major Responsibilities of the Three Branches of the Federal Government
The three branches of the Federal government each have specific roles and responsibilities:

- The **Legislative Branch** is largely concerned with law-making. All laws must be approved by Congress before they go into effect. They are also responsible for regulating money and trade, approving presidential appointments, and establishing organizations like the postal service and federal courts. Congress can also propose amendments to the Constitution, and can impeach, or bring charges against, the President. Only Congress can declare war.
- The **Executive Branch** carries out laws, treaties, and war declarations enacted by Congress. The President can also veto bills approved by Congress, and serves as commander-in-chief of the US military. The president appoints cabinet members, ambassadors to foreign countries, and federal judges.
- The **Judicial Branch** makes decisions on challenges as to whether laws passed by Congress meet the requirements of the US Constitution. The Supreme Court may also choose to review decisions made by lower courts to determine their constitutionality.

## US Citizenship

Qualifications of a US citizen How Citizenship May Be Lost
Anyone born in the US, born abroad to a US citizen, or who has gone through a process of naturalization is considered a **citizen** of the United States. It is possible to lose US citizenship as a result of conviction of certain crimes such as treason. Citizenship may also be lost if a citizen pledges an oath to another country or serves in the military of a country engaged in hostilities with the US. A US citizen can also choose to hold dual citizenship, work as an expatriate in another country without losing US citizenship, or even to renounce citizenship if he or she so chooses.

Rights, Duties, and Responsibilities Granted to or Expected from Citizens
Citizens are granted certain rights under the US government. The most important of these are defined in the **Bill of Rights**, and include freedom of speech, religion, assembly, and a variety of other rights the government is not allowed to remove. A US citizen also has a number of **duties**:

- Paying taxes
- Loyalty to the government (though the US does not prosecute those who criticize or seek to change the government)
- Support and defense of the Constitution
- Serving in the Armed Forces when required by law
- Obeying laws as set forth by the various levels of government.

**Responsibilities** of a US citizen include:

- Voting in elections
- Respecting one another's rights and not infringing on them
- Staying informed about various political and national issues
- Respecting one another's beliefs

## Bill of Rights

Importance of the Bill of Rights
The first ten amendments of the US Constitution are known as the **Bill of Rights**. These amendments prevent the government from infringing upon certain freedoms that the founding fathers felt were natural rights that already belonged to all people. These rights included freedom of speech, freedom of religion, the right to bear arms, and freedom of assembly. Many of the rights

were formulated in direct response to the way the colonists felt they had been mistreated by the British government.

<u>Rights Granted in the Bill of Rights</u>
The first ten amendments were passed by Congress in 1789. Three-fourths of the existing thirteen states had ratified them by December of 1791, making them official additions to the Constitution. The rights granted in the Bill of Rights are:

- **First Amendment**—freedom of religion, speech, freedom of the press, and the right to assemble and to petition the government
- **Second Amendment**—the right to bear arms
- **Third Amendment**—Congress cannot force individuals to house troops
- **Fourth Amendment**—protection from unreasonable search and seizure
- **Fifth Amendment**—no individual is required to testify against himself, and no individual may be tried twice for the same crime
- **Sixth Amendment**—right to criminal trial by jury, right to legal counsel
- **Seventh Amendment**—right to civil trial by jury
- **Eighth Amendment**—protection from excessive bail or cruel and unusual punishment
- **Ninth Amendment**—prevents rights not explicitly named in the Constitution from being taken away because they are not named
- **Tenth Amendment**—any rights not directly delegated to the national government, or not directly prohibited by the government from the states, belong to the states or to the people

## Situations Where the Government Restricts or Regulates First Amendment Freedoms

In some cases, the government restricts certain elements of First Amendment rights. Some examples include:

- **Freedom of religion**—when a religion espouses illegal activities, the government often restricts these forms of religious expression. Examples include polygamy, animal sacrifice, and use of illicit drugs or illegal substances.
- **Freedom of speech**—this can be restricted if exercise of free speech endangers other people.
- **Freedom of the press**—laws prevent the press from publishing falsehoods.

In **emergency situations** such as wartime, stricter restrictions are sometimes placed on these rights, especially rights to free speech and assembly, and freedom of the press, in order to protect national security.

## Constitution's Address of the Rights of Those Accused of Crimes

The US Constitution makes allowances for the **rights of criminals**, or anyone who has transgressed established laws. There must be laws to protect citizens from criminals, but those accused of crimes must also be protected and their basic rights as individuals preserved. In addition, the Constitution protects individuals from the power of authorities to prevent police forces and other enforcement organizations from becoming oppressive. The fourth, fifth, sixth and eighth amendments specifically address these rights.

## Supreme Court's Provision of Equal Protection Under the Law for All Individuals

When the Founding Fathers wrote in the Declaration of Independence that "all men are created equal," they actually were referring to men, and in fact defined citizens as white men who owned land. However, as the country has developed and changed, the definition has expanded to more wholly include all people.

"**Equality**" does not mean all people are inherently the same, but it does mean they all should be granted the same rights and should be treated the same by the government. Amendments to the Constitution have granted citizenship and voting rights to all Americans regardless of race or gender. The Supreme Court evaluates various laws and court decisions to determine if they properly represent the idea of **equal protection**. One sample case was Brown v. Board of Education in 1954, which declared separate-but-equal treatment to be unconstitutional.

## Civil Liberty Challenges Addressed in Current Political Discussions

The **civil rights movements** of the 1960s and ongoing struggle for the rights of women and other minorities have sparked **challenges to existing law**. In addition, debate has raged over how much information the government should be required to divulge to the public. Major issues in today's political climate include:
- Continued debate over women's rights, especially regarding equal pay for equal work
- Debate over affirmative action to encourage hiring of minorities
- Debate over civil rights of homosexuals, including marriage and military service
- Decisions as to whether minorities should be compensated for past discriminatory practices
- Balance between the public's right to know and the government's need to maintain national security
- Balance between the public's right to privacy and national security

## Civil Liberties vs. Civil Rights

While the terms "civil liberties" and "civil rights" are often used synonymously, in actuality their definitions are slightly different. The two concepts work together, however, to define the basics of a free state:
- "**Civil liberties**" defines the role of the state in providing equal rights and opportunities to individuals within that state.  An example is non-discrimination policies with regards to granting citizenship.
- "**Civil rights**" defines the limitations of governmental rights, describing those rights that belong to individuals and which cannot be infringed upon by the government. Examples of these rights include freedom of religion, political freedom, and overall freedom to live as one chooses.

## Suffrage, Franchise and the Change of Voting Rights Over the Course of American History

Suffrage and franchise both refer to the right to **vote**. As the US developed as a nation, there was much debate over which individuals should hold this right. In the early years, only white male landowners were granted suffrage. By the nineteenth century, most states had franchised, or granted the right to vote to, all adult white males. The **Fifteenth Amendment** of 1870 granted suffrage to former slave men. The **Nineteenth Amendment** gave women the right to vote in 1920, and in 1971 the **Twenty-sixth Amendment** expanded voting rights to include any US citizen over the age of eighteen. However, those who have not been granted full citizenship and citizens who have committed certain crimes do not have voting rights.

## Ways in Which the Voting Process Has Changed Over the Years

The first elections in the US were held by **public ballot**. However, election abuses soon became common, since public ballot made it easy to intimidate, threaten, or otherwise influence the votes of individuals or groups of individuals. New practices were put into play, including **registering voters** before elections took place, and using a **secret or Australian ballot**. In 1892, the introduction of the **voting machine** further privatized the voting process, since it allowed complete privacy for voting. Today debate continues about the accuracy of various voting methods, including high-tech voting machines and even low-tech punch cards.

## Effect of Political Parties on the Functioning of an Individual Government

Different types and numbers of political parties can have a significant effect on how a government is run. If there is a **single party**, or a one-party system, the government is defined by that one party, and all policy is based on that party's beliefs. In a **two-party system**, two parties with different viewpoints compete for power and influence. The US is basically a two-party system, with checks and balances to make it difficult for one party to gain complete power over the other. There are also **multi-party systems**, with three or more parties. In multiparty systems, various parties will often come to agreements in order to form a majority and shift the balance of power.

## Development of Political Parties in the US

George Washington was adamantly against the establishment of **political parties**, based on the abuses perpetrated by such parties in Britain. However, political parties developed in US politics almost from the beginning. Major parties throughout US history have included:
- **Federalists and Democratic-Republicans**—these parties formed in the late 1700s and disagreed on the balance of power between national and state government.
- **Democrats and Whigs**—these developed before the Civil War, based on disagreements about various issues such as slavery.
- **Democrats and Republicans**—the Republican Party developed after the Civil War, and the two parties debated issues centering on the treatment of the post-war South.

While third parties sometimes enter the picture in US politics, the government is basically a two-party system, dominated by the Democrats and Republicans.

## Functions of Political Parties

Political parties form organizations at all levels of government. Activities of individual parties include:
- Recruiting and backing candidates for offices
- Discussing various issues with the public, increasing public awareness
- Working toward compromise on difficult issues
- Staffing government offices and providing administrative support

At the administrative level, parties work to ensure that viable candidates are available for elections and that offices and staff are in place to support candidates as they run for office and afterwards, when they are elected.

## Processes of Selecting Political Candidates

Historically, in the quest for political office, a potential candidate has followed one of the following four processes:

- **Nominating convention**—an official meeting of the members of a party for the express purpose of nominating candidates for upcoming elections. The Democratic National Convention and the Republican National Convention, convened to announce candidates for presidency, are examples of this kind of gathering.
- **Caucus**—a meeting, usually attended by a party's leaders. Some states still use caucuses, but not all.
- **Primary election**—the most common method of choosing candidates today, the primary is a publicly held election to choose candidates.
- **Petition**—signatures are gathered to place a candidate on the ballot. Petitions can also be used to place legislation on a ballot.

## Ways the Average Citizen Participates in the Political Process

In addition to voting for elected officials, American citizens are able to participate in the political process through several other avenues. These include:

- Participating in local government
- Participating in caucuses for large elections
- Volunteering to help political parties
- Running for election to local, state, or national offices

Individuals can also donate money to political causes, or support political groups that focus on specific causes such as abortion, wildlife conservation or women's rights. These groups often make use of **representatives** who lobby legislators to act in support of their efforts.

## Ways in Which Political Campaign Gains Funding

Political campaigns are very expensive. In addition to the basic necessities of a campaign office, including office supplies, office space, etc., a large quantity of the money that funds a political campaign goes toward **advertising**. Money to fund a political campaign can come from several sources including:

- The candidate's personal funds
- Donations by individuals
- Special interest groups

The most significant source of campaign funding is **special interest groups**. Groups in favor of certain policies will donate money to candidates they believe will support those policies. Special interest groups also do their own advertising in support of candidates they endorse.

## Importance of Free Press and the Media

The right to free speech guaranteed in the first amendment to the Constitution allows the media to report on **government and political activities** without fear of retribution. Because the media has access to information about the government, its policies and actions, as well as debates and discussions that occur in Congress, it can keep the public informed about the inner workings of the government. The media can also draw attention to injustices, imbalances of power, and other transgressions the government or government officials might commit. However, media outlets may, like special interest groups, align themselves with certain political viewpoints and skew their reports to fit that viewpoint. The rise of the **Internet** has made media reporting even more complex, as news can be found from an infinite variety of sources, both reliable and unreliable.

## Forms of Government

### Anarchism, Communism and Dictatorship
**Anarchists** believe that all government should be eliminated and that individuals should rule themselves. Historically, anarchists have used violence and assassination to further their beliefs.

**Communism** is based on class conflict, revolution and a one-party state. Ideally, a communist government would involve a single government for the entire world. Communist government controls the production and flow of goods and services rather than leaving this to companies or individuals.

**Dictatorship** involves rule by a single individual. If rule is enforced by a small group, this is referred to as an oligarchy. Dictators tend to rule with a violent hand, using a highly repressive police force to ensure control over the populace.

### Fascism and Monarchy
Fascism centers on a single leader and is, ideologically, an oppositional belief to communism. **Fascism** includes a single party state and centralized control. The power of the fascist leader lies in the "cult of personality," and the fascist state often focuses on expansion and conquering of other nations. **Monarchy** was the major form of government for Europe through most of its history.

A monarchy is led by a king or a queen. This position is hereditary, and the rulers are not elected. In modern times, constitutional monarchy has developed, where the king and queen still exist but most of the governmental decisions are made by democratic institutions such as a parliament.

## Presidential System and Socialism

A presidential system, like a parliamentary system, has a legislature and political parties, but there is no difference between the head of state and the head of government. Instead of separating these functions, an elected president performs both. Election of the president can be direct or indirect, and the president may not necessarily belong to the largest political party. In **socialism**, the state controls production of goods, though it does not necessarily own all means of production. The state also provides a variety of social services to citizens and helps guide the economy. A democratic form of government often exists in socialist countries.

## Totalitarian and Authoritarian Systems

A totalitarian system believes everything should be under the control of the government, from resource production to the press to religion and other social institutions. All aspects of life under a totalitarian system must conform to the ideals of the government. **Authoritarian** governments practice widespread state authority, but do not necessarily dismantle all public institutions. If a church, for example, exists as an organization but poses no threat to the authority of the state, an authoritarian government might leave it as it is. While all totalitarian governments are by definition authoritarian, a government can be authoritarian without becoming totalitarian

## Parliamentary and Democratic Systems

In a parliamentary system, government involves a legislature and a variety of political parties. The head of government, usually a Prime Minister, is typically the head of the dominant party. A head of state can be elected, or this position can be taken by a monarch, as in Great Britain's constitutional monarchy system.

In a **democratic system** of government, the people elect their government representatives. The word "democracy" is a Greek term that means "rule of the people." There are two forms of democracy—direct and indirect. In a direct democracy, each issue or election is decided by a vote where each individual is counted separately. An indirect democracy employs a legislature that votes on issues that affect large numbers of people whom the legislative members represent. Democracy can exist as a parliamentary system or a presidential system. The US is a presidential, indirect democracy.

## Realism, Liberalism, Institutionalism and Constructivism in International Relations

The theory of realism states that nations are by nature aggressive, and work in their own self-interest. Relations between nations are determined by military and economic strength. The nation is seen as the highest authority. **Liberalism** believes states can cooperate, and that they act based on capability rather than power. This term was originally coined to describe Woodrow Wilson's theories on international cooperation. In **institutionalism**, institutions provide structure and incentive for cooperation among nations. Institutions are defined as a set of rules used to make international decisions. These institutions also help distribute power and determine how nations will interact. **Constructivism**, like liberalism, is based on international cooperation, but recognizes that perceptions countries have of each other can affect their relations.

## Effects of Foreign Policy on a Country's Position in World Affairs

Foreign policy is a set of goals, policies and strategies that determine how an individual nation will interact with other countries. These strategies shift, sometimes quickly and drastically, according to actions or changes occurring in the other countries. However, a nation's **foreign policy** is often based on a certain set of ideals and national needs. Examples of US foreign policy include isolationism versus internationalism. In the 1800s, the US leaned more toward isolationism, exhibiting a reluctance to become involved in foreign affairs. The World Wars led to a period of internationalism, as the US entered these wars in support of other countries and joined the United Nations. Today's foreign policy tends more toward **interdependence**, or **globalism**, recognizing the widespread affects of issues like economic health.

## Major Figures Involved in Determining and Enacting US Foreign Policy

US foreign policy is largely determined by Congress and the president, influenced by the secretary of state, secretary of defense, and the national security adviser. Executive officials carry out policies. The main departments in charge of these day-to-day issues are the **US Department of State**, also referred to as the State Department. The Department of State carries out policy, negotiates treaties, maintains diplomatic relations, assists citizens traveling in foreign countries, and ensures that the president is properly informed of any international issues. The **Department of Defense**, the largest executive department in the US, supervises the armed forces and provides assistance to the President in his role as Commander-in-chief.

## Major Types of International Organizations

Two types of international organizations are:
- **Intergovernmental organizations (IGOs)**. These organizations are made up of members from various national governments. The UN is an example of an intergovernmental organization. Treaties among the member nations determine the functions and powers of these groups.
- **Nongovernmental organizations (NGOs)**. An NGO lies outside the scope of any government and is usually supported through private donations. An example of an NGO is the International Red Cross, which works with governments all over the world when their countries are in crisis, but is formally affiliated with no particular country or government.

## Role of Diplomats in International Relations

Diplomats are individuals who reside in foreign countries in order to maintain communications between that country and their home country. They help negotiate trade agreements and environmental policies, as well as conveying official information to foreign governments. They also help to resolve conflicts between the countries, often working to sort out issues without making the conflicts official in any way. **Diplomats**, or **ambassadors**, are appointed in the US by the president. Appointments must be approved by Congress.

## Role of the United Nations in International Relations and Diplomacy

The United Nations (**UN**) helps form international policies by hosting representatives of various countries who then provide input into policy decisions. Countries who are members of the UN must agree to abide by all final UN resolutions, but this is not always the case in practice, as dissent is not uncommon. If countries do not follow UN resolutions, the UN can decide on sanctions against those countries, often economic sanctions, such as trade restriction. The UN can also send military forces to problem areas, with "peace keeping" troops brought in from member nations. An example of this function is the Korean War, the first war in which an international organization played a major role.

## Economics

Economics is the study of the ways specific societies **allocate** resources to individuals and groups within that society. Also important are the choices society makes regarding what efforts or initiatives are funded and which are not. Since resources in any society are finite, allocation becomes a vivid reflection of that society's values. In general, the economic system that drives an individual society is based on:

- What goods are produced
- How those goods are produced
- Who acquires the goods or benefits from them

Economics consists of two main categories: **macroeconomics**, which studies larger systems, and **microeconomics**, which studies smaller systems.

## Market Economy

A market economy is based on supply and demand. **Demand** has to do with what customers want and need, as well as what quantity those consumers are able to purchase based on other economic factors. **Supply** refers to how much can be produced to meet demand, or how much suppliers are willing and able to sell. Where the needs of consumers meet the needs of suppliers is referred to as a market equilibrium price. This price varies depending on many factors, including the overall health of a society's economy, overall beliefs and considerations of individuals in society. The following is a list of terms defined in the context of a market economy:

- **Elasticity**—this is based on how the quantity of a particular product responds to the price demanded for that product. If quantity responds quickly to changes in price, the supply/demand for that product is said to be elastic. If it does not respond quickly, then the supply/demand is inelastic.
- **Market efficiency**—this occurs when a market is capable of producing output high enough to meet consumer demand, that market is efficient.
- **Comparative advantage**—in the field of international trade, this refers to a country focusing on a specific product that it can produce it more efficiently and more cheaply, or at a lower opportunity cost, than another country, thus giving it a comparative advantage in production.

## Planned Economy vs. Market Economy

In a **market economy**, supply and demand are determined by consumers. In a **planned economy**, a public entity or planning authority makes the decisions about what resources will be produced, how they will be produced, and who will be able to benefit from them. The means of production, such as factories, are also owned by a public entity rather than by private interests. In **market socialism**, the economic structure falls somewhere between the market economy and the planned economy. Planning authorities determine allocation of resources at higher economic levels, while consumer goods are driven by a market economy.

## Microeconomics

While economics generally studies how resources are allocated, **microeconomics** focuses on economic factors such as the way consumers behave, how income is distributed, and output and input markets. Studies are limited to the industry or firm level, rather than an entire country or society.  Among the elements studied in microeconomics are factors of production, costs of production, and factor income. These factors determine production decisions of individual firms, based on resources and costs.

## Classification of Various Markets by Economists

The conditions prevailing in a given market are used to **classify** markets. Conditions considered include:
- Existence of competition
- Number and size of suppliers
- Influence of suppliers over price
- Variety of available products
- Ease of entering the market

Once these questions are answered, an economist can classify a certain market according to its structure and the nature of competition within the market.

## Market Failure

When any of the elements for a successfully competitive market are missing, this can lead to a **market failure**. Certain elements are necessary to create what economists call "**perfect competition**." If one of these factors is weak or lacking, the market is classified as having "**imperfect competition**." Worse than imperfect competition, though, is a market failure. There are five major types of market failure:
- Inadequate competition
- Inadequate information
- Immobile resources
- Negative externalities, or side effects
- Failure to provide public goods

**Externalities** are side effects of a market that affect third parties. These effects can be either negative or positive.

## Factors of Production and Costs of Production

Every good and service requires certain resources, or **inputs**. These inputs are referred to as **factors of production**. Every good and service requires four factors of production:
- Labor
- Capital
- Land
- Entrepreneurship

These factors can be fixed or variable, and can produce fixed or variable costs. Examples of **fixed costs** include land and equipment. **Variable costs** include labor. The total of fixed and variable costs makes up the cost of production.

## Factor Income

Factors of production each have an associated **factor income**. Factors that earn income include:
- **Labor**—earns wages
- **Capital**—earns interest
- **Land**—earns rent
- **Entrepreneurship**—earns profit

Each factor's income is determined by its **contribution**. In a market economy, this income is not guaranteed to be equal. How scarce the factor is and the weight of its contribution to the overall production process determines the final factor income.

## Kinds of Market Structures in an Output Market

The four kinds of market structures in an output market are:
- **Perfect competition**—all existing firms sell an identical product. The firms are not able to control the final price. In addition, there is nothing that makes it difficult to become involved in or leave the industry. Anything that would prevent entering or leaving an industry is called a barrier to entry. An example of this market structure is agriculture.
- **Monopoly**—a single seller controls the product and its price. Barriers to entry, such as prohibitively high fixed cost structures, prevent other sellers from entering the market.
- **Monopolistic competition**—a number of firms sell similar products, but they are not identical, such as different brands of clothes or food. Barriers to entry are low.
- **Oligopoly**—only a few firms control the production and distribution of products, such as automobiles. Barriers to entry are high, preventing large numbers of firms from entering the market.

## Types of Monopolies

Four types of monopolies are:
- **Natural monopoly**—a single supplier has a distinct advantage over the others.
- **Geographic monopoly**—only one business offers the product in a certain area.
- **Technological monopoly**—a single company controls the technology necessary to supply the product.
- **Government monopoly**—a government agency is the only provider of a specific good or service.

### Actions Taken by the US Government to Control Monopolies
The US government has passed several acts to regulate businesses, including:
- **Sherman Antitrust Act (1890)**—this prohibited trusts, monopolies, and any other situations that eliminated competition.
- **Clayton Antitrust Act (1914)**—this prohibited price discrimination.
- **Robinson-Patman Act (1936)**—this strengthened provisions of the Clayton Antitrust Act, requiring businesses to offer the same pricing on products to any customer.

The government has also taken other actions to ensure competition, including requirements for public disclosure. The **Securities and Exchange Commission (SEC)** requires companies that provide public stock to provide financial reports on a regular basis. Because of the nature of their business, banks are further regulated and required to provide various information to the government.

## Marketing and Utility

Marketing consists of all of the activity necessary to convince consumers to acquire goods. One major way to move products into the hands of consumers is to convince them that any single product will satisfy a need. The ability of a product or service to satisfy the need of a consumer is called **utility**. There are four types of utility:

- **Form utility**—a product's desirability lies in its physical characteristics.
- **Place utility**—a product's desirability is connected to its location and convenience.
- **Time utility**—a product's desirability is determined by its availability at a certain time.
- **Ownership utility**—a product's desirability is increased because ownership of the product passes to the consumer.

Marketing behavior will stress any or all of these types of utility when marketing to the consumer.

## Producers Determining What Customers Desire for Their Products

Successful marketing depends not only on convincing customers they need the product, but also on focusing the marketing towards those who already have a need or desire for the product. Before releasing a product into the general marketplace, many producers will **test** markets to determine which will be the most receptive to the product. There are three steps usually taken to evaluate a product's market:

- **Market research**—this involves researching a market to determine if it will be receptive to the product.
- **Market surveys**—a part of market research, market surveys ask consumers specific questions to help determine the marketability of a product to a specific group.
- **Test marketing**—this includes releasing the product into a small geographical area to see how it sells. Often test marketing is followed by wider marketing if the product does well.

## Major Elements of a Marketing Plan

The four major elements of a marketing plan are:

- **Product**—this includes any elements pertaining directly to the product, such as packaging, presentation, or services to include along with it.
- **Price**—this calculates cost of production, distribution, advertising, etc., as well as the desired profit to determine the final price.
- **Place**—this determines which outlets will be used to sell the product, whether traditional outlets such as brick and mortar stores or through direct mail or Internet marketing.
- **Promotion**—this involves ways to let consumers know the product is available, through advertising and other means.

Once these elements have all been determined, the producer can proceed with production and distribution of his product.

## Distribution Channels

Distribution channels determine the route a product takes on its journey from producer to consumer, and can also influence the final price and availability of the product. There are two major forms of distributions: wholesale and retail. A **wholesale distributor** buys in large quantities and then resells smaller amounts to other businesses. **Retailers** sell directly to the consumers rather than to businesses.  In the modern marketplace, additional distribution channels have grown up with the rise of markets such as club warehouse stores as well as purchasing through catalogs or over the Internet. Most of these newer distribution channels bring products more directly to the consumer, eliminating the need for middlemen.

## Distribution of Income in a Society

Distribution of income in any society ranges from poorest to richest. In most societies, income is not distributed evenly. To determine **income distribution**, family incomes are ranked from lowest to highest. These rankings are divided into five sections called **quintiles**, which are compared to each other.  The uneven distribution of income is often linked to higher levels of education and ability in the upper classes, but can also be due to other factors such as discrimination and existing monopolies. The **income gap** in America continues to grow, largely due to growth in the service industry, changes in the American family unit and reduced influence of labor unions.  **Poverty** is defined by comparing incomes to poverty guidelines. Poverty guidelines determine the level of income necessary for a family to function. Those below the poverty line are often eligible for assistance from government agencies.

## Macroeconomics

Macroeconomics examines economies on a much larger level than microeconomics. While **microeconomics** studies economics on a firm or industry level, **macroeconomics** looks at economic trends and structures on a national level. Variables studied in macroeconomics include:
- Output
- Consumption
- Investment
- Government spending
- Net exports

The overall economic condition of a nation is defined as the **Gross Domestic Product**, or GDP. GDP measures a nation's economic output over a limited time period, such as a year.

## Types of Consumer Behavior

The two major types of consumer behavior as defined in macroeconomics are:
- **Marginal propensity** to consume defines the tendency of consumers to increase spending in conjunction with increases in income. In general, individuals with greater income will buy more. As individuals increase their income through job changes or growth of experience, they will also increase spending.
- **Utility** is a term that describes the satisfaction experienced by a consumer in relation to acquiring and using a good or service. Providers of goods and services will stress utility to convince consumers they want the products being presented.

## Ways to Measure the Gross Domestic Product of a Country

The two major ways to measure the Gross Domestic Product of a country are:
- The **expenditures approach** calculates the GDP based on how much money is spent in each individual sector.
- The **income approach** calculates the GDP based on how much money is earned in each sector.

Both methods yield the same results and both of these calculation methods are based on four **economic sectors** that make up a country's macro-economy:
- Consumers
- Business
- Government
- Foreign sector

## Types of Earnings Generated by an Economy Considered to Calculate GDP

Several factors must be considered in order to accurately calculate the GDP using the incomes approach. **Income factors** are:
- Wages paid to laborers, or Compensation of Employees
- Rental income derived from land
- Interest income derived from invested capital
- Entrepreneurial income

**Entrepreneurial income** consists of two forms. **Proprietor's income** is income that comes back to the entrepreneur himself. **Corporate profit** is income that goes back into the corporation as a whole. Corporate profit is divided by the corporation into corporate profits taxes, dividends, and retained earnings.  Two other figures must be subtracted in the incomes approach. These are **indirect business taxes**, including property and sales taxes, and **depreciation**.

## Effects of Population of a Country on the Gross Domestic Product

Changes in population can affect the calculation of a nation's **GDP**, particularly since GDP and GNP (Gross National Product) are generally measured per capita. If a country's economic production is low, but the population is high, the income per individual will be lower than if the income is high and the population is lower. Also, if the population grows quickly and the income grows slowly, individual income will remain low or even drop drastically.

**Population growth** can also affect overall **economic growth**. Economic growth requires both that consumers purchase goods and workers produce them. A population that does not grow quickly enough will not supply enough workers to support rapid economic growth.

## Ideal Balance to be Obtained in an Economy

Ideally, an economy functions efficiently, with the **aggregate supply**, or the amount of national output, equal to the **aggregate demand**, or the amount of the output that is purchased. In these cases, the economy is stable and prosperous. However, economies more typically go through **phases**. These phases are:
- **Boom**—GDP is high and the economy prospers

- **Recession**—GDP falls, unemployment rises
- **Trough**—the recession reaches its lowest point
- **Recovery**—unemployment lessens, prices rise, and the economy begins to stabilize again

These phases tend to repeat in cycles that are not necessarily predictable or regular.

## Unemployment and Inflation

When demand outstrips supply, prices are driven artificially high, or **inflated**. This occurs when too much spending causes an imbalance in the economy. In general, inflation occurs because an economy is growing too quickly. When there is too little spending and supply has moved far beyond demand, a **surplus** of product results. Companies cut back on production, reduce the number of employees, and **unemployment** rises as people lose their jobs. This imbalance occurs when an economy becomes sluggish. In general, both these economic instability situations are caused by an imbalance between supply and demand. Government intervention may be necessary to stabilize an economy when either inflation or unemployment becomes too serious.

## Different Forms of Unemployment

- **Frictional**—when workers change jobs and are unemployed while waiting for new jobs
- **Structural**—when economic shifts reduce the need for workers
- **Cyclical**—when natural business cycles bring about loss of jobs
- **Seasonal**—when seasonal cycles reduce the need for certain jobs
- **Technological**—when advances in technology result in elimination of certain jobs

Any of these factors can increase unemployment in certain sectors.

Inflation is classified by the overall rate at which it occurs:
- **Creeping inflation**—this is an inflation rate of about 1-3% annually.
- **Walking inflation**—this is an inflation rate of 3-10% annually.
- **Galloping inflation**—this is a high inflation rate of more than 10% but less than 1000% annually.
- **Hyperinflation**—this is an inflation rate over 1000% per year. Hyperinflation usually leads to complete monetary collapse in a society, as individuals become unable to generate sufficient income to purchase necessary goods.

## Government Intervention Policies that Can Help Mitigate Inflation and Unemployment

When an economy becomes too imbalanced, either due to excessive spending or not enough spending, **government intervention** often becomes necessary to put the economy back on track. Government Fiscal Policy can take several forms, including:
- Contractionary policy
- Expansionary policy
- Monetary policy

**Contractionary policies** help counteract inflation. These include increasing taxes and decreasing government spending to slow spending in the overall economy. **Expansionary policies** increase government spending and lower taxes in order to reduce unemployment and increase the level of spending in the economy overall. **Monetary policy** can take several forms, and affects the amount of funds available to banks for making loans.

## Study and Quantification of Populations and Population Growth

Populations are studied by **size**, rates of **growth** due to immigration, the overall **fertility rate**, and **life expectancy**. For example, though the population of the United States is considerably larger than it was two hundred years ago, the rate of population growth has decreased greatly, from about three percent per year to less than one percent per year.

In the US, the fertility rate is fairly low, with most choosing not to have large families, and life expectancy is high, creating a projected imbalance between older and younger people in the near future. In addition, immigration and the mixing of racially diverse cultures are projected to increase the percentages of Asians, Hispanics and African-Americans.

## Functions and Types of Money

Money is used in three major ways:
- As an accounting unit
- As a store of value
- As an exchange medium

In general, money must be acceptable throughout a society in exchange for debts or to purchase goods and services. Money should be relatively scarce, its value should remain stable, and it should be easily carried, durable, and easy to divide up.  There are three basic types of money: commodity, representative and fiat. **Commodity money** includes gems or precious metals. **Representative money** can be exchanged for items such as gold or silver which have inherent value. **Fiat money**, or legal tender, has no inherent value but has been declared to function as money by the government. It is often backed by gold or silver, but not necessarily on a one-to-one ratio.

## Types of Money Available in the US and Economists' Measure of It

Money in the US is not just currency. When economists calculate the amount of money available, they must take into account other factors such as deposits that have been placed in checking accounts, debit cards and "near moneys" such as savings accounts, that can be quickly converted into cash. Currency, checkable deposits and traveler's checks, referred to as **M1**, are added up, and then **M2** is calculated by adding savings deposits, CDs and various other monetary deposits. The final result is the total quantity of available money.

## Aspects of Monetary Policy and the Role of the Federal Reserve System

The Federal Reserve System, also known as the **Fed**, implements all monetary policy in the US. Monetary policy regulates the amount of money available in the American banking system. The Fed can decrease or increase the amount of available money for loans, thus helping regulate the national economy.  Monetary policies implemented by the Fed are part of expansionary or contractionary monetary policies that help counteract inflation or unemployment.  The **discount rate** is an interest rate charged by the Fed when banks borrow money from them. A lower discount rate leads banks to borrow more money, leading to increased spending. A higher discount rate has the opposite effect.

## How Banks Function

Banks earn their income by **loaning** out money and charging **interest** on those loans. If less money is available, fewer loans can be made, which affects the amount of spending in the overall economy. While banks function by making loans, they are not allowed to loan out all the money they hold in deposit. The amount of money they must maintain in reserve is known as the **reserve ratio**. If the reserve ratio is raised, less money is available for loans and spending decreases. A lower reserve ratio increases available funds and increases spending. This ratio is determined by the Federal Reserve System.

## Open Market Operations

The Federal Reserve System can also expand or contract the overall money supply through **open market operations**. In this case, the Fed can buy or sell **bonds** it has purchased from banks or individuals. When the Fed buys bonds, more money is put into circulation, creating an expansionary situation to stimulate the economy. When the Fed sells bonds, money is withdrawn from the system, creating a **contractionary** situation to slow an economy suffering from inflation. Because of international financial markets, however, American banks often borrow and lend money in markets outside the US. By shifting their attention to international markets, domestic banks and other businesses can circumvent whatever contractionary policies the Fed may have put into place.

## Major Characteristics of International Trade

International trade can take advantage of broader markets, bringing a wider variety of products within easy reach. By contrast, it can also allow individual countries to specialize in particular products that they can produce easily, such as those for which they have easy access to raw materials. Other products, more difficult to make domestically, can be acquired through trade with other nations. **International trade** requires efficient use of **native resources** as well as sufficient **disposable income** to purchase native and imported products. Many countries in the world engage extensively in international trade, but others still face major economic challenges.

## Major Characteristics of a Developing Nation

The five major characteristics of a developing nation are:
- Low GDP
- Rapid growth of population
- Economy that depends on subsistence agriculture
- Poor conditions, including high infant mortality rates, high disease rates, poor sanitation, and insufficient housing
- Low literacy rate

**Developing nations** often function under oppressive governments that do not provide private property rights and withhold education and other rights from women. They also often feature an extreme disparity between upper and lower classes, with little opportunity for the lower classes to improve their position.

## Stages of Economic Development

Economic development occurs in three stages that are defined by the activities that drive the economy:
- Agricultural stage
- Manufacturing stage
- Service sector stage

In developing countries, it is often difficult to acquire the necessary funding to provide equipment and training to move into the advanced stages of economic development. Some can receive help from developed countries via foreign aid and investment or international organizations such as the **International Monetary Fund** or the **World Bank**. Having developed countries provide monetary, technical, or military assistance can help developing countries move forward to the next stage in their development.

## Obstacles Developing Nations Face Regarding Economic Growth

Developing nations typically struggle to overcome obstacles that prevent or slow economic development. Major **obstacles** can include:
- Rapid, uncontrolled population growth
- Trade restrictions
- Misused resources, often perpetrated by the government
- Traditional beliefs that can slow or reject change

Corrupt, oppressive governments often hamper the economic growth of developing nations, creating huge **economic disparities** and making it impossible for individuals to advance, in turn preventing overall growth. Governments sometimes export currency, called **capital flight**, which is detrimental to a country's economic development. In general, countries are more likely to experience economic growth if their governments encourage entrepreneurship and provide private property rights.

## Problems When Industrialization Occurs Too Quickly

Rapid growth throughout the world leaves some nations behind, and sometimes spurs their governments to move forward too quickly into **industrialization** and **artificially rapid economic growth**. While slow or nonexistent economic growth causes problems in a country, overly rapid industrialization carries its own issues. Four major problems encountered due to rapid industrialization are:
- Use of technology not suited to the products or services being supplied
- Poor investment of capital
- Lack of time for the population to adapt to new paradigms
- Lack of time to experience all stages of development and adjust to each stage

Economic failures in Indonesia were largely due to rapid growth that was poorly handled.

## Importance of E-Commerce in Today's Marketplace

The growth of the Internet has brought many changes to our society, not the least of which is the modern way of business. Where supply channels used to move in certain necessary ways, many of

*- 30 -*

these channels are now bypassed as **e-commerce** makes it possible for nearly any individual to set up a direct market to consumers, as well as direct interaction with suppliers. Competition is fierce. In many instances e-commerce can provide nearly instantaneous gratification, with a wide variety of products. Whoever provides the best product most quickly often rises to the top of a marketplace. How this added element to the marketplace will affect the economy in the future remains to be seen. Many industries are still struggling with the best ways to adapt to the rapid, continuous changes.

## Knowledge Economy and Possible Effect on Future Economic Growth

The knowledge economy is a growing sector in the economy of developed countries, and includes the trade and development of:
- Data
- Intellectual property
- Technology, especially in the area of communications

Knowledge as a resource is steadily becoming more and more important. What is now being called the **Information Age** may prove to bring about changes in life and culture as significant as those brought on by the Agricultural and Industrial Revolutions.

## Cybernomics

Related to the knowledge economy is what has been dubbed "**cybernomics**," or economics driven by e-commerce and other computer-based markets and products. Marketing has changed drastically with the growth of cyber communication, allowing suppliers to connect one-on-one with their customers. Other issues coming to the fore regarding cybernomics include:
- Secure online trade
- Intellectual property rights
- Rights to privacy
- Bringing developing nations into the fold

As these issues are debated and new laws and policies developed, the face of many industries continues to undergo drastic change. Many of the old ways of doing business no longer work, leaving industries scrambling to function profitably within the new system.

## Geography

Geography literally means the study of the earth. Geographers study **physical characteristics** of the earth as well as man-made borders and boundaries. They also study the **distribution of life** on the planet, such as where certain species of animals can be found or how different forms of life interact. Major elements of the study of geography include:
- Locations
- Regional characteristics
- Spatial relations
- Natural and manmade forces that change elements of the earth

These elements are studied from regional, topical, physical and human perspectives. Geography also focuses on the origins of the earth as well as the history and backgrounds of different human populations.

## Physical vs. Cultural Geography

Physical geography is the study of the physical characteristics of the earth: how they relate to each other, how they were formed, and how they develop. These characteristics include climate, land, and water, and also how they affect human population in various areas. Different landforms in combination with various climates and other conditions determine characteristics of various cultures.

**Cultural geography** is the study of how the various aspects of physical geography affect individual cultures. Cultural geography also compares various cultures: how their lifestyles and customs are affected by their geographical location, climate, and other factors, and how they interact with their environment.

## Divisions of Geographical Study and Tools Used

The four divisions of geographical study and tools used are:
- **Topical**—the study of a single feature of the earth or one specific human activity that occurs world-wide.
- **Physical**—the various physical features of the earth, how they are created, the forces that change them, and how they are related to each other and to various human activities.
- **Regional**—specific characteristics of individual places and regions.
- **Human**—how human activity affects the environment. This includes study of political, historical, social, and cultural activities.

Tools used in geographical study include special research methods like mapping, field studies, statistics, interviews, mathematics, and use of various scientific instruments.

## Important Ancient Geographers

The following are three important ancient geographers and their contributions to the study of geography:
- **Eratosthenes** lived in ancient Greek times, and mathematically calculated the circumference of the earth and the tilt of the earth's axis. He also created the first map of the world.
- **Strabo** wrote a description of the ancient world called *Geographica* in seventeen volumes.
- **Ptolemy**, primarily an astronomer, was also an experienced mapmaker. He wrote a treatise entitled *Geography*, which was used by Christopher Columbus in his travels.

## Ways Geographers Analyze Areas of Human Population

In cities, towns, or other areas where many people have settled, geographers focus on **distribution** of populations, neighborhoods, industrial areas, transportation, and other elements important to the society in question. For example, they would map out the locations of hospitals, airports, factories, police stations, schools, and housing groups. They would also make note of how these facilities are distributed in relation to the areas of habitation, such as the number of schools in a certain neighborhood, or how many grocery stores are located in a specific suburban area. Another area of study and discussion is the distribution of **towns** themselves, from widely spaced rural towns to large cities that merge into each other to form a megalopolis.

## Role of a Cartographer

A cartographer is a mapmaker. Mapmakers produce detailed illustrations of geographic areas to record where various features are located within that area. These illustrations can be compiled into maps, charts, graphs, and even globes. When constructing maps, **cartographers** must take into account the problem of **distortion**. Because the earth is round, a flat map does not accurately represent the correct proportions, especially if a very large geographical area is being depicted. Maps must be designed in such a way as to minimize this distortion and maximize accuracy. Accurately representing the earth's features on a flat surface is achieved through **projection**.

## Types of Projection Used in Creating World Maps

The three major types of projection used in creating world maps are:
- **Cylindrical projection**—this is created by wrapping the globe of the Earth in a cylindrical piece of paper, then using a light to project the globe onto the paper. The largest distortion occurs at the outermost edges.
- **Conical projection**—the paper is shaped like a cone and contacts the globe only at the cone's base. This type of projection is most useful for middle latitudes.
- **Flat-Plane projections**—also known as a Gnomonic projection, this type of map is projected onto a flat piece of paper that only touches the globe at a single point. Flat-plane projections make it possible to map out Great-Circle Routes, or the shortest route between one point and another on the globe, as a straight line.

## Specific Types of Map Projections

Four specific types of map projections that are commonly used today are:
- **Winkel tripel projection**—this is the most common projection used for world maps, since it was accepted in 1998 by the National Geographic Society as a standard. The Winkel tripel projection balances size and shape, greatly reducing distortion.
- **Robinson projection**—east and west sections of the map are less distorted, but continental shapes are somewhat inaccurate.
- **Goode homolosine projection**—sizes and shapes are accurate, but distances are not. This projection basically represents a globe that has been cut into connected sections so that it can lie flat.
- **Mercator projection**—though distortion is high, particularly in areas farther from the equator, this cylindrical projection is commonly used by seafarers.

## Major Elements of Any Map

The five major elements of any map are:
- **Title**—this tells basic information about the map, such as the area represented.
- **Legend**—also known as the key, the legend explains what symbols used on a particular map represent, such as symbols for major landmarks.
- **Grid**—this most commonly represents the Geographic Grid System, or latitude and longitude marks used to precisely locate specific locations.
- **Directions**—a compass rose or other symbol is used to indicate the cardinal directions.

- **Scale**—this shows the relation between a certain distance on the map and the actual distance. For example, one inch might represent one mile, or ten miles, or even more depending on the size of the map.

## Equal Area Maps vs. Conformal Maps

An equal area map is designed such that the proportional sizes of various areas are accurate. For example, if one land mass is one-fifth the size of another, the lines on the map will be shifted to accommodate for distortion so that the proportional size is accurate. In many maps, areas farther from the equator are greatly distorted; this type of map compensates for this phenomenon. A **conformal map** focuses on representing the correct shape of geographical areas, with less concern for comparative size.

## Consistent Scale Maps and Thematic Maps

With a consistent scale map, the same scale, such as one inch=ten miles, is used throughout the entire map. This is most often used for maps of smaller areas, as maps that cover larger areas, such as the full globe, must make allowances for distortion. Maps of very large areas often make use of more than one scale, with scales closer to the center representing a larger area than those at the edges.

A **thematic map** is constructed to show very specific information about a chosen theme. For example, a thematic map might represent political information, such as how votes were distributed in an election, or could show population distribution or climatic features.

## Relief Maps

A relief map is constructed to show details of various **elevations** across the area of the map. Higher elevations are represented by different colors than lower elevations. **Relief maps** often also show additional details, such as the overall ruggedness or smoothness of an area. Mountains would be represented as ridged and rugged, while deserts would be shown as smooth.

Elevation in relief maps can also be represented by contour lines, or lines that connect points of the same elevation. Some relief maps even feature textures, reconstructing details in a sort of miniature model.

## Geographical Features

- **Mountains** are elevated areas that measure 2,000 feet or more above sea level. Often steep and rugged, they usually occur in groups called chains or ranges. Six of the seven continents on Earth contain at least one range.
- **Hills** are of lower elevation than mountains, at about 500-2,000 feet. Hills are usually more rounded, and are found throughout every continent.
- **Plains** are large, flat areas and are usually very fertile. The majority of the Earth's population is supported by crops grown on vast plains.
- **Valleys** lie between hills and mountains. Depending on their location, their specific features can vary greatly, from fertile and habitable to rugged and inhospitable.
- **Plateaus** are elevated, but flat on top. Some plateaus are extremely dry, such as the Kenya Plateau, because surrounding mountains prevent them from receiving moisture.

- **Deserts** receive less than ten inches of rain per year. They are usually large areas, such as the Sahara Desert in Africa or the Australian Outback.
- **Deltas** occur at river mouths. Because the rivers carry sediment to the deltas, these areas are often very fertile.
- **Mesas** are flat, steep-sided mountains or hills. The term is sometimes used to refer to plateaus.
- **Basins** are areas of low elevation where rivers drain.
- **Foothills** are the transitional area between the plains and the mountains, usually consisting of hills that gradually increase in size as they approach the mountain range.
- **Marshes** and **swamps** are also lowlands, but they are very wet and largely covered in vegetation such as reeds and rushes.

### Geographical Terms Referring to Bodies of Water

- **Oceans** are the largest bodies of water on Earth. They are salt water, and cover about two-thirds of the earth's surface. The four major oceans are the Atlantic, Pacific, Indian and Arctic.
- **Seas** are generally also salt water, but are smaller than oceans and surrounded by land. Examples include the Mediterranean Sea, the Caribbean Sea, and the Caspian Sea.
- **Lakes** are bodies of freshwater found inland. Sixty percent of all lakes are located in Canada.
- **Rivers** are moving bodies of water that flow from higher elevations to lower. They usually start as rivulets or streams, and grow until they finally empty into a sea or an ocean.
- **Canals**, such as the Panama Canal and the Suez Canal, are manmade waterways connecting two large bodies of water.

### Community Development

Communities, or groups of people who settle together in a specific area, typically gather where certain conditions exists. These conditions include:
- Easy access to resources such as food, water, and raw materials
- Ability to easily transport raw materials and goods, such as access to a waterway
- Room to house a sufficient work force

People also tend to form groups with others who are similar to them. In a typical **community**, people can be found who share values, a common language, and common or similar cultural characteristics and religious beliefs. These factors will determine the overall composition of a community as it develops.

### Differences Between Cities in Various Areas of the World

Cities develop and grow as an area develops. Modern statistics show that over half of the world's people live in **cities**. That percentage is even higher in developed areas of the globe. Cities are currently growing more quickly in developing regions, and even established cities continue to experience growth throughout the world. In developing or developed areas, cities often are surrounded by a metropolitan area made up of both urban and suburban sections. In some places, cities have merged into each other and become a **megalopolis**—a single, huge city.

Cities develop differently in different areas of the world. The area available for cities to grow, as well as cultural and economic forces, drives how cities develop. For example, North American cities tend to cover wider areas. European cities tend to have better developed transportation systems. In Latin America, the richest inhabitants can be found in the city centers, while in North America wealthier inhabitants tend to live in suburban areas.

In other parts of the world, transportation and communication between cities is less developed. Recent technological innovations such as the cell phone have increased communication even in these areas. Urban areas must also maintain communication with rural areas in order to procure food, resources, and raw materials that cannot be produced within the city limits.

## Weather vs. Climate

Weather and climate are physical systems that affect geography. Though they deal with similar information, the way this information is measured and compiled is different.

**Weather** involves daily conditions in the atmosphere that affect temperature, precipitation (rain, snow, hail, or sleet), wind speed, air pressure, and other factors. Weather focuses on the short-term—what the conditions will be today, tomorrow, or over the next few days.

In contrast, **climate** aggregates information about daily and seasonal weather conditions in a region over a long period of time. The climate takes into account average monthly and yearly temperatures, average precipitation over long periods of time, and the growing season of an area. Climates are classified according to latitude, or how close they lie to the earth's equator. The three major divisions are:
- **Low Latitudes**, lying from 0 to approximately 23.5 degrees latitude
- **Middle Latitudes**, found from approximately 23.5 to 66.5 degrees
- **High Latitudes**, found from approximately 66.5 degrees to the poles

## Climates Found in the Low Latitudes

Rainforests, savannas, and deserts occur in low latitudes:
- **Rainforest** climates, near the equator, experience high average temperatures and humidity, as well as relatively high rainfall.
- **Savannas** are found on either side of the rainforest region. Mostly grasslands, they typically experience dry winters and wet summers.
- Beyond the savannas lie the **desert** regions, with hot, dry climates, sparse rainfall, and temperature fluctuations of up to fifty degrees from day to night.

## Climate Regions Found in the Middle Latitudes

The climate regions found in the middle latitudes are:
- **Mediterranean**—the Mediterranean climate occurs between 30 and 40 degrees latitude, both north and south, on the western coasts of continents. Characteristics include a year-long growing season, hot, dry summers followed by mild winters, and sparse rainfall that occurs mostly during the winter months.
- **Humid-subtropical**—humid-subtropical regions are located on southeastern coastal areas. Winds that blow in over warm ocean currents produce long summers, mild winters, and a long growing season. These areas are highly productive, and support a larger part of the earth's population than any other climate.

- **Humid-continental**—the humid continental climate produces the familiar four seasons typical of a good portion of the US. Some of the most productive farmlands in the world lie in these climates. Winters are cold, summers are hot and humid.

## Marine, Steppe, and Desert Climates

The climate regions found in the middle latitudes are:
- **Marine**—marine climates are found near water or on islands. Ocean winds help make these areas mild and rainy. Summers are cooler than humid-subtropical summers, but winters also bring milder temperatures due to the warmth of the ocean winds.
- **Steppe**—steppe climates, or prairie climates, are found far inland on large continents. Summers are hot and winters are cold, but rainfall is sparser than in continental climates.
- **Desert**—desert climates occur where steppe climates receive even less rainfall. Examples include the Gobi desert in Asia as well as desert areas of Australia and the southwestern US.

## Climates Found in the High Latitudes

The high latitudes consist of two major climate areas, the tundra and taiga:
- **Tundra** means "marshy plain." Ground is frozen throughout long, cold winters, but there is little snowfall. During the short summers, it becomes wet and marshy. Tundras are not amenable to crops, but many plants and animals have adapted to the conditions.
- **Taigas** lie south of tundra regions, and include the largest forest areas in the world, as well as swamps and marshes. Large mineral deposits exist here, as well as many animals valued for their fur. In the winter, taiga regions are colder than the tundra, and summers are hotter. The growing season is short.

A **vertical climate** exists in high mountain ranges. Increasing elevation leads to varying temperatures, growing conditions, types of vegetation and animals, and occurrence of human habitation, often encompassing elements of various other climate regions.

## Factors Affecting Climate

Because the earth is tilted, its **rotation** brings about changes in **seasons**. Regions closer to the equator, and those nearest the poles, experience very little change in seasonal temperatures. Mid-range latitudes are most likely to experience distinct seasons. Large bodies of water also affect climate. Ocean currents and wind patterns can change the climate for an area that lies in typically cold latitude, such as England, to a much more temperate climate. Mountains can affect both short-term weather and long-term climates. Some deserts occur because precipitation is stopped by the wall of a mountain range.

Over time, established **climate patterns** can shift and change. While the issue is hotly debated, it has been theorized that human activity has also led to climate change.

## Effect of Human Systems

Human Systems that Geographers Incorporate into the Study of the Earth
Human systems affect geography in the way in which they settle, form groups that grow into large-scale habitations, and even create permanent changes in the landscape. **Geographers** study movements of people, how they distribute goods among each other and to other settlements or

cultures, and how ideas grow and spread. Migrations, wars, forced relocations, and trade can all spread cultural ideas, language, goods and other practices to wide-spread areas. Some major migrations or the conquering of one people by another have significantly changed cultures throughout history. In addition, **human systems** can lead to various conflicts or alliances to control access to and the use of natural resources.

## Human Systems that Form the Basis of Cultures in North America
North America consists of 23 countries, including (in decreasing population order) the United States of America, Mexico, Canada, Guatemala, Cuba, Haiti, and the Dominican Republic. The US and Canada support similarly diverse cultures, as both were formed from groups of native races as well as large numbers of immigrants. Many **North American cultures** come from a mixture of indigenous and colonial European influences. Agriculture is important to North American countries, while service industries and technology also play a large part in the economy. On average, North America supports a high standard of living and a high level of development and supports trade with countries throughout the world.

## Human Systems that Shape South America
Including Brazil (largest in area and population), Colombia, Argentina, Venezuela, Peru, and 10 more countries or territories, **South America** is largely defined by its prevailing languages. The majority of countries in South America speak Spanish or Portuguese. Most of South America has experienced a similar history, having been originally dominated by Native cultures, conquered by European nations. The countries of South America have since gained independence, but there is a wide disparity between various countries' economic and political factors. Most South American countries rely on only one or two exports, usually agricultural, with suitable lands often controlled by rich families. Most societies in South America feature major separations between classes, both economically and socially. Challenges faced by developing South American countries include geographical limitations, economic issues, and sustainable development, including the need to preserve the existing rainforests.

## Human Systems Influencing Europe
Europe contains a wide variety of cultures, ethnic groups, physical geographical features, climates, and resources, all of which have influenced the distribution of its varied population. **Europe** in general is industrialized and developed, with cultural differences giving each individual country its own unique characteristics. Greek and Roman influences played a major role in European culture, as did Christianity. European countries spread their beliefs and cultural elements throughout the world by means of migration and colonization. They have had a significant influence on nearly every other continent in the world. While Western Europe has been largely democratic, Eastern Europe functioned under communist rule for many years. The recent formation of the European Union (EU) has increased stability and positive diplomatic relations among European nations. Like other industrialized regions, Europe is now focusing on various environmental issues.

## Human Systems that Have Shaped Russia
After numerous conflicts, Russia became a Communist state, known as the **USSR**. With the collapse of the USSR in 1991, the country has struggled in its transition to a market-driven economy. Attempts to build a workable system have led to the destruction of natural resources as well as problems with nuclear power, including accidents such as Chernobyl. To complete the transition to a market economy, Russia needs to improve its transportation and communication systems, and find a way to more efficiently use its natural resources.

The population of Russia is not distributed evenly, with three quarters of the population living west of the Ural Mountains. The people of Russia encompass over a hundred different ethnic groups. Over eighty percent of the population is ethnically Russian, and Russian is the official language of the country.

## Human Systems that Have Shaped North Africa, Southwest and Central Asia

The largely desert climate of these areas has led most population centers to rise around sources of **water**, such as the Nile River. This area is the home of the **earliest known civilizations** and the origin of Christianity, Judaism, and Islam.  After serving as the site of huge, independent civilizations in ancient times, North Africa and Southwest and Central Asia were largely parceled out as **European colonies** during the eighteenth and nineteenth centuries. The beginning of the twentieth century saw many of these countries gain their independence.  **Islam** has served as a unifying force for large portions of these areas, and many of the inhabitants speak Arabic. In spite of the arid climate, agriculture is a large business, but the most valuable resource is **oil**. Centuries of conflict throughout this area have led to ongoing political problems. These political problems have also contributed to environmental issues.

## Human Systems that Shape and Influence the Culture of Sub-Saharan Africa

South of the Sahara Desert, **Africa** is divided into a number of culturally diverse nations. The inhabitants are unevenly distributed due to geographical limitations that prevent settlement in vast areas. **AIDS** has become a major plague throughout this part of Africa, killing millions, largely due to restrictive beliefs that prevent education about the disease, as well as abject poverty and unsettled political situations that make it impossible to manage the pandemic.  The population of this area of Africa is widely diverse due to extensive **migration**. Many of the people still rely on **subsistence farming** for their welfare. Starvation and poverty are rampant due to drought and political instability. Some areas are far more stable than others due to greater availability of resources. These have been able to begin the process of **industrialization**.

## Human Systems that Determine the Cultural Makeup of South Asia

South Asia is home to one of the first human civilizations, which grew up in the **Indus River Valley**. With a great deal of disparity between rural and urban life, South Asia has much to do to improve the quality of life for its lower classes.  Two major religions, **Hinduism** and **Buddhism**, have their origins in this region. Parts of South Asia, most notably India, were subject to **British rule** for several decades, and are still working to improve independent governments and social systems. Overall, South Asia is very culturally diverse, with a wide mix of religions and languages throughout. Many individuals are **farmers**, but a growing number have found prosperity in the spread of **high-tech industries**. Industrialization is growing in South Asia, but continues to face environmental, social, religious and economic challenges.

## Human Systems Shaping the Culture of East Asia

Governments in East Asia are varied, ranging from communist to democratic governments, with some governments that mix both approaches. **Isolationism** throughout the area limited the countries' contact with other nations until the early twentieth century. The unevenly distributed population of East Asia consists of over one and a half billion people with widely diverse ethnic backgrounds, religions and languages. More residents live in **urban** areas than in **rural** areas, creating shortages of farm workers at times. Japan, Taiwan and South Korea are overall more urban, while China and Mongolia are more rural. Japan stands as the most industrial country of East Asia.  Some areas of East Asia are suffering from major environmental issues. Japan has dealt with many of these problems and now has some of the strictest environmental laws in the world.

Human Systems that Have Influenced Southeast Asia
Much of Southeast Asia was **colonized** by European countries during the eighteenth and nineteenth centuries, with the exception of Siam, now known as Thailand. All Southeast Asian countries are now independent, but the twentieth century saw numerous conflicts between **communist** and **democratic** forces.

Southeast Asia has been heavily influenced by both Buddhist and Muslim religions. Industrialization is growing, with the population moving in large numbers from rural to urban areas. Some have moved to avoid conflict, oppression, and poverty.

**Natural disasters**, including volcanoes, typhoons, and flash flooding, are fairly common in Southeast Asia, creating extensive economic damage and societal disruption.

Human Systems that Affect the Development and Culture of Australia, Oceana and Antarctica
**South Pacific** cultures originally migrated from Southeast Asia, creating hunter-gatherer or sometimes settled agricultural communities. **European** countries moved in during later centuries, seeking the plentiful natural resources of the area. Today, some South Pacific islands remain under the control of foreign governments, and culture in these areas mixes modern, industrialized society with indigenous culture. Population is unevenly distributed, largely due to the inhabitability of many parts of the South Pacific, such as the extremely hot desert areas of Australia. **Agriculture** still drives much of the economy, with **tourism** growing. **Antarctica** remains the only continent not claimed by a single country. There are no permanent human habitations in Antarctica, but scientists and explorers visit the area on a temporary basis.

**Human-Environment Interaction**

Geography also studies the ways people interact with, use, and change their **environment**. The effects, reasons, and consequences of these changes are studied, as are the ways the environment limits or influences human behavior. This kind of study can help determine the best course of action when a nation or group of people are considering making changes to the environment, such as building a dam or removing natural landscape to build or expand roads. Study of the **consequences** can help determine if these actions are manageable and how long-term, detrimental results can be mitigated.

**Physical Geography and Climates**

Physical Geography and Climate of North America
The largest amount of North America is the US and Canada, which have a similar distribution of geographical features, mountain ranges in both east and west, stretches of fertile plains through the center, and lakes and waterways. Both areas were shaped by **glaciers**, which also deposited highly fertile soil. Because they are so large, Canada and the US experience several varieties of **climate**, including continental climates with four seasons in median areas, tropical climates in the southern part of the US, and arctic climes in the far north. The remaining area of North America is comprised primarily of islands, including the Caribbean Isles and Greenland.

Physical Geography and Climate of South America
South America contains a wide variety of geographical features including high **mountains** such as the Andes, wide **plains**, and high altitude **plateaus**. The region contains numerous natural resources, but many of them have remained unused due to various obstacles, including political issues, geographic barriers, and lack of sufficient economic power. Climate zones in South America

- 40 -

are largely **tropical**, with rainforests and savannas, but vertical climate zones and grasslands also exist in places.

## Physical Geography and Climate of Europe
Europe spans a wide area with a variety of climate zones. In the east and south are **mountain** ranges, while the north is dominated by a **plains** region. The long coastline and the island nature of some countries, such as Britain, mean the climate is often warmer than other lands at similar latitudes, as the area is warmed by **ocean currents**. Many areas of western Europe have a moderate climate, while areas of the south are dominated by the classic Mediterranean climate. Europe carries a high level of natural resources. Numerous waterways help connect the inner regions with the coastal areas. Much of Europe is **industrialized**, and **agriculture** has been developed for thousands of years.

## Physical Geography and Climate of Russia
Russia's area encompasses part of Asia and Europe. From the standpoint of square footage alone, **Russia** is the largest country in the world. Due to its size, Russia encompasses a wide variety of climatic regions, including **plains**, **plateaus**, **mountains**, and **tundra**.

Russia's **climate** can be quite harsh, with rivers that are frozen most of the year, making transportation of the country's rich natural resources more difficult. Siberia, in northern Russia, is dominated by **permafrost**. Native peoples in this area still follow a hunting and gathering lifestyle, living in portable yurts and subsisting largely on herds of reindeer or caribou. Other areas include taiga with extensive, dense woods in north central Russia and more temperate steppes and grasslands in the southwest.

## Physical Geography and Climate of North Africa, Southwest, and Central Asia
This area of the world is complex in its geographical structure and climate, incorporating seas, peninsulas, rivers, mountains, and numerous other features. **Earthquakes** are common, with tectonic plates in the area remaining active. Much of the world's **oil** lies in this area. The tendency of the large rivers of North Africa, especially the Nile, to follow a set pattern of **drought** and extreme **fertility**, led people to settle there from prehistoric times. As technology has advanced, people have tamed this river, making its activity more predictable and the land around it more productive. The extremely arid nature of many other parts of this area has also led to **human intervention** such as irrigation to increase agricultural production.

## Physical Geography and Climate of the Southern Portion of Africa
South of the Sahara Desert, the high elevations and other geographical characteristics have made it very difficult for human travel or settlement to occur. The geography of the area is dominated by a series of **plateaus**. There are also mountain ranges and a large rift valley in the eastern part of the country. Contrasting the wide desert areas, sub-Saharan Africa contains numerous lakes, rivers, and world-famous waterfalls. The area has **tropical** climates, including rainforests, savannas, steppes, and desert areas. The main natural resources are minerals, including gems and water.

## Physical Geography and Climate of South Asia
The longest **alluvial plain,** a plain caused by shifting floodplains of major rivers and river systems over time, exists in South Asia. South Asia boasts three major **river systems** in the Ganges, Indus, and Brahmaputra. It also has large deposits of **minerals**, including iron ore that is in great demand internationally. South Asia holds mountains, plains, plateaus, and numerous islands. The climates range from tropical to highlands and desert areas. South Asia also experiences monsoon winds that

cause a long rainy season. Variations in climate, elevation and human activity influence agricultural production.

## Geography and Climate of East Asia

East Asia includes North and South Korea, Mongolia, China, Japan, and Taiwan. Mineral resources are plentiful but not evenly distributed throughout. The coastlines are long, and while the population is large, farmlands are sparse. As a result, the surrounding **oceans** have become a major source of sustenance. East Asia is large enough to also encompass several climate regions. **Ocean currents** provide milder climates to coastal areas, while **monsoons** provide the majority of the rainfall for the region. **Typhoons** are somewhat common, as are **earthquakes**, **volcanoes**, and **tsunamis**. The latter occur because of the tectonic plates that meet beneath the continent and remain somewhat active.

## Geography and Climate of Southeast Asia

Southeast Asia lies largely on the **equator**, and roughly half of the countries of the region are island nations. These countries include Indonesia, the Philippines, Vietnam, Thailand, Myanmar, and Malaysia (which is partially on the mainland and partially an island country). The island nations of Southeast Asia feature mountains that are considered part of the **Ring of Fire**, an area where tectonic plates remain active, leading to extensive volcanic activity as well as earthquakes and tsunamis. Southeast Asia boasts many rivers as well as abundant natural resources, including gems, fossil fuels and minerals. There are basically two seasons—wet and dry. The wet season arrives with the **monsoons**. In general, Southeast Asia consists of **tropical rainforest climates**, but there are some mountain areas and tropical savannas.

## Geography and Climate of Australia, Oceania and Antarctica

In the far southern hemisphere of the globe, Australia and Oceania present their own climatic combinations. **Australia**, the only island on earth that is also a continent, has extensive deserts as well as mountains and lowlands. The economy is driven by agriculture, including ranches and farms, and minerals. While the steppes bordering extremely arid inland areas are suitable for livestock, only the coastal areas receive sufficient rainfall for crops without using irrigation. **Oceania** refers to over 10,000 Pacific islands created by volcanic activity. Most of these have tropical climates with wet and dry seasons. **New Zealand**, Australia's nearest neighbor, boasts rich forests as well as mountain ranges and relatively moderate temperatures, including rainfall throughout the year. **Antarctica** is covered with ice. Its major resource consists of scientific information. It supports some wildlife, such as penguins, and little vegetation, mostly mosses or lichens.

## Theory of Plate Tectonics

According to the geological theory of plate tectonics, the earth's crust is made up of ten major and several minor **tectonic plates**. These plates are the solid areas of the crust. They float on top of the earth's mantle, which is made up of molten rock. Because the plates float on this liquid component of the earth's crust, they move, creating major changes in the earth's surface. These changes can happen very slowly over a long time period, such as in continental drift, or rapidly, such as when earthquakes occur. **Interaction** between the different continental plates can create mountain ranges, volcanic activity, major earthquakes, and deep rifts.

<u>Types of Plate Boundaries</u>

Plate tectonics defines three types of plate boundaries, determined by the way in which the edges of the plates interact. These **plate boundaries** are:

- **Convergent boundaries**—the bordering plates move toward one another. When they collide directly, this is known as continental collision, which can create very large, high mountain ranges such as the Himalayas and the Andes. If one plate slides under the other, this is called subduction. Subduction can lead to intense volcanic activity. One example is the Ring of Fire that lies along the northern Pacific coastlines.
- **Divergent boundaries**—plates move away from each other. This movement leads to rifts such as the Mid-Atlantic Ridge and east Africa's Great Rift Valley.
- **Transform boundaries**—plate boundaries slide in opposite directions against each other. Intense pressure builds up along transform boundaries as the plates grind along each other's edges, leading to earthquakes. Many major fault lines, including the San Andreas Fault, lie along transform boundaries.

## Erosion, Weathering, Transportation, and Deposition

Erosion involves movement of any loose material on the earth's surface. This can include soil, sand, or rock fragments. These loose fragments can be displaced by natural forces such as wind, water, ice, plant cover, and human factors. **Mechanical erosion** occurs due to natural forces. **Chemical erosion** occurs as a result of human intervention and activities. **Weathering** occurs when atmospheric elements affect the earth's surface. Water, heat, ice, and pressure all lead to weathering. **Transportation** refers to loose material being moved by wind, water or ice. Glacial movement, for example, carries everything from pebbles to boulders, sometimes over long distances. **Deposition** is the result of transportation. When material is transported, it is eventually deposited, and builds up to create formations like moraines and sand dunes.

## Effects of Human Interaction and Conflict on Geographical Boundaries

Human societies and their interaction have led to divisions of territories into **countries** and various other subdivisions. While these divisions are at their root artificial, they are important to geographers in the discussion of interactions of various populations.

**Geographical divisions** often occur through conflict between different human populations. The reasons behind these divisions include:

- Control of resources
- Control of important trade routes
- Control of populations

**Conflict** often occurs due to religious, political, language, or race differences. Natural resources are finite and so often lead to conflict over how they are distributed among populations.

## State Sovereignty

State sovereignty recognizes the division of geographical areas into areas controlled by various governments or groups of people. These groups control not only the territory, but also all its natural resources and the inhabitants of the area. The entire planet Earth is divided into **political** or **administratively sovereign areas** recognized to be controlled by a particular government with the exception of the continent of Antarctica.

## Alliances

Alliances form between different countries based on similar interests, political goals, cultural values, or military issues. Six existing **international alliances** include:
- North Atlantic Treaty Organization (NATO)
- Common Market
- European Union (EU)
- United Nations (UN)
- Caribbean Community
- Council of Arab Economic Unity

In addition, very large **companies** and **multi-national corporations** can create alliances and various kinds of competition based on the need to control resources, production, and the overall marketplace.

## Ways Agricultural Revolution Changed Society

The agricultural revolution began approximately six thousand years ago when the **plow** was invented in **Mesopotamia**. Using a plow drawn by animals, people were able to cultivate crops in large quantities rather than gathering available seeds and grains and planting them by hand. Because large-scale agriculture was labor intensive, this led to the development of stable communities where people gathered to make farming possible. As **stable farming communities** replaced groups of nomadic hunter-gatherers, human society underwent profound changes. Societies became dependent on limited numbers of crops as well as subject to the vagaries of weather. Trading livestock and surplus agricultural output led to the growth of large-scale **commerce** and **trade routes**.

## Ways Human Populations Modify Their Surrounding Environment

The agricultural revolution led human societies to begin changing their surroundings in order to accommodate their needs for shelter and room to cultivate food and to provide for domestic animals. Clearing ground for crops, redirecting waterways for irrigation purposes, and building permanent settlements all create major changes in the **environment**. Large-scale agriculture can lead to loose topsoil and damaging erosion. Building large cities leads to degraded air quality, water pollution from energy consumption, and many other side effects that can severely damage the environment. Recently, many countries have taken action by passing laws to **reduce human impact** on the environment and reduce the potentially damaging side effects. This is called **environmental policy**.

## Ecology

Ecology is the study of the way living creatures interact with their environment. **Biogeography** explores the way physical features of the earth affect living creatures.
**Ecology** bases its studies on three different levels of the environment:
- **Ecosystem**—this is a specific physical environment and all the organisms that live there.
- **Biome**—this is a group of ecosystems, usually consisting of a large area with similar flora and fauna as well as similar climate and soil. Examples of biomes include deserts, tropical rain forests, taigas, and tundra.

- **Habitat**—this is an area in which a specific species usually lives. The habitat includes the necessary soil, water, and resources for that particular species, as well as predators and other species that compete for the same resources.

## Types of Interactions Occurring Between Species in an Individual Habitat

Different interactions occur among species and members of single species within a habitat. These **interactions** fall into three categories:
- **Competition** — competition occurs when different animals, either of the same species or of different species, compete for the same resources. Robins can compete with other robins for available food, but other insectivores also compete for these same resources.
- **Predation**— predation occurs when one species depends on the other species for food, such as a fox who subsists on small mammals.
- **Symbiosis** — symbiosis occurs when two different species exist in the same environment without negatively affecting each other. Some symbiotic relationships are beneficial to one or both organisms without harm occurring to either.

## Importance of an Organism's Ability to Adapt

If a species is relocated from one habitat to another, it must **adapt** in order to survive. Some species are more capable of adapting than others. Those that cannot adapt will not survive. There are different ways a creature can adapt, including behavior modification as well as structure or physiological changes. Adaptation is also vital if an organism's environment changes around it. Although the creature has not been relocated, it finds itself in a new environment that requires changes in order to survive. The more readily an organism can adapt, the more likely it is to survive. The almost infinite ability of **humans** to adapt is a major reason why they are able to survive in almost any habitat in any area of the world.

## Biodiversity

Biodiversity refers to the variety of habitats that exist on the planet, as well as the variety of organisms that can exist within these habitats. A greater level of **biodiversity** makes it more likely that an individual habitat will flourish along with the species that depend upon it. Changes in habitat, including climate change, human intervention, or other factors, can reduce biodiversity by causing the extinction of certain species.

## Importance of Socialization to Individuals Within a Specific Culture

Individuals learn how to function within a specific culture, group, or society via a process called **socialization**. Social contact with other human beings is vitally important to early development so that children can grow up to function in society as expected.

During the early years, children receive socialization from their families, siblings, peers, schoolmates, and from exposure to mass media when applicable. Observing the behavior of others and adapting it to their own use helps children learn to interact with others. This process continues throughout life as individuals learn to adapt to various situations and interact with new groups.

## Processes Bringing About Cultural Change and Traits that Appear in All Cultures

Three major processes bring about the majority of changes in a culture:
- **Discovery**—finding things that already exist, such as fire, a major cultural transformer
- **Invention**—creating new equipment, machinery, etc., that changes the way tasks are accomplished
- **Diffusion**—borrowing elements from other cultures

Over 70 **traits** have been identified that are found in nearly every culture to some level. These traits can be divided into four categories that determine the basic structure, mores, norms, and other characteristics of a culture.
- Language and cognition
- Society
- Myth, ritual, and aesthetics
- Technology

## Culture

"Culture" refers to all learned human behaviors and behavioral patterns and is made up of:
- **Cultural universals**—traits shared by all human beings such as language
- **Culture**—all traditions that define a society
- **Subculture**—groups within a culture that share specific traits

While culture serves as a survival mechanism by bringing people together in groups and helping individuals identify with each other, it also undergoes frequent and sometimes profound **change** as groups respond to new technologies, knowledge, or contact with other cultures.

## Characteristics and Importance of Religion in an Anthropological Sense

Strictly defined, **religion** consists of a belief system and usually a set of rituals involving worship of a supernatural force or forces that have some effect on both everyday life and the overall structure and functioning of the world around us. Religion provides meaning and explanation for various life events and profoundly affects a culture's **worldviews**. Religion provides emotional support for individuals and a sense of **community** within a group that has shared religious views. Religious organization also provides structured sets of **moral norms** and motivation to abide by these norms and rules.

Increased **secularization**, particularly in developed countries, has reduced the role of religion in everyday life, leading individuals to find other systems to fill these basic human needs.

## Behaviorism

**John B. Watson**, an American, developed the idea of **behaviorism**. In his theory, growth, learning, and training would always win out over any possible inborn tendencies. He believed that any person, regardless of origin, could learn to perform any type of art, craft or enterprise with sufficient training and experience.

## Science of Sociology

Sociology is a scientific discipline that focuses on the study of societies. Human societies are made up of institutions, groups, and finally individuals. How all these levels of organization **interact** is the major interest of sociologists. The way individuals organize themselves, how they interact with each other, and the attitudes and beliefs different groups develop, all define those groups' cultural backgrounds. Groups of people in the same geographical area often develop similar organizational structures, beliefs and attitudes.

## Major Study Areas Covered by Sociology

The five major study areas covered by sociology are:
- **Population studies**—these studies involve observing social patterns of groups of people who live in the same area.
- **Social behaviors**—sociology studies how general behaviors change over time, as well as attitudes such as morale, need for conformity, and other elements of social interaction.
- **Cultural influences**—the influences of culture on social groups include art, religion, language, and overall knowledge and learning.
- **Social change**—this involves the ways societies change over time, including major events such as wars and revolutions, or the way technology changes how people interact.
- **Social institutions**—large groups of people are organized to fit specific niches in society, such as churches, hospitals, government, businesses, and schools. These organizations change over time and according to the overall needs and beliefs of an individual society.

## How Sociologists Gather and Test Data

The three major methods of gathering data for sociological studies are:
- **Surveys**—gathering information via direct questioning of members of the social group being studied
- **Controlled experiments**—performing experiments that change an element of society
- **Field observations**—living among members of a particular group or culture and observing how they interact and live their everyday lives

## Major Classifications of Social Groups

Social groups are defined based on how they come into being, how they develop, and how they interact with wider society. The five major classifications are:
- **Primary groups**—focused on members' need for support, such as a family or friend grouping
- **Secondary groups**—form around the need to complete a task
- **Reference groups**—help form an individual's identity
- **In-groups and out-groups**—oppose each other or exclude members of other groups
- **Social networks**—provide multiple links to an often large number of other individuals

## Major Types of Social Interaction

Five main forms of social interaction help define social groups:
- Cooperation
- Coercion

- 47 -

- Conflict
- Conformity
- Social exchange

All of these elements can bring a group into existence, break it apart, or transform it.

## Major Social Institutions that Characterize and Meet the Needs of Any Society

Six major social institutions that characterize and meet the needs of any society are:
- **Family**—this is the basic unit of any society and the most important social institution in all sociological study.
- **Education**—in many societies, the values and norms of culture are communicated through institutionalized education as well as via the family.
- **Political institutions**—political institutions in a society determine the distribution of power.
- **Economic institutions**—these institutions determine distribution of wealth.
- **Religion**—this provides mores and beliefs that help unify a culture. Unfortunately many religions also function in an in-group/out-group capacity.
- **Sport**—this reflects values of society, promotes unity, and provides an outlet for aggression.

## Various Patterns Used by Sociologists to Define Relationships Involving Race and Ethnicity

In general, relationships within cultures involving race and ethnicity are defined by either assimilation or conflict. **Assimilation** in the US can involve:
- **Anglo-conformity**—immigrants and racial minorities conform to the expectations of Anglo-American society, whether by choice, necessity, or force.
- **Cultural pluralism**—this involves acceptance of varieties of racial and ethnic groups.
- **Accommodation**—this is mutual adaptation between majority and minority groups.
- **Melting pot**—the mixing together of various ethnic groups will bring about a new cultural group.

Patterns of **conflict** include:
- **Population transfer**—one group is required or forced to leave by another group.
- **Subjugation**—one group exercises control over the other.
- **Genocide**—one group slaughters another.

## Ways Gender and Age Lead to Discrimination

In spite of legislation, education, and other attempts to bring about a higher level of equality, **discrimination** still exists against women and the elderly, particularly as involves law, politics and economic standing. Discrimination against **women** is particularly profound in most developing countries. It is believed that increasing the standing of women in a society is a major element in increasing the overall livelihood of that society.

While some societies value the **elderly** for their knowledge and experience, others discriminate against older people because of their decreased physical ability and ability to contribute economically. In the US, the poverty level for the elderly still stands at about ten percent. As lifespan increases, all societies must find a way to accommodate the needs of the elderly population.

## Importance of Auguste Comte

Auguste Comte, a French philosopher, first used the term "**sociology**" to describe the study of human organizations and culture. His major theory was **positivism**. Positivism relies entirely on physical and sensory data to describe and evaluate human experience, completely discounting anything metaphysical. **Social behavior**, according to Comte, could be measured scientifically, as could major events that occurred in different populations. Comte is considered to be the first sociologist in the Western world.

## Influence of Emile Durkheim on Sociology and Sociological Study

Through Durkheim's efforts, sociology eventually came to be considered a discipline in major universities. Heavily influenced by Comte's views of positivism, Durkheim felt the larger world was influenced by group beliefs, attitudes, and cultural aspects rather than by individuals. He performed in-depth studies on the cause of higher suicide rates among certain social groups. In the course of this study, he discussed **anomie**, a condition when people are affected by larger changes in society, such as unemployment or alienation of social groups, and receive little moral guidance from society.

## Philosophy of Karl Marx and Friedrich Engels

According to Marx and Engels, society worldwide could be boiled down to a constant struggle between **classes**. This socioeconomic battle, as explained in *The Communist Manifesto*, would eventually lead to a revolution by the working class, since work itself is a social organization that involves large groups of people

## Herbert Spencer

Herbert Spencer is credited with the idea known as **Social Darwinism**. Though he and Darwin were technically rivals, Spencer applied Darwin's idea of "**survival of the fittest**" (a term actually coined by Spencer) to the way society develops. According to Spencer, **competition** is the major driving force behind the development and changes inherent in human society.

## Max Weber

**Weber's** major thesis stated that the differing **religions** of East and West led to differences in societal development. Weber believed **Protestantism** as a religion influenced the development of **capitalism** in the West. He also stated that the organization of the state felt **violence** was a legitimate means of protecting citizenry or enforcing rule. Police action, military action, and violence of individuals against each other in order to protect themselves or property demonstrate the state's propensity to solve problems through violence.

## Science of Anthropology

While archeology studies the physical remains of populations, **anthropology** in contrast studies human culture, its development, and how various cultural groups are similar or different. Anthropologists often engage in direct study of cultures by living among them, observing and participating in everyday activities. This is referred to as "**participant observation**." Anthropologists also perform cross-cultural and comparative research.

Anthropology can be divided into four major areas of study. Each one addresses a slightly different approach to culture and how it affects human beings, as well as how culture develops over time:

- **Archeology**—studies materials and physical items left behind by human settlements
- **Social-cultural anthropology**—focuses on cultural standards, beliefs, values and norms
- **Biological anthropology**—studies specific genetic characteristics of different populations
- **Linguistics**—studies the development of languages over time

## Subsistence Patterns and Its Major Classifications

The term "subsistence pattern" refers to ways in which societies obtain the necessities of life such as food and shelter. The **subsistence pattern** of a society often directly correlates to its economy, population size, political systems, and overall technological development. Certain subsistence patterns can only support lower levels of societal development, while others can support a much more developed culture. The four major subsistence patterns are:

- **Foraging**—the hunter-gatherer lifestyle
- **Pastoralism**—herding
- **Horticulture**—small-scale farming
- **Intensive agriculture**—large-scale farming

Hunter-gatherer societies by nature are nomadic and do not tend to support highly developed cultures. Intensive agriculture, in contrast, can support a large population to a high subsistence level, allowing for the development of a sophisticated, modern culture.

## Margaret Mead

Margaret Mead studied sexual beliefs and norms among **South Pacific** and **Southeast Asian** cultures. She acquired a Ph.D. from Columbia University, and her work popularized sociology, bringing it to the attention of a wide number of people. She also studied how children were treated and brought up in different cultures, and how breastfeeding was viewed in different population groups. Among other works, she wrote a book called *Coming of Age in Samoa*, about the culture of these Pacific Islanders.

## Mary and Louis Leakey and Discoveries at Olduvai Gorge

The Leakeys made major discoveries regarding the **origin of the human species** during their excavations in Olduvai Gorge in Tanzania, Africa, excavating wide varieties of stone tools and other artifacts dating back as far as two million years. Mary Leakey discovered footprints of **Laetoli** and developed a system to classify early human tools. The Leakeys also discovered prehistoric remains of **humans**, including early humans dating to nearly four million years ago, fifteen new species, and one new genus of early human ancestors. They also discovered the first fossil ape skull, and only three similar specimens exist to this day. Their findings fundamentally changed theories regarding development and evolution of ancient humans.

## Psychology

Psychology studies **human behavior** and how the **mind** works. Some psychologists pursue scientific psychology, while others focus on applied psychology. Psychology correlates human behavior and can make use of this data to predict behavior or determine why a particular behavior has occurred. Psychologists also help work with people who have specific problems with relationships or with how they perceive the world. By observing patterns and recording them in detail, psychologists can apply these patterns to predictions about human behavior in individuals, groups, cultures, and even countries.

## Techniques Used by Psychologists in Research

Psychological researchers study their discipline in various ways. Based on what they are studying, they generally use one of the following methods:
- **Naturalistic observation**—much as with sociological study, psychologists observe people and their natural behavior without interfering.
- **Survey method**—surveys are distributed among a wide range of people and the answers are correlated.
- **Case studies**—specific individuals or groups are studied in depth over a period of time, sometimes for many years.
- **Experimental method**—this involves experimental and control groups and use of specific experiments to prove or disprove a theory.
- **Correlational design**—this is concerned with relationships between variables, such as whether one factor causes or influences another.

## Importance of Aristotle to the Science of Psychology

Aristotle is often cited as founding the science of **psychology** through his overall interest in the working of the human mind. His beliefs stated that the mind was part of the body, while the psyche functioned as a receiver of knowledge. He felt psychology's major focus was to uncover the soul. Later philosophers and scientists built on these ideas to eventually develop the modern science of psychology.

## Nativism

Nativism is a theory that states that there is a certain **body of knowledge** all people are born with. This knowledge requires no learning or experience on the part of the individual. **René Descartes**, a French philosopher, developed this concept. He believed the body and mind affected each other profoundly, largely because they are separate from each other. The physical site of this interaction took place in the **pineal gland** (a small gland in the brain), according to his theory. Descartes developed several theories in the fields of philosophy and psychology that are still studied in modern universities.

## Empiricism

Empiricism is in direct opposition to Descartes' theory of nativism. Nativism states that people are born with a certain body of knowledge that they do not have to learn. **Empiricism** theorizes that all knowledge is acquired through **life experience**, impressing itself on a mind and brain that are **blank** at the time of birth. Major proponents of empiricism were Thomas Hobbes, John Locke, David Hume and George Berkeley.

## Johannes P. Muller, Hermann L.F. von Hemholtz, William James and William Wundt

Johannes P. Müller and Hermann L.F. von Helmholtz conducted scientific, organized studies of sensation and perception. As the first psychologists to attempt this kind of study, they showed that it was possible to study actual physical processes that work to produce mental activity.

**William James** was the founder of the world's first psychology laboratory. **Wilhelm Wundt**, a student of Helmholtz, published the first experimental psychology journal and is known as the father of modern psychology. Together, James and Wundt helped bring psychology into its own, separating it from philosophy. The method of psychological study called introspection grew out of their work.

## Sigmund Freud

An Austrian doctor, Freud developed a number of theories regarding human mental processes and behavior. He believed the **subconscious** to hold numerous repressed experiences and feelings that drive behavior without the individual's awareness, and that these subconscious motivators could lead to severe personality problems and disorders. He particularly stressed sexual desire as a motivating force. Freud developed the method of **psychoanalysis** to help discover the hidden impulses driving individual behavior. Freud's psychoanalytic theory proposed three major components to an individual's psychological makeup:
- **Id**—driven by instinct and basic drives
- **Ego**—most conscious and producing self-awareness
- **Superego**—strives for perfection and appropriate behavior

The **ego** acts as mediator between the **id** and **superego**, which function in opposition to each other.

## Carl Jung

A student of Freud, Jung eventually developed different theories regarding the workings of the human mind. With an intense interest in both Eastern and Western philosophy, he incorporated ideas from both into his psychological explorations. He developed the theories of **extroversion** and **introversion**, as well as proposing the existence of the **collective unconscious** and the occurrence of **synchronicity**.

## Ivan Pavlov and B.F. Skinner

Ivan Pavlov and B.F. Skinner both built on Watson's theories of behaviorism. This work came about largely as a counter to the growing importance of introspective techniques to psychological study. Believing **environment** strongly influenced individual behavior, Pavlov and Skinner searched for connections between outside stimuli and behavioral patterns. Pavlov's experiments proved the existence of **conditioned response**. His most famous experiment conditioned dogs to salivate at the sound of a ringing bell. Skinner went on to build further on these ideas, developing the "Skinner box," a device used to develop and study conditioned response in rats.

## Gestalt Psychology, Social Psychology, and Modern Psychology

Gestalt psychology is a theory developed by **Max Wertheimer**. In **Gestalt theory**, events are not considered individually, but as part of a larger pattern. **Social psychology** is the study of how social conditions affect individuals. **Modern psychology**, as it has developed, combines earlier schools of psychology, including Freudian, Jungian, behaviorism, cognitive, humanistic, and stimulus-response theories.

## Divisions of the Human Lifespan

Developmental psychologists divide the human lifespan into stages, and list certain developmental milestones that generally take place during these stages:

- **Infancy and childhood**—this is the most rapid period of human development, during which the child learns to experience its world, relate to other people, and perform tasks necessary to function in its native culture. Debate exists as to which characteristics are inborn and which are learned.
- **Adolescence**—this period represents the shift from child to adult. Changes are rapid and can involve major physical and emotional shifts.
- **Adulthood**—individuals take on new responsibilities, become self-sufficient, and often form their own families and other social networks.
- **Old age**—priorities shift again as children become adults and no longer require support and supervision.

## Types of Learning

Psychologists define learning as a **permanent change in behavior**. Learning is divided into three basic categories, based on how the behavioral change is acquired:

1. **Classical conditioning**—this is a learning process in which a specific stimulus is associated with a specific response over time.
2. **Operant conditioning**—this is a learning process in which behavior is punished or rewarded, leading to a desired long-term behavior.
3. **Social learning**—this refers to learning based on observation of others and modeling others' behavior.

These three learning processes work together to produce the wide variety of human behavior.

## Factors Involved in Social Psychology and Effects on Various Groups of People

Social psychology studies how people **interact** as well as why and how they decide whom to interact with. The ways people react with each other are defined in several ways, including:

- **Social perception**—this describes how we perceive others and their behavior as we make judgments based on our own experiences and prejudices.
- **Personal relationships**—close relationships develop among people for various reasons, including the desire to reproduce and form a family unit.
- **Group behavior**—people gather into groups with similar beliefs, needs, or other characteristics. Sometimes group behavior differs greatly from behavior that would be practiced by individuals.
- **Attitudes**—individual attitudes toward others develop over time based on individual history, experience, knowledge, and other factors. Attitudes can change over time, but some are deeply ingrained and can lead to prejudice.

# Historical Concepts and World History

## Different Periods of Prehistory

Prehistory is the period of human history before writing was developed. The three major periods of prehistory are:
- **Lower Paleolithic**—Humans used crude tools.
- **Upper Paleolithic**—Humans began to develop a wider variety of tools. These tools were better made and more specialized. They also began to wear clothes, organize in groups with definite social structures, and to practice art. Most lived in caves during this time period.
- **Neolithic**—Social structures became even more complex, including growth of a sense of family and the ideas of religion and government. Humans learned to domesticate animals and produce crops, build houses, start fires with friction tools, and to knit, spin and weave.

## Anthropology

Anthropology is the study of human culture. Anthropologists study groups of humans, how they relate to each other, and the similarities and differences between these different groups and cultures. Anthropological research takes two approaches: **cross-cultural research** and **comparative research**. Most anthropologists work by living among different cultures and participating in those cultures in order to learn about them.
There are four major **divisions** within anthropology:
- Biological anthropology
- Cultural anthropology
- Linguistic anthropology
- Archaeology

## Science of Archeology

Archeology studies past human cultures by evaluating what they leave behind. This can include bones, buildings, art, tools, pottery, graves, and even trash. Archeologists maintain detailed notes and records of their findings and use special tools to evaluate what they find. Photographs, notes, maps, artifacts, and surveys of the area can all contribute to evaluation of an archeological site. By studying all these elements of numerous archeological sites, scientists have been able to theorize that humans or near-humans have existed for about 600,000 years. Before that, more primitive humans are believed to have appeared about one million years ago. These humans eventually developed into **Cro-Magnon man**, and then **Homo sapiens**, or modern man.

## Human Development from the Lower Paleolithic to the Iron Age

Human development has been divided into several phases:
- **Lower Paleolithic or Early Stone Age**, beginning two to three million years ago—early humans used tools like needles, hatchets, awls, and cutting tools.
- **Middle Paleolithic or Middle Stone Age**, beginning approximately 300,000 BCE—sophisticated stone tools were developed, along with hunting, gathering, and ritual practices.
- **Upper Paleolithic or Late Stone Age**, beginning approximately 40,000 BCE—including the Mesolithic and Neolithic eras, textiles and pottery are developed. Humans of this era

discovered the wheel, began to practice agriculture, made polished tools, and had some domesticated animals.
- **Bronze Age**, beginning in approximately 3,000 BCE—metals are discovered and the first civilizations emerge as humans become more technologically advanced.
- **Iron Age**, beginning in 1,200 to 1,000 BCE—metal tools replace stone tools as humans develop knowledge of smelting.

## Requirements for Civilization and the Earliest Civilizations

Civilizations are defined as having the following characteristics:
- Use of metal to make weapons and tools
- Written language
- A defined territorial state
- A calendar

The **earliest civilizations** developed in river valleys where reliable, fertile land was easily found, including:
- The Nile River Valley in Egypt
- Mesopotamia
- The Indus Valley
- Hwang Ho in China

The very earliest civilizations developed in the **Tigris-Euphrates valley** in Mesopotamia, which is now part of Iraq, and in Egypt's **Nile valley**. These civilizations arose between 5,000 and 3,000 BCE The area where these civilizations grew is known as the Fertile Crescent. Geography and the availability of water made large-scale human habitation possible.

## Importance of Rivers and Water to the Growth of Early Civilizations

The earliest civilizations are also referred to as **fluvial civilizations** because they were founded near rivers. Rivers and the water they provide were vital to these early groupings, offering:
- Water for drinking, cultivating crops, and caring for domesticated animals
- A gathering place for wild animals that could be hunted
- Rich soil deposits as a result of regular flooding

**Irrigation techniques** helped direct water where it was most needed, to sustain herds of domestic animals and to nourish crops of increasing size and quality.

## Fertile Crescent

**James Breasted**, an archeologist from the University of Chicago, popularized the term "**Fertile Crescent**" to describe the area in the Near East where the earliest civilizations arose. The region includes modern day Iraq, Syria, Lebanon, Israel, Palestine, and Jordan. It is bordered on the south by the Syrian and Arabian Deserts, the west by the Mediterranean Sea, and to the north and east by the Taurus and Zagros Mountains respectively. This area not only provided the raw materials for the development of increasingly advanced civilizations, but also saw waves of migration and invasion, leading to the earliest wars and genocides as groups conquered and absorbed each other's cultures and inhabitants.

**Accomplishments of the Egyptian, Sumerian, Babylonian and Assyrian Cultures**

The **Egyptians** were one of the most advanced ancient cultures, having developed construction methods to build the great pyramids, as well as a form of writing known as hieroglyphics. Their religion was highly developed and complex, and included advanced techniques for the preservation of bodies after death. They also made paper by processing papyrus, a plant commonly found along the Nile, invented the decimal system, devised a solar calendar, and advanced overall knowledge of mathematics.

> ➢ **Review Video:** Egyptians
> *Visit mometrix.com/academy and enter Code:* **939880**

The **Sumerians** were the first to invent the wheel, and also brought irrigation systems into use. Their cuneiform writing was simpler than Egyptian hieroglyphs, and they developed the timekeeping system we still use today.

> ➢ **Review Video:** Early Mesopotamia: The Sumerians
> *Visit mometrix.com/academy and enter Code:* **939880**

The **Babylonians** are best known for the Code of Hammurabi, an advanced law code.

> ➢ **Review Video:** Early Mesopotamia: The Babylonians
> *Visit mometrix.com/academy and enter Code:* **340325**

The **Assyrians** developed horse-drawn chariots and an organized military.

**Accomplishments of the Hebrew, Persian, Minoan, and Mycenaean cultures**

The **Hebrew** or ancient Israelite culture developed the monotheistic religion that eventually developed into modern Judaism and Christianity.

The **Persians** were conquerors, but those they conquered were allowed to keep their own laws, customs, and religious traditions rather than being forced to accept those of their conquerors. They also developed an alphabet and practiced Zoroastrianism and Mithraism, religions that have influenced modern religious practice.

The **Minoans** used a syllabic writing system and built large, colorful palaces. These ornate buildings included sewage systems, running water, bathtubs, and even flushing toilets. Their script, known as Linear A, has yet to be deciphered.

The **Mycenaeans** practiced a religion that grew into the Greek pantheon, worshipping Zeus and other Olympian gods. They developed Linear B, a writing system used to write the earliest known form of Greek.

**Phoenicians and Early Culture in India and Ancient China**

Skilled seafarers and navigators, the **Phoenicians** used the stars to navigate their ships at night. They developed a purple dye that was in great demand in the ancient world, and worked with glass and metals. They also devised a phonetic alphabet, using symbols to represent individual sounds rather than whole words or syllables.

In the **Indus Valley**, an urban civilization arose in what is now India. These ancient humans developed the concept of zero in mathematics, practiced an early form of the Hindu religion, and developed the caste system which is still prevalent in India today. Archeologists are still uncovering information about this highly developed ancient civilization.

In ancient **China**, human civilization developed along the **Yangtze River**. These people produced silk, grew millet, and made pottery, including Longshan black pottery.

### Civilizations of Mesopotamia

The major civilizations of Mesopotamia, in what is now called the **Middle East**, were:
- Sumerians
- Amorites
- Hittites
- Assyrians
- Chaldeans
- Persians

These cultures controlled different areas of Mesopotamia during various time periods, but were similar in that they were **autocratic**: a single ruler served as the head of the government and often was the main religious ruler as well. These rulers were often tyrannical, militaristic leaders who controlled all aspects of life, including law, trade, and religious activity. Portions of the legacies of these civilizations remain in cultures today. These include mythologies, religious systems, mathematical innovations and even elements of various languages.

### Sumerians

Sumer, located in the southern part of Mesopotamia, consisted of a dozen **city-states**. Each city-state had its own gods, and the leader of each city-state also served as the high priest. Cultural legacies of Sumer include:
- The invention of writing
- Invention of the wheel
- The first library—established in Assyria by Ashurbanipal
- The Hanging Gardens of Babylon—one of the Seven Wonders of the Ancient World
- First written laws—Ur-Nammu's Codes and the Codes of Hammurabi
- The *Epic of Gilgamesh*—the first recorded epic story

### Kushites

Kush, or Cush, was located in Nubia, south of ancient Egypt, and the earliest existing records of this civilization were found in Egyptian texts. At one time, Kush was the largest empire on the Nile River, ruling not only Nubia but Upper and Lower Egypt as well.

In Neolithic times, Kushites lived in villages, with buildings made of mud bricks. They were settled rather than nomadic, and practiced hunting and fishing, cultivated grain, and also herded cattle. **Kerma**, the capital, was a major center of trade.

Kush determined leadership through **matrilineal descent** of their kings, as did Egypt. Their heads of state, the Kandake or Kentake, were female. Their polytheistic religion included the primary Egyptian gods as well as regional gods, including a lion-headed god, which is commonly found in African cultures.

Archeological evidence indicates the Kushites were a mix of Mediterranean and Negroid peoples. Kush was conquered by the **Aksumite Empire** in the 4th century CE.

### Minoans

The Minoans lived on the island of Crete, just off the coast of Greece. This civilization reigned from approximately 4000 to 1400 BCE and is considered to be the first advanced civilization in Europe. The Minoans developed writing systems known to linguists as **Linear A** and **Linear B**. Linear A has not yet been translated; Linear B evolved into classical Greek script. "Minoans" is not the name they used for themselves, but is instead a variation on the name of King Minos, a king in Greek mythology believed by some to have been a denizen of Crete. The Minoan civilization subsisted on trade, and their way of life was often disrupted by earthquakes and volcanoes. Much is still unknown about the Minoans, and archeologists continue to study their architecture and archeological remains. The Minoan culture eventually fell to Greek invaders and was supplanted by the **Mycenaean civilization**.

### Ancient India

The civilizations of ancient India gave rise to both **Hinduism** and **Buddhism**, major world religions that have influenced countries far from their place of origin. Practices such as yoga, increasingly popular in the West, can trace their roots to these earliest Indian civilizations, and the poses are still formally referred to by Sanskrit names. Literature from ancient India includes the *Mahabharata* containing the *Bhagavad Gita*, the *Ramayana*, *Arthashastra*, and the *Vedas*, a collection of sacred texts. Indo-European languages, including English, find their beginnings in these ancient cultures. Ancient Indo-Aryan languages such as Sanskrit are still used in some formal Hindu practices.

### Earliest Civilizations in China

Many historians believe **Chinese civilization** is the oldest uninterrupted civilization in the world. The **Neolithic age** in China goes back to 10,000 BCE, with agriculture in China beginning as early as 5,000 BCE. Their system of writing dates to 1,500 BCE. The Yellow River served as the center for the earliest Chinese settlements. In Ningxia, in northwest China, there are carvings on cliffs that date back to the Paleolithic Period, indicating the extreme antiquity of Chinese culture. Literature from ancient China includes Confucius' *Analects*, the *Tao Te Ching*, and a variety of poetry.

### Ancient Cultures in the Americas

Less is known of ancient American civilizations since less was left behind. Some of the more well-known cultures include:
- The **Norte Chico civilization** in Peru, an agricultural society of up to 30 individual communities, existed over 5,000 years ago. This culture is also known as the Caral-Supe civilization, and is the oldest known civilization in the Americas.

- The **Anasazi**, or Ancestral Pueblo People, lived in what is now the southwestern United States. Emerging about 1200 BCE, the Anasazi built complex adobe dwellings and were the forerunners of later Pueblo Indian cultures.
- The **Maya** emerged in southern Mexico and northern Central America as early as 2,600 BCE They developed a written language and a complex calendar.

> ➢ **Review Video:** American Civilizations: Early Cultures
> Visit **mometrix.com/academy** and enter **Code**: **575452**

> ➢ **Review Video:** American Civilizations: The Mayas
> Visit **mometrix.com/academy** and enter **Code**: **556527**

## Mycenaeans

In contrast to the Minoans, whom they displaced, the **Mycenaeans** relied more on conquest than on trade. Mycenaean states included Sparta, Athens, and Corinth. The history of this civilization, including the **Trojan War**, was recorded by the Greek poet, **Homer**. His work was largely considered mythical until archeologists discovered evidence of the city of **Troy** in Hisarlik, Turkey. Archeologists continue to add to the body of information about this ancient culture, translating documents written in Linear B, a script derived from the Minoan Linear A. It is theorized that the Mycenaean civilization was eventually destroyed in either a Dorian invasion or an attack by Greek invaders from the north.

## Dorian Invasion

A Dorian invasion does not refer to an invasion by a particular group of people, but rather is a hypothetical theory to explain the end of the **Mycenaean civilization** and the growth of **classical Greece**. Ancient tradition refers to these events as "the return of the Heracleidae," or the sons (descendents) of Hercules. Archeologists and historians still do not know exactly who conquered the Mycenaeans, but it is believed to have occurred around 1200 BCE, contemporaneous with the destruction of the **Hittite civilization** in what is now modern Turkey. The Hittites speak of an attack by people of the Aegean Sea, or the "Sea People." Only Athens was left intact.

## Spartans vs. Athenians

Both powerful city-states, Sparta and Athens fought each other in the **Peloponnesian War** (431-404 BCE). Despite their proximity, the Spartans and the Athenians nurtured contrasting cultures:
- The **Spartans**, located in Peloponnesus, were ruled by an oligarchic military state. They practiced farming, disallowed trade for Spartan citizens, and valued military arts and strict discipline. They emerged as the strongest military force in the area, and maintained this status for many years. In one memorable encounter, a small group of Spartans held off a huge army of Persians at Thermopylae.
- The **Athenians** were centered in Attica, where the land was rocky and unsuitable for farming. Like the Spartans, they descended from invaders who spoke Greek. Their government was very different from Sparta's; it was in Athens that democracy was created by Cleisthenes of Athens in 508 BCE Athenians excelled in art, theater, architecture, and philosophy.

## Contributions of Ancient Greece that Still Exist Today

Ancient Greece made numerous major contributions to cultural development, including:
- **Theater**—Aristophanes and other Greek playwrights laid the groundwork for modern theatrical performance.
- **Alphabet**—the Greek alphabet, derived from the Phoenician alphabet, developed into the Roman alphabet, and then into our modern-day alphabet.
- **Geometry**—Pythagoras and Euclid pioneered much of the system of geometry still taught today. Archimedes made various mathematical discoveries, including calculating a very accurate value of pi.
- **Historical writing**—much of ancient history doubles as mythology or religious texts. Herodotus and Thucydides made use of research and interpretation to record historical events.
- **Philosophy**—Socrates, Plato, and Aristotle served as the fathers of Western philosophy. Their work is still required reading for philosophy students.

## Alexander the Great

Born to Philip II of Macedon and tutored by Aristotle, **Alexander the Great** is considered one of the greatest conquerors in history. He conquered Egypt, the Achaemenid/Persian Empire, a powerful empire founded by Cyrus the Great that spanned three continents, and he traveled as far as India and the Iberian Peninsula. Though Alexander died from malaria at age 32, his conquering efforts spread **Greek culture** into the east. This cultural diffusion left a greater mark on history than did his empire, which fell apart due to internal conflict not long after his death. Trade between the East and West increased, as did an exchange of ideas and beliefs that influenced both regions greatly. The **Hellenistic traditions** his conquest spread were prevalent in Byzantine culture until as late as the 15th century.

## Hittites

The Hittites were centered in what is now Turkey, but their empire extended into Palestine and Syria. They conquered the Babylonian civilization, but adopted their religion, laws, and literature. Overall, the Hittites tended to tolerate other religions, unlike many other contemporary cultures, and absorbed foreign gods into their own belief systems rather than forcing their religion onto peoples they conquered. The **Hittite Empire** reached its peak in 1600-1200 BCE After a war with Egypt, which weakened them severely, they were eventually conquered by the **Assyrians**.

## Persian Wars

The Persian Empire, ruled by **Cyrus the Great**, encompassed an area from the Black Sea to Afghanistan, and beyond into Central Asia. After the death of Cyrus, **Darius I** became king in 522 BCE. The empire reached its zenith during his reign and Darius attempted to conquer Greece as well. From 499-449 BCE, the Greeks and Persians fought in the **Persian Wars**. The **Peace of Callias** brought an end to the fighting, after the Greeks were able to repel the invasion.

Battles of the Persian Wars included:
- The **Battle of Marathon**—heavily outnumbered Greek forces managed to achieve victory.
- The **Battle of Thermopylae**—a small band of Spartans held off a throng of Persian troops for several days before Persia defeated the Greeks and captured an evacuated Athens.

- The **Battle of Salamis**—this was a naval battle that again saw outnumbered Greeks achieving victory.
- The **Battle of Plataea**—this was another Greek victory, but one in which they outnumbered the Persians. This ended the invasion of Greece.

## Maurya Empire

The Maurya Empire was a large, powerful empire established in India. It was one of the largest ever to rule in the Indian subcontinent, and existed from 322 to 185 BCE, ruled by **Chandragupta Maurya** after the withdrawal from India of Alexander the Great. The Maurya Empire was highly developed, including a standardized economic system, waterways, and private corporations. Trade to the Greeks and others became common, with goods including silk, exotic foods, and spices. Religious development included the rise of Buddhism and Jainism. The laws of the Maurya Empire protected not only civil and social rights of the citizens, but also protected animals, establishing protected zones for economically important creatures such as elephants, lions and tigers. This period of time in Indian history was largely peaceful, perhaps due to the strong Buddhist beliefs of many of its leaders. The empire finally fell after a succession of weak leaders, and was taken over by **Demetrius**, a Greco-Bactrian king who took advantage of this lapse in leadership to conquer southern Afghanistan and Pakistan around 180 BCE, forming the **Indo-Greek Kingdom**.

## Development and Growth of the Chinese Empires

In China, history was divided into a series of **dynasties**. The most famous of these, the **Han dynasty**, existed from 206 BCE to 220 CE. Accomplishments of the Chinese Empires included:
- Building the Great Wall of China
- Numerous inventions, including paper, paper money, printing, and gunpowder
- High level of artistic development
- Silk production

The Chinese dynasties were comparable to Rome as far as their artistic and intellectual accomplishments, as well as the size and scope of their influence.

## Roman Empire and Republic

Rome began humbly, in a single town that grew out of Etruscan settlements and traditions, founded, according to legend, by twin brothers Romulus and Remus, who were raised by wolves. Romulus killed Remus, and from his legacy grew Rome. A thousand years later, the **Roman Empire** covered a significant portion of the known world, from what is now Scotland, across Europe, and into the Middle East. **Hellenization**, or the spread of Greek culture throughout the world, served as an inspiration and a model for the spread of Roman culture. Rome brought in belief systems of conquered peoples as well as their technological and scientific accomplishments, melding the disparate parts into a Roman core. Rome began as a **republic** ruled by consuls, but after the assassination of **Julius Caesar**, it became an **empire** led by emperors. Rome's overall government was autocratic, but local officials came from the provinces where they lived. This limited administrative system was probably a major factor in the long life of the empire.

## Development of the Byzantine Empire from the Roman Empire

In the early fourth century, the Roman Empire split, with the eastern portion becoming the Eastern Empire, or the **Byzantine Empire**. In 330 CE, **Constantine** founded the city of **Constantinople**, which became the center of the Byzantine Empire. Its major influences came from Mesopotamia and Persia, in contrast to the Western Empire, which maintained traditions more closely linked to Greece and Carthage. Byzantium's position gave it an advantage over invaders from the west and the east, as well as control over trade from both regions. It protected the Western empire from invasion from the Persians and the Ottomans, and practiced a more centralized rule than in the West. The Byzantines were famous for lavish art and architecture, as well as the Code of Justinian, which collected Roman law into a clear system. The Byzantine Empire finally fell to the **Ottomans** in 1453.

## Significance of the Nicene Creed

The **Byzantine Empire** was Christian-based but incorporated Greek language, philosophy and literature and drew its law and government policies from Rome. However, there was as yet no unified doctrine of Christianity, as it was a relatively new religion that had spread rapidly and without a great deal of organization. In 325, the **First Council of Nicaea** addressed this issue. From this conference came the **Nicene Creed**, addressing the Trinity and other basic Christian beliefs. The **Council of Chalcedon** in 451 further defined the view of the Trinity.

## Factors that Led to the Fall of the Western Roman Empire

**Germanic tribes**, including the Visigoths, Ostrogoths, Vandals, Saxons and Franks, controlled most of Europe. The Roman Empire faced major opposition on that front. The increasing size of the empire also made it harder to manage, leading to dissatisfaction throughout the empire as Roman government became less efficient. Germanic tribes refused to adhere to the Nicene Creed, instead following **Arianism**, which led the Roman Catholic Church to declare them heretics. The **Franks** proved a powerful military force in their defeat of the Muslims in 732. In 768, **Charlemagne** became king of the Franks. These tribes waged several wars against Rome, including the invasion of Britannia by the Angles and Saxons. Far-flung Rome lost control over this area of its Empire, and eventually Rome itself was **invaded**.

## Iconoclasm and the Conflict Between the Roman Catholic and Eastern Orthodox Churches

**Emperor Leo III** ordered the destruction of all icons throughout the Byzantine Empire. Images of Jesus were replaced with crosses, and images of Jesus, Mary or other religious figures were considered blasphemy on grounds of idolatry. **Pope Gregory II** called a synod to discuss the issue. The synod declared that the images were not heretical, and that strong disciplinary measures would result for anyone who destroyed them. Leo's response was an attempt to kill Pope Gregory, but this plan ended in failure.

## Effect of the Viking Invasions on the Culture of England and Europe

Vikings invaded Northern France in the tenth century, eventually becoming the **Normans**. Originating in Scandinavia, the **Vikings** were accomplished seafarers with advanced knowledge of trade routes. With overpopulation plaguing their native lands, they began to travel. From the eighth to the eleventh centuries, they spread throughout Europe, conquering and colonizing. Vikings invaded and colonized England in several waves, including the **Anglo-Saxon invasions** that displaced Roman control. Their influence remained significant in England, affecting everything from the language of the country to place names and even the government and social structure.  By 900, Vikings had settled in **Iceland**. They proceeded then to **Greenland** and eventually to **North America**, arriving in the New World even before the Spanish and British who claimed the lands several centuries later. They also traded with the Byzantine Empire until the eleventh century when their significant level of activity came to an end.

## West vs. East Tenth Century Events

In **Europe**, the years 500-1000 CE are largely known as the **Dark Ages**. In the tenth century, numerous Viking invasions disrupted societies that had been more settled under Roman rule. Vikings settled in Northern France, eventually becoming the Normans. By the eleventh century, Europe would rise again into the **High Middle Ages** with the beginning of the **Crusades**.

In **China**, wars also raged. This led the Chinese to make use of gunpowder for the first time in warfare.

In the **Americas**, the **Mayan Empire** was winding down while the **Toltec** became more prominent. **Pueblo** Indian culture was also at its zenith.

In the **East**, the **Muslims** and the **Byzantine Empire** were experiencing a significant period of growth and development.

## Feudalism in Europe in the Middle Ages

A major element of the social and economic life of Europe, **feudalism** developed as a way to ensure European rulers would have the wherewithal to quickly raise an army when necessary. **Vassals** swore loyalty and promised to provide military service for lords, who in return offered a **fief**, or a parcel of land, for them to use to generate their livelihood. Vassals could work the land themselves, have it worked by **peasants** or **serfs**—workers who had few rights and were little more than slaves—or grant the fief to someone else. The king legally owned all the land, but in return promised to protect the vassals from invasion and war. Vassals returned a certain percentage of their income to the lords, who in turn passed a portion of their income on to the king.  A similar practice was **manorialism**, in which the feudal system was applied to a self-contained manor. These manors were often owned by the lords who ran them, but were usually included in the same system of loyalty and promises of protection that drove feudalism.

## Influence of the Roman Catholic Church over Medieval Society

The Roman Catholic Church extended significant influence both politically and economically throughout medieval society. The church supplied **education**, as there were no established schools or universities. To a large extent, the church had filled a power void left by various invasions throughout the former Roman Empire, leading it to exercise a role that was far more **political** than religious. Kings were heavily influenced by the Pope and other church officials, and churches controlled large amounts of land throughout Europe.

## Effect of Black Death on Medieval Politics and Economic Conditions

The Black Death, believed to be **bubonic plague**, most likely came to Europe on fleas carried by rats on sailing vessels. The plague killed more than a third of the entire population of Europe and effectively ended **feudalism** as a political system. Many who had formerly served as peasants or serfs found different work, as a demand for skilled labor grew. Nation-states grew in power, and in the face of the pandemic, many began to turn away from faith in God and toward the ideals of ancient Greece and Rome for government and other beliefs.

## Progression of the Crusades and Major Figures Involved

The Crusades began in the eleventh century and continued into the fifteenth. The major goal of these various military ventures was to slow the progression of Muslim forces into Europe and to expel them from the **Holy Land**, where they had taken control of Jerusalem and Palestine. Alexius I, the Byzantine emperor, called for helped from **Pope Urban** II when Palestine was taken. In 1095, the Pope, hoping to reunite Eastern and Western Christianity, encouraged all Christians to help the cause. Amidst great bloodshed, this Crusade recaptured **Jerusalem**, but over the next centuries, Jerusalem and other areas of the Holy Land changed hands numerous times. The **Second Crusade** (1147-1149) consisted of an unsuccessful attempt to retake Damascus. The **Third Crusade**, under Pope Gregory VIII, attempted to recapture Jerusalem, but failed. The **Fourth Crusade**, under Pope Innocent III, attempted to come into the Holy Land via Egypt. The Crusades led to greater power for the Pope and the Catholic Church in general and also opened numerous trading and cultural routes between Europe and the East.

## Political Developments in India Through the 11th Century

After the Mauryan dynasty, the **Guptas** ruled India, maintaining a long period of peace and prosperity in the area. During this time, the Indian people invented the decimal system as well as the concept of zero. They produced cotton and calico, as well as other products in high demand in Europe and Asia, and developed a complex system of medicine. The Gupta Dynasty ended in the sixth century. First the **Huns** invaded, and then the **Hephthalites** (an Asian nomadic tribe) destroyed the weakened empire. In the fourteenth century, **Tamerlane**, a Muslim who envisioned restoring Genghis Khan's empire, expanded India's borders and founded the **Mogul Empire**. His grandson Akbar promoted freedom of religion and built a wide-spread number of mosques, forts, and other buildings throughout the country.

## Development of Chinese and Japanese Governments Through the 11th Century

After the Mongols, led by Genghis Khan and his grandson Kublai Khan, unified the Mongol Empire, **China** was led by the **Ming Dynasty** (1368-1644) and the **Manchu (also known as Qing) Dynasty** (1644-1912). Both dynasties were isolationist, ending China's interaction with other countries until the eighteenth century. The Ming Dynasty was known for its porcelain, while the Manchus focused on farming and road construction as the population grew.

**Japan** developed independently of China, but borrowed the Buddhist religion, the Chinese writing system, and other elements of Chinese society. Ruled by the divine emperor, Japan basically functioned on a feudal system led by **daimyo**, or warlords, and soldiers known as **samurai**. Japan remained isolationist, not interacting significantly with the rest of the world until the 1800s.

## Ming Dynasty

The Ming dynasty lasted in China from A.D. 1368 to 1644. This dynasty was established by a Buddhist monk, **Zhu Yuanzhang**, who quickly became obsessed with consolidating power in the central government and was known for the brutality with which he achieved his ends. It was during the **Ming dynasty** that China developed and introduced its famous civil service examinations, rigorous tests on the **Confucian classics**. The future of an ambitious Chinese youth depended on his performance on this exam. The capital was transferred from Nanjing to Beijing during this period, and the **Forbidden City** was constructed inside the new capital. The Ming period, despite its constant expansionary wars, also continued China's artistic resurgence; the porcelain of this period is especially admired.

## Developments in Africa Through the 11th Century

Much of Africa was difficult to traverse early on, due to the large amount of desert and other inhospitable terrain. **Egypt** remained important, though most of the northern coast became Muslim as their armies spread through the area. **Ghana** rose as a trade center in the ninth century, lasting into the twelfth century, primarily trading in gold, which it exchanges for Saharan salt. **Mali** rose somewhat later, with the trade center Timbuktu becoming an important exporter of goods such as iron, leather and tin. Mali also dealt in agricultural trade, becoming one of the most significant trading centers in West Africa. The Muslim religion dominated, and technological advancement was sparse.

African culture was largely defined through migration, as Arab merchants and others settled on the continent, particularly along the east coast. Scholars from the Muslim nations gravitated to Timbuktu, which in addition to its importance in trade, had also become a magnet for those seeking Islamic knowledge and education.

## History of Islam and Its Role in Bringing Unity to the Middle East

Born in 570 CE, **Muhammad** began preaching around 613, leading his followers in a new religion called **Islam**, which means "submission to God's will." Before this time, the Arabian Peninsula was inhabited largely by Bedouins, nomads who battled amongst each other and lived in tribal organizations. But by the time Muhammad died in 632, most of Arabia had become Muslim to some extent.

Muhammad conquered **Mecca**, where a temple called the **Kaaba** had long served as a center of the nomadic religions. He declared this temple the most sacred of Islam, and Mecca as the holy city. His writings became the **Koran**, or **Qur'an**, divine revelations he said had been delivered to him by the angel Gabriel.

Muhammad's teachings gave the formerly tribal Arabian people a sense of unity that had not existed in the area before. After his death, the converted Muslims of Arabia conquered a vast territory, creating an empire and bringing advances in literature, technology, science and art as Europe was declining under the scourge of the Black Death. Literature from this period includes the *Arabian Nights* and the *Rubaiyat* of Omar Khayyam.

Later in its development, Islam split into two factions, the **Shiite** and the **Sunni** Muslims. Conflict continues today between these groups.

> ➤ **Review Video:** Islam
> *Visit **mometrix.com/academy** and enter **Code:* **359164**

> ➤ **Review Video:** The Islamic Empire
> *Visit **mometrix.com/academy** and enter **Code:* **511181**

## Ottoman Empire

By 1400, the Ottomans had grown in power in Anatolia and had begun attempts to take Constantinople. In 1453 they finally conquered the Byzantine capital and renamed it **Istanbul**. The **Ottoman Empire's** major strength, much like Rome before it, lay in its ability to unite widely disparate people through religious tolerance. This tolerance, which stemmed from the idea that Muslims, Christians, and Jews were fundamentally related and could coexist, enabled the Ottomans to develop a widely varied culture. They also believed in just laws and just government, with government centered in a monarch, known as the **sultan**.

## Renaissance

Renaissance literally means "rebirth." After the darkness of the Dark Ages and the Black Plague, interest rose again in the beliefs and politics of ancient Greece and Rome. Art, literature, music, science, and philosophy all burgeoned during the Renaissance.

Many of the ideas of the Renaissance began in **Florence, Italy**, in the fourteenth century, spurred by the **Medici** family. Education for the upper classes expanded to include law, math, reading, writing, and classical Greek and Roman works. As the Renaissance progressed, the world was presented through art and literature in a realistic way that had never been explored before. This **realism** drove culture to new heights.

## Renaissance Artists, Authors and Scientists

**Artists** of the Renaissance included Leonardo da Vinci, also an inventor, Michelangelo, also an architect, and others who focused on realism in their work. In **literature**, major contributions came from humanist authors like Petrarch, Erasmus, Sir Thomas More, and Boccaccio, who believed man should focus on reality rather than on the ethereal. Shakespeare, Cervantes and Dante followed in their footsteps, and their works found a wide audience thanks to Gutenberg's development of the printing press.

**Scientific developments** of the Renaissance included the work of Copernicus, Galileo and Kepler, who challenged the geocentric philosophies of the day by proving that the earth was not the center of the solar system.

> ➤ **Review Video:** Renaissance
> *Visit **mometrix.com/academy** and enter **Code:* **123100**

## Two Phases of the Reformation Period

The Reformation consisted of both the Protestant and the Catholic Reformation. The **Protestant Reformation** rose in Germany when **Martin Luther** protested abuses of the Catholic Church. **John Calvin** led the movement in Switzerland, while in England King Henry VIII made use of the Reformation's ideas to further his own political goals. The **Catholic Reformation**, or **Counter-Reformation**, occurred in response to the Protestant movement, leading to various changes in the Catholic Church. Some provided wider tolerance of different religious viewpoints, but others actually increased the persecution of those deemed to be heretics.

From a **religious** standpoint, the Reformation occurred due to abuses by the Catholic Church such as indulgences and dispensations, religious offices being offered up for sale, and an increasingly dissolute clergy. **Politically**, the Reformation was driven by increased power of various ruling monarchs, who wished to take all power to themselves rather than allowing power to remain with the church. They also had begun to chafe at papal taxes and the church's increasing wealth. The ideas of the Protestant Revolution removed power from the Catholic Church and the Pope himself, playing nicely into the hands of those monarchs, such as Henry VIII, who wanted out from under the church's control.

> ➤ **Review Video:** The Reformation: The Protestants
> *Visit **mometrix.com/academy** and enter **Code**: 583582*

## Developments of the Scientific Revolution

In addition to holding power in the political realm, church doctrine also governed scientific belief. During the **Scientific Revolution**, astronomers and other scientists began to amass evidence that challenged the church's scientific doctrines. Major figures of the Scientific Revolution included:

- **Nicolaus Copernicus**—wrote *On the Revolutions of the Celestial Spheres*, arguing that the earth revolved around the sun
- **Tycho Brahe**—catalogued astronomical observations
- **Johannes Kepler**—developed laws of planetary motion
- **Galileo Galilei**—defended the heliocentric theories of Copernicus and Kepler, discovered four moons of Jupiter, and died under house arrest by the church, charged with heresy
- **Isaac Newton**—discovered gravity, studied optics, calculus and physics, and believed the workings of nature could be studied and proven through observation

> ➤ **Review Video:** The Scientific Revolution
> *Visit **mometrix.com/academy** and enter **Code**: 974600*

## Major Ideas of the Enlightenment

During the Enlightenment, philosophers and scientists began to rely more and more on **observation** to support their ideas, rather than building on past beliefs, particularly those held by the church. A focus on **ethics and logic** drove their work. Major philosophers of the **Enlightenment** included:

- **Rene Descartes**—he famously wrote, "I think, therefore I am." He believed strongly in logic and rules of observation.
- **David Hume**—he pioneered empiricism and skepticism, believing that truth could only be found through direct experience, and that what others said to be true was always suspect.

- **Immanuel Kant**—he believed in self-examination and observation, and that the root of morality lay within human beings.
- **Jean-Jacques Rousseau**—he developed the idea of the social contract, that government existed by the agreement of the people, and that the government was obligated to protect the people and their basic rights. His ideas influenced John Locke and Thomas Jefferson.

> ➤ **Review Video:** The Enlightenment
> Visit *mometrix.com/academy* and enter *Code*: **540039**

## American Revolution vs. French Revolution

Both the American and French Revolution came about as a protest against the excesses and overly controlling nature of their respective monarchs. In **America**, the British colonies had been left mostly to self-govern until the British monarchs began to increase control, spurring the colonies to revolt. In **France**, the nobility's excesses had led to increasingly difficult economic conditions, with inflation, heavy taxation and food shortages creating great burdens on the lower classes. Both revolutions led to the development of republics to replace the monarchies that were displaced. However, the French Revolution eventually led to the rise of the dictator **Napoleon Bonaparte**, while the American Revolution produced a working **republic** from the beginning.

## Events and Figures of the French Revolution

In 1789, **King Louis XVI**, faced with a huge national debt, convened parliament. The **Third Estate**, or Commons, a division of the French parliament, then claimed power, and the king's resistance led to the storming of the **Bastille**, the royal prison. The people established a constitutional monarchy. When King Louis XVI and Marie Antoinette attempted to leave the country, they were executed on the guillotine. From 1793 to 1794, **Robespierre** and extreme radicals, the **Jacobins**, instituted a **Reign of Terror**, executing tens of thousands of nobles as well as anyone considered an enemy of the Revolution. Robespierre was then executed, as well, and the **Directory** came into power, leading to a temporary return to bourgeois values. This governing body proved incompetent and corrupt, allowing **Napoleon Bonaparte** to come to power in 1799, first as a dictator, then as emperor. While the French Revolution threw off the power of a corrupt monarchy, its immediate results were likely not what the original perpetrators of the revolt had intended.

> ➤ **Review Video:** The Revolutionary War
> Visit *mometrix.com/academy* and enter *Code*: **935282**

> ➤ **Review Video:** The French Revolution: Napoleon Bonaparte
> Visit *mometrix.com/academy* and enter *Code*: **876330**

## Causes and Progression of the Russian Revolution of 1905

In Russia, rule lay in the hands of the **Czars**, and the overall structure was **feudalistic**. Beneath the Czars was a group of rich nobles, landowners whose lands were worked by peasants and serfs. The **Russo-Japanese War** (1904-1905) made conditions much worse for the lower classes. When peasants demonstrated outside the Czar's Winter Palace, the palace guard fired upon the crowd. The demonstration had been organized by a trade union leader, and after the violent response, many unions as well as political parties blossomed and began to lead numerous strikes. When the economy ground to a halt, Czar Nicholas II signed a document known as the **October Manifesto**, which established a constitutional monarchy and gave legislative power to parliament. However, he violated the Manifesto shortly thereafter, disbanding parliament and ignoring the civil liberties granted by the Manifesto. This eventually led to the **Bolshevik Revolution**.

## Bolshevik Revolution

Factors Leading to the Bolshevik Revolution of 1917
Throughout its modern history, Russia had lagged behind other countries in development. The continued existence of a feudal system, combined with harsh conditions and the overall size of the country, led to massive food shortages and increasingly harsh conditions for the majority of the population. The tyrannical rule of the Czars only made this worse, as did repeated losses in various military conflicts. Increasing poverty, decreasing supplies, and the Czar's violation of the **October Manifesto** which had given some political power and civil rights to the people finally came to a head with the **Bolshevik Revolution**.

Events of the Bolshevik Revolution
A **workers' strike in Petrograd** in 1917 set the revolutionary wheels in motion when the army sided with the workers. While parliament set up a provisional government made up of nobles, the workers and military joined to form their own governmental system known as **soviets**, which consisted of local councils elected by the people. The ensuing chaos opened the doors for formerly exiled leaders Vladimir Lenin, Joseph Stalin and Leon Trotsky to move in and gain popular support as well as the support of the Red Guard. Overthrowing parliament, they took power, creating a **communist** state in Russia. This development led to the spread of communism throughout Eastern Europe and elsewhere, greatly affecting diplomatic policies throughout the world for several decades.

## Industrial Revolution

Effects of the Industrial Revolution on Society
The Industrial Revolution began in Great Britain, bringing coal- and steam-powered machinery into widespread use. Industry began a period of rapid growth with these developments. Goods that had previously been produced in small workshops or even in homes were produced more efficiently and in much larger quantities in **factories**. Where society had been largely agrarian-based, the focus swiftly shifted to an **industrial** outlook. As electricity and internal combustion engines replaced coal and steam as energy sources, even more drastic and rapid changes occurred. Western European countries in particular turned to colonialism, taking control of portions of Africa and Asia to ensure access to the raw materials needed to produce factory goods. Specialized labor became very much in demand, and businesses grew rapidly, creating monopolies, increasing world trade, and developing large urban centers. Even agriculture changed fundamentally as the Industrial Revolution led to a second **Agricultural Revolution** with the addition of new technology to advance agricultural production.

> ➤ **Review Video:** The Industrial Revolution
> *Visit **mometrix.com/academy** and enter **Code**: **372796***

First and Second Phases of the Industrial Revolution
The **first phase** of the Industrial Revolution took place from roughly 1750 to 1830. The textile industry experienced major changes as more and more elements of the process became mechanized. Mining benefited from the steam engine. Transportation became easier and more widely available as waterways were improved and the railroad came into prominence. In the

**second phase**, from 1830 to 1910, industries further improved in efficiency and new industries were introduced as photography, various chemical processes, and electricity became more widely available to produce new goods or new, improved versions of old goods. Petroleum and hydroelectricity became major sources of power. During this time, the Industrial Revolution spread out of Western Europe and into the US and Japan.

Political, Social and Economic Side Effects of the Industrial Revolution

The Industrial Revolution led to widespread education, a wider franchise, and the development of mass communication in the political arena. **Economically**, conflicts arose between companies and their employees, as struggles for fair treatment and fair wages increased. Unions gained power and became more active. Government regulation over industries increased, but at the same time, growing businesses fought for the right to free enterprise. In the **social** sphere, populations increased and began to concentrate around centers of industry. Cities became larger and more densely populated. Scientific advancements led to more efficient agriculture, greater supply of goods, and increased knowledge of medicine and sanitation, leading to better overall health.

## Nationalism and Its Effect on Society Through the 18th and 19th Centuries

Nationalism, put simply, is a strong belief in, identification with, and allegiance to a particular nation and people. **Nationalistic belief** unified various areas that had previously seen themselves as fragmented, which led to **patriotism** and, in some cases, **imperialism**. As nationalism grew, individual nations sought to grow, bringing in other, smaller states that shared similar characteristics such as language and cultural beliefs. Unfortunately, a major side effect of these growing nationalistic beliefs was often conflict and outright **war**.

In Europe, imperialism led countries to spread their influence into Africa and Asia. **Africa** was eventually divided among several European countries that wanted the raw materials. **Asia** also came under European control, with the exception of China, Japan and Siam (now Thailand). In the US, **Manifest Destiny** became the rallying cry as the country expanded west. Italy and Germany formed larger nations from a variety of smaller states.

> ➢ **Review Video:** Nationalism
> *Visit **mometrix.com/academy** and enter **Code**: 865693*

## Events of World War I in the European Theater

WWI began in 1914 with the assassination of **Archduke Franz Ferdinand**, heir to the throne of Austria-Hungary, by a Serbian national. This led to a conflict between Austria-Hungary and Serbia that quickly escalated into the First World War. Europe split into the **Allies**—Britain, France, and Russia, and later Italy, Japan, and the US, against the **Central Powers**—Austria-Hungary, Germany, the Ottoman Empire, and Bulgaria. As the war spread, countries beyond Europe became involved. The war left Europe deeply in debt, and particularly devastated the German economy. The ensuing **Great Depression** made matters worse, and economic devastation opened the door for communist, fascist, and socialist governments to gain power.

## Trench Warfare and Its Use in World War I

Fighting during WWI largely took place in a series of **trenches** built along the Eastern and Western Fronts. These trenches added up to more than 24,000 miles. This produced fronts that stretched over 400 miles, from the coast of Belgium to the border of Switzerland. The Allies made use of straightforward open-air trenches with a front line, supporting lines, and communications lines. By contrast, the German trenches sometimes included well-equipped underground living quarters.

> ➢ **Review Video:** World War I
> *Visit **mometrix.com/academy** and enter **Code**: **659767***

## Communism vs. Socialism

At their roots, socialism and communism both focus on public ownership and distribution of goods and services. However, **communism** works toward revolution by drawing on what it sees to be inevitable class antagonism, eventually overthrowing the upper classes and the systems of capitalism. **Socialism** makes use of democratic procedures, building on the existing order. This was particularly true of the utopian socialists, who saw industrial capitalism as oppressive, not allowing workers to prosper. While socialism struggled between the World Wars, communism took hold, especially in Eastern Europe. After WWII, **democratic socialism** became more common. Later, **capitalism** took a stronger hold again, and today most industrialized countries in the western world function under an economy that mixes elements of capitalism and socialism.

> ➢ **Review Video:** Socialism
> *Visit **mometrix.com/academy** and enter **Code**: **917677***

## Conditions that Led to the Rise of the Nazi Party in Germany

The **Great Depression** had a particularly devastating effect on Germany's economy, especially after the US was no longer able to supply reconstruction loans to help the country regain its footing. With unemployment rising rapidly, dissatisfaction with the government grew. Fascist and Communist parties rose, promising change and improvement.

Led by **Adolf Hitler**, the fascist **Nazi Party** eventually gained power in Parliament based on these promises and the votes of desperate German workers. When Hitler became Chancellor, he launched numerous expansionist policies, violating the peace treaties that had ended WWI. His military buildup and conquering of neighboring countries sparked the aggression that soon led to WWII.

## Importance of the German Blitzkrieg to the Progression of World War II

The blitzkrieg, or "lightning war," consisted of fast, powerful surprise attacks that disrupted communications, made it difficult if not impossible for the victims to retaliate, and demoralized Germany's foes. The "blitz," or the aerial bombing of England in 1940, was one example, with bombings occurring in London and other cities 57 nights in a row. The **Battle of Britain** in 1940 also brought intense raids by Germany's air force, the **Luftwaffe**, mostly targeting ports and British air force bases. Eventually, Britain's Royal Air Force blocked the Luftwaffe, ending Germany's hopes for conquering Britain.

## Battle of the Bulge

Following the **D-Day Invasion**, Allied forces gained considerable ground and began a major campaign to push through Europe. In December of 1944, Hitler launched a counteroffensive, attempting to retake Antwerp, an important port. The ensuing battle became the largest land battle on the war's Western Front, and was known as the Battle of the Ardennes, or the **Battle of the**

**Bulge**. The battle lasted from December 16, 1944 to January 25, 1945. The Germans pushed forward, making inroads into Allied lines, but in the end the Allies brought the advance to a halt. The Germans were pushed back, with massive losses on both sides. However, those losses proved crippling to the German army.

## Holocaust

As Germany sank deeper and deeper into dire economic straits, the tendency was to look for a person or group of people to blame for the problems of the country. With distrust of the Jewish people already ingrained, it was easy for German authorities to set up the **Jews** as scapegoats for Germany's problems. Under the rule of Hitler and the Nazi party, the "Final Solution" for the supposed Jewish problem was devised. Millions of Jews, as well as Gypsies, homosexuals, communists, Catholics, the mentally ill, and others, simply named as criminals, were transported to concentration camps during the course of the war. At least six million were slaughtered in death camps such as **Auschwitz**, where horrible conditions and torture of prisoners were commonplace. The Allies were aware of rumors of mass slaughter throughout the war, but many discounted the reports. Only when troops went in to liberate the prisoners was the true horror of the concentration camps brought to light. The **Holocaust** resulted in massive loss of human life, but also in the loss and destruction of cultures. Because the genocide focused on specific ethnic groups, many traditions, histories, knowledge, and other cultural elements were lost, particularly among the Jewish and Gypsy populations. After World War II, the United Nations recognized **genocide** as a "crime against humanity." The UN passed the **Universal Declaration of Human Rights** in 1948 in order to further specify what rights the organization protected. Nazi war criminals faced justice during the **Nuremberg Trials**. There individuals, rather than their governments, were held accountable for war crimes.

> ➢ **Review Video:** The Holocaust
> *Visit **mometrix.com/academy** and enter **Code**:* **350695**

## World War II and the Ensuing Diplomatic Climate that Led to the Cold War

With millions of military and civilian deaths and over 12 million persons displaced, **WWII** left large regions of Europe and Asia in disarray. **Communist** governments moved in with promises of renewed prosperity and economic stability. The **Soviet Union** backed communist regimes in much of Eastern Europe. In China, **Mao Zedong** led communist forces in the overthrow of the Chinese Nationalist Party and instituted a communist government in 1949. While the new communist governments restored a measure of stability to much of Eastern Europe, it brought its own problems, with dictatorial governments and an oppressive police force. The spread of communism also led to several years of tension between communist countries and the democratic west, as the west fought to slow the spread of oppressive regimes throughout the world. With both sides in possession of nuclear weapons, tensions rose. Each side feared the other would resort to nuclear attack. This standoff lasted until 1989, when the **Berlin Wall** fell. The Soviet Union was dissolved two years later.

## Origins of the United Nations

The United Nations (**UN**) came into being toward the end of World War II. A successor to the less-than-successful League of Nations formed after World War I, the UN built and improved on those ideas. Since its inception, the UN has worked to bring the countries of the world together for **diplomatic solutions** to international problems, including sanctions and other restrictions. It has also initiated military action, calling for peacekeeping troops from member countries to move against countries violating UN policies. The **Korean War** was the first example of UN involvement in an international conflict.

## Effects of Decolonization on the Post-War Period

A rise of nationalism among European colonies led to many of them declaring independence. **India** and **Pakistan** became independent of Britain in 1947, and numerous African and Asian colonies declared independence as well. This period of **decolonization** lasted into the 1960s. Some colonies moved successfully into independence but many, especially in Africa and Asia, struggled to create stable governments and economies, and suffered from ethnic and religious conflicts, some of which continue today.

## Factors and Shifts in Power that Led to the Korean War

In 1910, Japan annexed Korea and maintained this control until 1945. After WWII, Soviet and US troops occupied Korea, with the **Soviet Union** controlling North Korea and the **US** controlling South Korea. In 1947, the UN ordered elections in Korea to unify the country but the Soviet Union refused to allow them to take place in North Korea, instead setting up a communist government. In 1950, the US withdrew troops, and the North Korean troops moved to invade South Korea. The **Korean War** was the first war in which the UN—or any international organization—played a major role. The US, Australia, Canada, France, Netherlands, Great Britain, Turkey, China, USSR and other countries sent troops at various times, for both sides, throughout the war. In 1953, the war ended in a truce, but no peace agreement was ever achieved, and Korea remains divided.

## Events that Led to the Vietnam War

Vietnam had previously been part of a French colony called French Indochina. The **Vietnam War** began with the **First Indochina War** from 1946-1954, in which France battled with the Democratic Republic of Vietnam, ruled by Ho Chi Minh.

In 1954, a siege at Dien Bien Phu ended in a Vietnamese victory. Vietnam was then divided into North and South, much like Korea. Communist forces controlled the North and the South was controlled by South Vietnamese forces, supported by the US. Conflict ensued, leading to another war. US troops eventually led the fight, in support of South Vietnam. The war became a major political issue in the US, with many citizens protesting American involvement. In 1975, South Vietnam surrendered, and Vietnam became the **Socialist Republic of Vietnam**.

## Globalism

In the modern era, globalism has emerged as a popular political ideology. **Globalism** is based in the idea that all people and all nations are **interdependent**. Each nation is dependent on one or more other nations for production of and markets for goods, and for income generation. Today's ease of international travel and communication, including technological advances such as the airplane, has heightened this sense of interdependence. The global economy, and the general idea of globalism, has shaped many economic and political choices since the beginning of the twentieth century. Many of today's issues, including environmental awareness, economic struggles, and continued warfare, often require the cooperation of many countries if they are to be dealt with effectively.

**Effect of Globalization on the Way Countries Interact with Each Other**

Countries worldwide often seek the same resources, leading to high demand, particularly for **nonrenewable resources**. This can result in heavy fluctuations in price. One major example is the demand for petroleum products such as oil and natural gas. Increased travel and communication make it possible to deal with diseases in remote locations; however, this also allows diseases to be spread via travelers.

A major factor contributing to increased globalization over the past few decades has been the **Internet**. By allowing instantaneous communication with anyone nearly anywhere on the globe, the Internet has led to interaction between far-flung individuals and countries, and an ever increasing awareness of events all over the world.

**Role of the Middle East in International Relations and Economics**

The location on the globe, with ease of access to Europe and Asia, and its preponderance of oil deposits, makes the **Middle Eastern countries** crucial in many international issues, both diplomatic and economic. Because of its central location, the Middle East has been a hotbed for violence since before the beginning of recorded history. Conflicts over land, resources, and religious and political power continue in the area today, spurred by conflict over control of the area's vast oil fields as well as over territories that have been disputed for thousands of years.

> ➢ **Review Video:** Globalization: The Middle East
> *Visit **mometrix.com/academy** and enter **Code**: **655231***

**Major Occurrences of Genocide in Modern History**

The three major occurrences of genocide in modern history other than the Holocaust are:
- **Armenian genocide**—from 1914 to 1918, the Young Turks, heirs to the Ottoman Empire, slaughtered between 800,000 and 1.5 million Armenians. This constituted approximately half of the Armenian population at the time.
- **Russian purges under Stalin**—scholars have attributed deaths between 3 and 60 million, both directly and indirectly, to the policies and edicts of Joseph Stalin's regime. The deaths took place from 1921 to 1953, when Stalin died. In recent years, many scholars have settled on a number of deaths near 20 million but this is still disputed today.
- **Rwandan genocide**—in 1994, hundreds of thousands of Tutsi, as well as Hutu who sympathized with them, were slaughtered during the Rwandan Civil War. The UN did not act or authorize intervention during these atrocities

# U.S. and Illinois History

## Well-Known Native Americans

The following are five well-known Native Americans and their roles in early US history:
- **Squanto**, an Algonquian, helped early English settlers survive the hard winter by teaching them the native methods of planting corn, squash, and pumpkins.
- **Pocahontas**, also Algonquian, became famous as a liaison with John Smith's Jamestown colony in 1607.
- **Sacagawea**, a Shoshone, served a vital role in the Lewis and Clark expedition when the two explorers hired her as their guide in 1805.
- **Crazy Horse** and **Sitting Bull** led Sioux and Cheyenne troops in the Battle of the Little Bighorn in 1876, soundly defeating George Armstrong Custer.
- **Chief Joseph**, a leader of the Nez Perce who supported peaceful interaction with white settlers, attempted to relocate his tribe to Canada rather than move them to a reservation.

## Major Regional Native American Groups

The major regional Native American groups and the major traits of each are as follows:
- The **Algonquians** in the eastern part of the United States lived in wigwams. The northern tribes subsisted on hunting and gathering, while those who were farther south grew crops such as corn.
- The **Iroquois**, also an east coast tribe, spoke a different language from the Algonquians, and lived in rectangular longhouses.
- The **Plains tribes** lived between the Mississippi River and the Rocky Mountains. These nomadic tribes lived in teepees and followed the buffalo herds. Plains tribes included the Sioux, Cheyenne, Comanche and Blackfoot.
- **Pueblo tribes** included the Zuni, Hopi, and Acoma. They lived in the Southwest deserts in homes made of stone or adobe. They domesticated animals and cultivated corn and beans.
- On the Pacific coast, tribes such as the **Tlingit**, **Chinook**, and **Salish** lived on fish as well as deer, native berries and roots. Their rectangular homes housed large family groups, and they used totem poles.
- In the far north, the **Aleuts** and **Inuit** lived in skin tents or igloos. Talented fishermen, they built kayaks and umiaks and also hunted caribou, seals, whales and walrus.

## Age of Exploration

The Age of Exploration is also called the **Age of Discovery**. It is generally considered to have begun in the early fifteenth century and continued into the seventeenth century. Major developments of the **Age of Exploration** included technological advances in navigation, mapmaking and shipbuilding. These advances led to expanded European exploration of the rest of the world. Explorers set out from several European countries, including Portugal, Spain, France and England, seeking new routes to Asia. These efforts led to the discovery of new lands, as well as colonization in India, Asia, Africa, and North America.

> ➤ **Review Video:** Age of Exploration
> *Visit **mometrix.com/academy** and enter **Code**: 612972*

## Impact of Technological Advances in Navigation and Seafaring Exploration

For long ocean journeys, it was important for sailors to be able to find their way home even when their vessels sailed far out to sea. A variety of navigational tools enabled them to launch ambitious journeys over long distances. The **compass** and **astrolabe** were particularly important advancements. The magnetic compass was used by Chinese navigators from approximately 200 BCE, and knowledge of the astrolabe came to Europe from Arab navigators and traders who had refined designs developed by the ancient Greeks. The Portuguese developed a ship called a **caravel** in the 1400s that incorporated navigational advancements with the ability to make long sea journeys. Equipped with this advanced vessel, the Portuguese achieved a major goal of the Age of Exploration by discovering a **sea route** from Europe to Asia in 1498.

## Significance of Christopher Columbus' Voyage

In 1492, Columbus, a Genoan explorer, obtained financial backing from King Ferdinand and Queen Isabella of Spain to seek a sea route to Asia. He sought a trade route with the Asian Indies to the west. With three ships, the *Niña*, the *Pinta* and the *Santa Maria*, he eventually landed in the **West Indies**. While Columbus failed in his effort to discover a western route to Asia, he is credited with the discovery of the **Americas**.

> ➢ **Review Video:** Christopher Columbus
> *Visit **mometrix.com/academy** and enter **Code**: 496598*

## French, Spanish, Dutch and British Goals in Colonization of the Americas

France, Spain, the Netherlands, and England each had specific goals in the colonization of the Americas:
- Initial **French colonies** were focused on expanding the fur trade. Later, French colonization led to the growth of plantations in Louisiana which brought numerous African slaves to the New World.
- **Spanish colonists** came to look for wealth, and to convert the natives to Christianity. For some, the desire for gold led to mining in the New World, while others established large ranches.
- The **Dutch** were also involved in the fur trade, and imported slaves as the need for laborers increased.
- **British colonists** arrived with various goals. Some were simply looking for additional income, while others were fleeing Britain to escape religious persecution.

## New England Colonies

The New England colonies were New Hampshire, Connecticut, Rhode Island and Massachusetts. These colonies were founded largely to escape **religious persecution** in England. The beliefs of the **Puritans**, who migrated to America in the 1600s, significantly influenced the development of these colonies. Situated in the northeast coastal areas of America, the New England colonies featured numerous harbors as well as dense forests. The soil, however, was rocky and had a very short growing season, so was not well suited for agriculture. The economy of New England during the colonial period centered around fishing, shipbuilding and trade along with some small farms and lumber mills. Although some groups congregated in small farms, life centered mainly in towns and cities where **merchants** largely controlled the trade economy. Coastal cities such as Boston grew and thrived.

## Middle or Middle Atlantic Colonies

The Middle or Middle Atlantic Colonies were New York, New Jersey, Pennsylvania and Delaware. Unlike the New England colonies, where most colonists were from England and Scotland, the Middle Colonies founders were from various countries including the Netherlands and Sweden. Various factors led these colonists to America. More fertile than New England, the Middle Colonies became major producers of **crops** including rye, oats, potatoes, wheat, and barley. Some particularly wealthy inhabitants owned large farms and/or businesses. Farmers in general were able to produce enough to have a surplus to sell. Tenant farmers also rented land from larger land owners.

## Southern Colonies

The Southern Colonies were Maryland, Virginia, North Carolina, South Carolina and Georgia. Of the Southern Colonies, Virginia was the first permanent English colony and Georgia the last. The warm climate and rich soil of the south encouraged **agriculture**, and the growing season was long. As a result, economy in the south was based largely on labor-intensive **plantations**. Crops included tobacco, rice and indigo, all of which became valuable cash crops. Most land in the south was controlled by wealthy plantation owners and farmers. Labor on the farms came in the form of indentured servants and African slaves. The first of these **African slaves** arrived in Virginia in 1619.

## Significance of the French and Indian Wars

The **British defeat of the Spanish Armada** in 1588 led to the decline of Spanish power in Europe. This in turn led the British and French into battle several times between 1689 and 1748. These wars were:
- King William's War, or the Nine Years War, 1689-1697. This war was fought largely in Flanders.
- The War of Spanish Succession, or Queen Anne's War, 1702-1713
- War of Austrian Succession, or King George's War, 1740-1748

The fourth and final war, the **French and Indian War** (1754-1763), was fought largely in the North American territory, and resulted in the end of France's reign as a colonial power in North America. Although the French held many advantages, including more cooperative colonists and numerous Indian allies, the strong leadership of **William Pitt** eventually led the British to victory. Costs incurred during the wars eventually led to discontent in the colonies and helped spark the **American Revolution**.

## Navigation Acts

The Navigation Acts, enacted in 1651, were an attempt by Britain to dominate international trade. Aimed largely at the Dutch, the **Acts** banned foreign ships from transporting goods to the British colonies, and from transporting goods to Britain from elsewhere in Europe. While the restrictions on trade angered some colonists, these Acts were helpful to other American colonists who, as members of the British Empire, were legally able to provide ships for Britain's growing trade interests and use the ships for their own trading ventures. By the time the French and Indian War had ended, one-third of British merchant ships were built in the American colonies. Many colonists amassed fortunes in the shipbuilding trade.

## Britain's Taxation of the American Colonies After the French and Indian War

The French and Indian War created circumstances for which the British desperately needed more revenue. These needs included:
- Paying off the war debt
- Defending the expanding empire
- Governing Britain's 33 far-flung colonies, including the American colonies

To meet these needs, the British passed additional laws, increasing revenues from the colonies. Because they had spent so much money to defend the American colonies, the British felt it was appropriate to collect considerably higher **taxes** from them. The colonists felt this was unfair, and many were led to protest the increasing taxes. Eventually, protest led to violence.

## Triangular Trade

Triangular trade began in the Colonies with ships setting off for **Africa**, carrying rum. In Africa, the rum was traded for gold or slaves. Ships then went from Africa to the **West Indies**, trading slaves for sugar, molasses, or money. To complete the triangle, the ships returned to the **colonies** with sugar or molasses to make more rum, as well as stores of gold and silver. This trade triangle violated the Molasses Act of 1733, which required the colonists to pay high duties to Britain on molasses acquired from French, Dutch, and Spanish colonies. The colonists ignored these duties, and the British government adopted a policy of salutary neglect by not enforcing them.

## Effects of New Laws on British-Colonial Relations

While earlier revenue-generating acts such as the Navigation Acts brought money to the colonists, the new laws after 1763 required colonists to pay money back to **Britain**. The British felt this was fair since the colonists were British subjects and since they had incurred debt protecting the Colonies. The colonists felt it was not only unfair, but illegal.

The development of **local government** in America had given the colonists a different view of the structure and role of government. This made it difficult for the British to understand the colonists' protests against what the British felt was a fair and reasonable solution to the mother country's financial problems.

## Factors that Led to Increasing Discontent in the American Colonies

More and more colonists were born on American soil, decreasing any sense of kinship with the far away British rulers. Their new environment had led to new ideas of government and a strong view of the colonies as a separate entity from Britain. Colonists were allowed to **self-govern** in domestic issues, but **Britain** controlled international issues. In fact, the American colonies were largely left to form their own local government bodies, giving them more freedom than any other colonial territory. This gave the colonists a sense of **independence**, which led them to resent control from Britain. Threats during the French and Indian War led the colonists to call for unification in order to protect themselves.

## Colonial Government and British Government Differences that Led to "No Taxation Without Representation"

As new towns and other legislative districts developed in America, the colonists began to practice **representative government**. Colonial legislative bodies were made up of elected representatives chosen by male property owners in the districts. These individuals represented the interests of the districts from which they had been elected.

By contrast, in Britain the **Parliament** represented the entire country. Parliament was not elected to represent individual districts. Instead, they represented specific classes. Because of this drastically different approach to government, the British did not understand the colonists' statement that they had no representation in the British Parliament.

## Acts of British Parliament that Occurred After the French and Indian Wars

After the French and Indian Wars, the British Parliament passed four major acts:
1. The **Sugar Act**, 1764—this act not only required taxes to be collected on molasses brought into the colonies, but gave British officials the right to search the homes of anyone suspected of violating it.
2. The **Stamp Act**, 1765—this act taxed printed materials such as newspapers and legal documents. Protests led the Stamp Act to be repealed in 1766, but the repeal also included the Declaratory Act, which stated that Parliament had the right to govern the colonies.
3. The **Quartering Act**, 1765—this act required colonists to provide accommodations and supplies for British troops. In addition, colonists were prohibited from settling west of the Appalachians until given permission by Britain.
4. The **Townshend Acts**, 1767—these acts taxed paper, paint, lead and tea that came into the colonies. Colonists led boycotts in protest, and in Massachusetts leaders like Samuel and John Adams began to organize resistance against British rule.

## Factors that Led to the Boston Massacre

With the passage of the **Stamp Act**, nine colonies met in New York to demand its repeal. Elsewhere, protest arose in New York City, Philadelphia, Boston and other cities. These protests sometimes escalated into violence, often targeting ruling British officials. The passage of the **Townshend Acts** in 1767 led to additional tension in the colonies. The British sent troops to New York City and Boston. On March 5, 1770, protesters began to taunt the British troops, throwing snowballs. The soldiers responded by firing into the crowd. This clash between protesters and soldiers led to five deaths and eight injuries, and was christened the **Boston Massacre**. Shortly thereafter, Britain repealed the majority of the Townshend Acts.

## Tea Act that Led to the Boston Tea Party

The majority of the **Townshend Acts** were repealed after the Boston Massacre in 1770, but Britain kept the tax on tea. In 1773, the **Tea Act** was passed. This allowed the East India Company to sell tea for much lower prices, and also allowed them to bypass American distributors, selling directly to shopkeepers instead. Colonial tea merchants saw this as a direct assault on their business. In December of 1773, the **Sons of Liberty** boarded ships in Boston Harbor and dumped 342 chests of tea into the sea in protest of the new laws. This act of protest came to be known as the **Boston Tea Party**.

## Coercive Acts Passed After the Boston Tea Party

The Coercive Acts passed by Britain in 1774 were meant to punish Massachusetts for defying British authority. The four acts, also known as the **Intolerable Acts**:
- Shut down ports in Boston until the city paid back the value of the tea destroyed during the Boston Tea Party
- Required that local government officials in Massachusetts be appointed by the governor rather than being elected by the people
- Allowed trials of British soldiers to be transferred to Britain rather than being held in Massachusetts
- Required locals to provide lodging for British soldiers any time there was a disturbance, even if lodging required them to stay in private homes

These Acts led to the assembly of the First Continental Congress in Philadelphia on September 5, 1774. Fifty-five delegates met, representing 12 of the American colonies. They sought compromise with England over England's increasingly harsh efforts to control the colonies.

## First Continental Congress

The First Continental Congress met in Philadelphia on September 5, 1774. Their goal was to achieve a peaceful agreement with Britain. Made up of delegates from 12 of the 13 colonies, the Congress affirmed loyalty to Britain and the power of Parliament to dictate foreign affairs in the colonies. However, they demanded that the **Intolerable Acts** be repealed, and instituted a trade embargo with Britain until this came to pass.

In response, George III of England declared that the American colonies must submit or face military action. The British sought to end assemblies that opposed their policies. These assemblies gathered weapons and began to form militias. On April 19, 1775, the British military was ordered to disperse a meeting of the Massachusetts Assembly. A battle ensued on Lexington Common as the armed colonists resisted. The resulting battles became the **Battle of Lexington and Concord**—the first battles of the **American Revolution**.

## Significance of the Second Continental Congress

The Second Continental Congress met in Philadelphia on May 10, 1775, a month after Lexington and Concord. Their discussions centered on defense of the American colonies and how to conduct the growing war, as well as local government. The delegates also discussed declaring independence from Britain, with many members in favor of this drastic move. They established an army, and on June 15, named **George Washington** as its commander-in-chief. By 1776, it was obvious that there was no turning back from full-scale war with Britain. The colonial delegates of the Continental Congress drafted the **Declaration of Independence** on July 4, 1776.

## Origins and Basic Ideas of the Declaration of Independence

Penned by Thomas Jefferson and signed on July 4, 1776, the **Declaration of Independence** stated that King George III had violated the rights of the colonists and was establishing a tyrannical reign over them. Many of Jefferson's ideas of natural rights and property rights were shaped by seventeenth-century philosopher **John Locke**. Jefferson asserted all people's rights to "life, liberty and the pursuit of happiness." Locke's comparable idea asserted "life, liberty, and private property."

Both felt that the purpose of government was to protect the rights of the people, and that individual rights were more important than individuals' obligations to the state.

## Battles of the Revolutionary War

The following are five major battles of the Revolutionary War and their significance:
- The **Battle of Lexington and Concord** (April 1775) is considered the first engagement of the Revolutionary War.
- The **Battle of Bunker Hill** (June 1775) was one of the bloodiest of the entire war. Although American troops withdrew, about half of the British army was lost. The colonists proved they could stand against professional British soldiers. In August, Britain declared that the American colonies were officially in a state of rebellion.
- The first colonial victory occurred in Trenton, New Jersey, when Washington and his troops **crossed the Delaware River** on Christmas Day, 1776 for a December 26 surprise attack on British and Hessian troops.
- The **Battle of Saratoga** effectively ended a plan to separate the New England colonies from their Southern counterparts. The surrender of British general John Burgoyne led to France joining the war as allies of the Americans, and is generally considered a turning point of the war.
- On October 19, 1781, General Cornwallis surrendered after a defeat in the **Battle of Yorktown**, ending the Revolutionary War.

## Significance of the Treaty of Paris

The Treaty of Paris was signed on September 3, 1783, bringing an official end to the Revolutionary War. In this document, Britain officially recognized the United States of America as an **independent nation**. The treaty established the Mississippi River as the country's western border. The treaty also restored Florida to Spain, while France reclaimed African and Caribbean colonies seized by the British in 1763. On November 25, 1783, the last British troops departed from the newly born United States of America.

## Significance of the Articles of Confederation

A precursor to the Constitution, the **Articles of Confederation** represented the first attempt of the newly independent colonies to establish the basics of government. The Continental Congress approved the Articles on November 15, 1777. They went into effect on March 1, 1781, following ratification by the thirteen states.  The Articles prevented a central government from gaining too much power, instead giving power to a **Congressional body** made up of **delegates** from all thirteen states. However, the individual states retained final authority.

Without a strong central **executive**, though, this weak alliance among the new states proved ineffective in settling disputes or enforcing laws. The idea of a weak central government needed to be revised. Recognition of these weaknesses eventually led to the drafting of a new document, the **Constitution**.

## Initial Proposition and Draft of the Constitution

Delegates from twelve of the thirteen states (Rhode Island was not represented) met in Philadelphia in May of 1787, initially intending to revise the Articles of Confederation. However, it quickly became apparent that a simple revision would not provide the workable governmental structure the newly formed country needed. After vowing to keep all the proceedings secret until the final document was completed, the delegates set out to draft what would eventually become the **Constitution of the United States of America**. By keeping the negotiations secret, the delegates were able to present a completed document to the country for ratification, rather than having every small detail hammered out by the general public.

## General Structure of Government Proposed by the Delegates

The delegates agreed that the new nation required a **strong central government**, but that its overall power should be **limited**. The various branches of the government should have **balanced power**, so that no one group could control the others. Final power belonged with the **citizens** who voted officials into office based on who would provide the best representation.

## Significance of the Virginia Plan, the New Jersey Plan, and the Great Compromise

Disagreement immediately occurred between delegates from large states and those from smaller states. James Madison and Edmund Randolph (the governor of Virginia) felt that representation in Congress should be based on state population. This was the **Virginia Plan**. The **New Jersey Plan**, presented by William Paterson, from New Jersey, proposed each state have equal representation. Finally, Roger Sherman from Connecticut formulated the **Connecticut Compromise**, also called the Great Compromise. The result was the familiar structure we have today. Each state has the equal representation of two Senators in the Senate, with the number of representatives in the House of Representatives based on population. This is called a **bicameral Congress**. Both houses may draft bills, but financial matters must originate in the House of Representatives.

## Effects of the Three-Fifths Compromise and the Number of Representatives for Each State

During debate on the US Constitution, a disagreement arose between the Northern and Southern states involving how **slaves** should be counted when determining a state's quota of representatives. In the South large numbers of slaves were commonly used to run plantations. Delegates wanted slaves to be counted to determine the number of representatives, but not counted to determine the amount of taxes the states would pay. The Northern states wanted exactly the opposite arrangement. The final decision was to count three-fifths of the slave population both for tax purposes and to determine representation. This was called the **three-fifths compromise**.

## Provisions of the Commerce Compromise

The Commerce Compromise also resulted from a North/South disagreement. In the North the economy was centered on **industry and trade**. The Southern economy was largely **agricultural**. The Northern states wanted to give the new government the ability to regulate exports as well as trade between the states. The South opposed this plan. Another compromise was in order. In the end, Congress received regulatory power over all trade, including the ability to collect **tariffs** on exported goods. In the South, this raised another red flag regarding the slave trade, as they were concerned about the effect on their economy if tariffs were levied on slaves. The final agreement allowed importing slaves to continue for twenty years without government intervention. Import taxes on slaves were limited, and after the year 1808, Congress could decide whether to allow continued imports of slaves.

## Objections Against the Constitution

Once the Constitution was drafted, it was presented for approval by the states. Nine states needed to approve the document for it to become official. However, debate and discussion continued. Major **concerns** included:
- The lack of a bill of rights to protect individual freedoms
- States felt too much power was being handed over to the central government
- Voters wanted more control over their elected representatives

Discussion about necessary changes to the Constitution was divided into two camps: Federalists and Anti-Federalists. **Federalists** wanted a strong central government. **Anti-Federalists** wanted to prevent a tyrannical government from developing if a central government held too much pow

## Major Players in the Federalist and Anti-Federalist camps

Major Federalist leaders included Alexander Hamilton, John Jay and James Madison. They wrote a series of letters, called the **Federalist Papers**, aimed at convincing the states to ratify the Constitution. These were published in New York papers. Anti-Federalists included Thomas Jefferson and Patrick Henry. They argued against the Constitution as it was originally drafted in a series of **Anti-Federalist Papers**.

The final compromise produced a strong central government controlled by checks and balances. A **Bill of Rights** was also added, becoming the first ten amendments to the Constitution. These amendments protected rights such as freedom of speech, freedom of religion, and other basic rights. Aside from various amendments added throughout the years, the United States Constitution has remained unchanged.

## Individuals Who Formed the First Administration of the New Government

The individuals who formed the first administration of the new government were:
- **George Washington**—elected as the first President of the United States in 1789
- **John Adams**—finished second in the election and became the first Vice President
- **Thomas Jefferson**—appointed by Washington as Secretary of State
- **Alexander Hamilton**—appointed Secretary of the Treasury

## Alien and Sedition Acts

When **John Adams** became president, a war was raging between Britain and France. While Adams and the **Federalists** backed the British, Thomas Jefferson and the **Republican Party** supported the French. The United States nearly went to war with France during this time period, while France worked to spread its international standing and influence under the leadership of **Napoleon Bonaparte**. The **Alien and Sedition Acts** grew out of this conflict, and made it illegal to speak in a hostile fashion against the existing government. They also allowed the president to deport anyone in the US who was not a citizen and who was suspected of treason or treasonous activity. When Jefferson became the third president in 1800, he repealed these four laws and pardoned anyone who had been convicted under them.

## Development of Political Parties in Early U.S. Government

Many in the US were against political parties after seeing the way parties, or factions, functioned in Britain. The factions in Britain were more interested in personal profit than the overall good of the country, and they did not want this to happen in the US.

However, the differences of opinion between Thomas Jefferson and Alexander Hamilton led to formation of **political parties**. Hamilton favored a stronger central government, while Jefferson felt that more power should remain with the states. Jefferson was in favor of strict Constitutional interpretation, while Hamilton believed in a more flexible approach. As others joined the two camps, Hamilton backers began to term themselves **Federalists** while those supporting Jefferson became identified as **Democratic-Republicans**.

## Development of the Whig, the Democratic, and the Republican Parties

**Thomas Jefferson** was elected president in 1800 and again in 1804. The **Federalist Party** began to decline, and its major figure, Alexander Hamilton, died in a duel with Aaron Burr in 1804. By 1816, the Federalist Party had virtually disappeared.

New parties sprang up to take its place. After 1824, the **Democratic-Republican Party** suffered a split. The **Whigs** rose, backing John Quincy Adams and industrial growth. The new Democratic Party formed, in opposition to the Whigs, and their candidate, Andrew Jackson, was elected as president in 1828.

By the 1850s, issues regarding slavery led to the formation of the **Republican Party**, which was anti-slavery, while the Democratic Party, with a larger interest in the South, favored slavery. This Republican/Democrat division formed the basis of today's **two-party system**.

## Significance of Marbury v. Madison

The main duty of the Supreme Court today is **judicial review**. This power was largely established by **Marbury v. Madison**. When John Adams was voted out of office in 1800, he worked, during his final days in office, to appoint Federalist judges to Supreme Court positions, knowing Jefferson, his replacement, held opposing views. As late as March 3, the day before Jefferson was to take office, Adams made last-minute appointments referred to as "Midnight Judges." One of the late appointments was William Marbury. The next day, March 4, Jefferson ordered his Secretary of State, James Madison, not to deliver Marbury's commission. This decision was backed by Chief Justice Marshall, who determined that the **Judiciary Act of 1789**, which granted the power to deliver commissions, was illegal in that it gave the Judicial Branch powers not granted in the Constitution. This case set precedent for the Supreme Court to nullify laws it found to be **unconstitutional**.

> ➢ **Review Video:** Marbury v. Madison
> *Visit **mometrix.com/academy** and enter **Code**: 573964*

## McCulloch v. Maryland

Judicial review was further exercised by the Supreme Court in **McCulloch v. Maryland**. When Congress chartered a national bank, the **Second Bank of the United States**, Maryland voted to tax any bank business dealing with banks chartered outside the state, including the federally chartered bank. Andrew McCulloch, an employee of the Second Bank of the US in Baltimore, refused to pay this tax. The resulting lawsuit from the State of Maryland went to the Supreme Court for judgment.

John Marshall, Chief Justice of the Supreme Court, stated that Congress was within its rights to charter a national bank. In addition, the State of Maryland did not have the power to levy a tax on the federal bank or on the federal government in general. In cases where state and federal government collided, precedent was set for the **federal government** to prevail.

### Effect of the Treaty of Paris on Native Americans

After the Revolutionary War, the **Treaty of Paris**, which outlined the terms of surrender of the British to the Americans, granted large parcels of land to the US that were occupied by Native Americans. The new government attempted to claim the land, treating the natives as a conquered people. This approach proved unenforceable.

Next, the government tried purchasing the land from the Indians via a series of **treaties** as the country expanded westward. In practice, however, these treaties were not honored, and Native Americans were simply dislocated and forced to move farther and farther west, often with military action, as American expansion continued.

### Indian Removal Act of 1830 and the Treaty of New Echota

The Indian Removal Act of 1830 gave the new American government power to form treaties with Native Americans. In theory, America would claim land east of the Mississippi in exchange for land west of the Mississippi, to which the natives would relocate voluntarily. In practice, many tribal leaders were forced into signing the treaties, and relocation at times occurred by force.

The **Treaty of New Echota** in 1835 was supposedly a treaty between the US government and Cherokee tribes in Georgia. However, the treaty was not signed by tribal leaders, but rather by a small portion of the represented people. The leaders protested and refused to leave, but President Martin Van Buren enforced the treaty by sending soldiers. During their forced relocation, more than 4,000 Cherokee Indians died on what became known as the **Trail of Tears**.

### Development of Economic Trends as the U.S. Continued to Grow

In the Northeast, the economy mostly depended on **manufacturing, industry, and industrial development**. This led to a dichotomy between rich business owners and industrial leaders and the much poorer workers who supported their businesses. The South continued to depend on **agriculture**, especially on large-scale farms or plantations worked mostly by slaves and indentured servants. In the West, where new settlements had begun to develop, the land was largely wild. Growing communities were essentially **agricultural**, raising crops and livestock. The differences between regions led each to support different interests both politically and economically.

### Political Motivations Behind France Selling the Louisiana Purchase

With tension still high between France and Britain, Napoleon was in need of money to support his continuing war efforts. To secure necessary funds, he decided to sell the **Louisiana Territory** to the US. President **Thomas Jefferson** wanted to buy New Orleans, feeling US trade was made vulnerable to both Spain and France at that port. Instead, Napoleon sold him the entire territory for the bargain price of fifteen million dollars. The Louisiana Territory was larger than all the rest of the United States put together, and it eventually became fifteen additional states.

**Federalists** in Congress were opposed to the purchase. They feared that the Louisiana Purchase would extend slavery, and that further western growth would weaken the power of the northern states.

## Major Ideas Driving American Foreign Policy

The three major ideas driving American foreign policy during its early years were:
- **Isolationism**—the early US government did not intend to establish colonies, though they did plan to grow larger within the bounds of North America.
- **No entangling alliances**—both George Washington and Thomas Jefferson were opposed to forming any permanent alliances with other countries or becoming involved in other countries' internal issues.
- **Nationalism**—a positive patriotic feeling about the United States blossomed quickly among its citizens, particularly after the War of 1812, when the US once again defeated Britain. The Industrial Revolution also sparked increased nationalism by allowing even the most far-flung areas of the US to communicate with each other via telegraph and the expanding railroad.

## Causes and Result of the War of 1812

The War of 1812 grew out of the continuing tension between France and Great Britain. Napoleon continued striving to conquer Britain, while the US continued trade with both countries, but favored France and the French colonies. Because of what Britain saw as an alliance between America and France, they determined to bring an end to trade between the two nations.

With the British preventing US trade with the French and the French preventing trade with the British, James Madison's presidency introduced acts to **regulate international trade**. If either Britain or France removed their restrictions, America would not trade with the other country. Napoleon acted first, and Madison prohibited trade with England. England saw this as the US formally siding with the French, and war ensued in 1812.

The **War of 1812** has been called the **Second American Revolution**. It established the superiority of the US naval forces and reestablished US independence from Britain and Europe.

The British had two major objections to America's continued trade with France. First, they saw the US as helping France's war effort by providing supplies and goods. Second, the United States had grown into a competitor, taking trade and money away from British ships and tradesmen. In its attempts to end American trade with France, the British put into effect the **Orders in Council**, which made any and all French-owned ports off-limits to American ships. They also began to seize American ships and conscript their crews.

> ➤ **Review Video:** Opinions About the War of 1812
> *Visit **mometrix.com/academy** and enter **Code**: **274558***

> ➤ **Review Video:** Results of the War of 1812
> *Visit **mometrix.com/academy** and enter **Code**: **993725***

## Major Military Events of the War of 1812

Two major naval battles, at **Lake Erie** and **Lake Champlain**, kept the British from invading the US via Canada. American attempts to conquer Canadian lands were not successful.

In another memorable British attack, the British invaded Washington DC and burned the White House on August 24, 1814. Legend has it that **Dolley Madison**, the First Lady, salvaged the portrait of George Washington from the fire. On Christmas Eve, 1814, the **Treaty of Ghent** officially ended the war. However, Andrew Jackson, unaware that the war was over, managed another victory at New Orleans on January 8, 1815. This victory improved American morale and led to a new wave of national pride and support known as the "**Era of Good Feelings.**"

## Monroe Doctrine

On December 2, 1823, President Monroe delivered a message to Congress in which he introduced the **Monroe Doctrine**. In this address, he stated that any attempts by European powers to establish new colonies on the North American continent would be considered interference in American politics. The US would stay out of European matters, and expected Europe to offer America the same courtesy. This approach to foreign policy stated in no uncertain terms that America would not tolerate any new European colonies in the New World, and that events occurring in Europe would no longer influence the policies and doctrines of the US.

## Lewis and Clark Expedition

The purchase of the **Louisiana Territory** from France in 1803 more than doubled the size of the United States. President Thomas Jefferson wanted to have the area mapped and explored, since much of the territory was wilderness. He chose Meriwether Lewis and William Clark to head an expedition into the Louisiana Territory. After two years, Lewis and Clark returned, having traveled all the way to the Pacific Ocean. They brought maps, detailed journals, and a multitude of information about the wide expanse of land they had traversed. The **Lewis and Clark Expedition** opened up the west in the Louisiana Territory and beyond for further exploration and settlement.

> ➤ **Review Video:** The Lewis and Clark Expedition
> Visit *mometrix.com/academy* and enter *Code*: **570657**

## Effects of Manifest Destiny on American Politics

In the 1800s, many believed America was destined by God to expand west, bringing as much of the North American continent as possible under the umbrella of US government. With the Northwest Ordinance and the Louisiana Purchase, over half of the continent became American. However, the rapid and relentless expansion brought conflict with the Native Americans, Great Britain, Mexico and Spain. One result of "**Manifest Destiny**" was the **Mexican-American War** from 1846 to 1848. By the end of the war, Texas, California, and a large portion of what is now the American Southwest joined the growing nation. Conflict also arose over the **Oregon territory**, shared by the US and Britain. In 1846, President James Polk resolved this problem by compromising with Britain, establishing a US boundary south of the 49th parallel.

> ➤ **Review Video:** Manifest Destiny
> Visit *mometrix.com/academy* and enter *Code*: **957409**

## Mexican-American War

Spain had held colonial interests in America since the 1540s—earlier even than Great Britain. In 1810, **Mexico** revolted against Spain and became a free nation in 1821. **Texas** followed suit, declaring its independence after an 1836 revolution. In 1844, the Democrats pressed President Tyler to annex Texas. Unlike his predecessor, Andrew Jackson, Tyler agreed to admit Texas into the Union and in 1845 Texas became a state.

During Mexico's war for independence, the nation incurred $4.5 million in war debts to the US. Polk offered to forgive the debts in return for New Mexico and Upper California, but Mexico refused. In 1846, war was declared in response to a Mexican attack on American troops along the southern border of Texas. Additional conflict arose in Congress over the **Wilmot Proviso**, which stated that slavery was prohibited in any territory the U.S. acquired from Mexico as a result of the **Mexican-American War**. The war ended in 1848.

## Gadsden Purchase and the 1853 Post-War Treaty with Mexico

After the Mexican-American war, a **second treaty** in 1853 determined hundreds of miles of America's southwest borders. In 1854, the **Gadsden Purchase** was finalized, providing even more territory to aid in the building of the transcontinental railroad. This purchase added what would eventually become the southernmost regions of Arizona and New Mexico to the growing nation. The modern outline of the United States was by this time nearly complete.

## Influence of the American System on American Economics

Spurred by the trade conflicts of the War of 1812, and supported by Henry Clay among others, the **American System** set up tariffs to help protect American interests from competition with overseas products. Reducing competition led to growth in employment and an overall increase in American industry. The higher tariffs also provided funds for the government to pay for various improvements. Congress passed high tariffs in 1816 and also chartered a federal bank. The **Second Bank of the United States** was given the job of regulating America's money supply.

## Jacksonian Democracy vs. Preceding Political Climate

Jacksonian Democracy is largely seen as a shift from politics favoring the wealthy to politics favoring the common man. All free white males were given the right to **vote**, not just property owners, as had been the case previously. Jackson's approach favored the patronage system, Laissez-faire economics, and relocation of the Indian tribes from the Southeast portion of the country. Jackson opposed the formation of a federal bank and allowed the Second Band of the United States to collapse by vetoing a bill to renew the charter. Jackson also faced the challenge of the **Nullification Crisis** when South Carolina claimed that it could ignore or nullify any federal law it considered unconstitutional. Jackson sent troops to the state to enforce the protested tariff laws, and a compromise engineered by Henry Clay in 1833 settled the matter for the time being.

> ➤ **Review Video:** <u>Andrew Jackson as President</u>
> *Visit **mometrix.com/academy** and enter **Code**: **667792**

> ➤ **Review Video:** <u>Major Issues Under Andrew Jackson</u>
> *Visit **mometrix.com/academy** and enter **Code**: **739251**

**Major Events and Developments that Brought the North and South into Conflict**

The conflict between North and South coalesced around the issue of **slavery**, but other elements contributed to the growing disagreement. Though most farmers in the South worked small farms with little or no slave labor, the huge plantations run by the South's rich depended on slaves or indentured servants to remain profitable. They had also become more dependent on **cotton**, with slave populations growing in concert with the rapid increase in cotton production. In the North, a more diverse agricultural economy and the growth of **industry** made slaves rarer. The **abolitionist movement** grew steadily, with Harriet Beecher Stowe's *Uncle Tom's Cabin* giving many an idea to rally around. A collection of anti-slavery organizations formed, with many actively working to free slaves in the South, often bringing them to the northern states or Canada.

> ➢ **Review Video:** Conflict between the North and South
> *Visit **mometrix.com/academy** and enter **Code**: **219819***

**Anti-Slavery Organizations**

Five anti-slavery organizations and their significance are:
- **American Colonization Society**—Protestant churches formed this group, aimed at returning black slaves to Africa. Former slaves subsequently formed Liberia, but the colony did not do well, as the region was not well-suited for agriculture.
- **American Anti-Slavery Society**—William Lloyd Garrison, a Quaker, was the major force behind this group and its newspaper, *The Liberator*.
- **Philadelphia Female Anti-Slavery Society**—a women-only group formed by Margaretta Forten because women were not allowed to join the Anti-Slavery Society formed by her father.
- **Anti-Slavery Convention of American Women**—this group continued meeting even after pro-slavery factions burned down their original meeting place.
- **Female Vigilant Society**—an organization that raised funds to help the Underground Railroad, as well as slave refugees.

**Attitudes Toward Education in the Early 19ᵗʰ Century**

**Horace Mann**, among others, felt that schools could help children become better citizens, keep them away from crime, prevent poverty, and help American society become more unified. His *Common School Journal* brought his ideas of the importance of education into the public consciousness and proposed his suggestions for an improved American education system. Increased literacy led to increased awareness of current events, Western expansion, and other major developments of the time period. Public interest and participation in the arts and literature also increased. By the end of the 19ᵗʰ century, all children had access to a **free public elementary education**.

**Developments in Transportation**

As America expanded its borders, it also developed new technology to travel the rapidly growing country. Roads and railroads traversed the nation, with the **Transcontinental Railroad** eventually allowing travel from one coast to the other. Canals and steamboats simplified water travel and made shipping easier and less expensive. The **Erie Canal** (1825) connected the Great Lakes with the Hudson River. Other canals connected other major waterways, further facilitating transportation and the shipment of goods.

With growing numbers of settlers moving into the West, **wagon trails** developed, including the Oregon Trail, California Trail and the Santa Fe Trail. The most common vehicles seen along these westbound trails were covered wagons, also known as **prairie schooners**.

## Industrial Activity Before and After 1800

During the eighteenth century, goods were often manufactured in houses or small shops. With increased technology allowing for the use of machines, **factories** began to develop. In factories a large volume of salable goods could be produced in a much shorter amount of time. Many Americans, including increasing numbers of **immigrants**, found jobs in these factories, which were in constant need of labor.  Another major invention was the **cotton gin**, which significantly decreased the processing time of cotton and was a major factor in the rapid expansion of cotton production in the South.

## Development of Labor Movements in the 1800s

In 1751, a group of bakers held a protest in which they stopped baking bread. This was technically the first American **labor strike**. In the 1830s and 1840s, labor movements began in earnest. Boston's masons, carpenters and stoneworkers protested the length of the workday, fighting to reduce it to ten hours. In 1844, a group of women in the textile industry also fought to reduce their workday to ten hours, forming the **Lowell Female Labor Reform Association**. Many other protests occurred and organizations developed through this time period with the same goal in mind.

## Second Great Awakening

Led by Protestant evangelical leaders, the **Second Great Awakening** occurred between 1800 and 1830. Several missionary groups grew out of the movement, including the **American Home Missionary Society**, which formed in 1826. The ideas behind the Second Great Awakening focused on personal responsibility, both as an individual and in response to injustice and suffering. The **American Bible Society** and the **American Tract Society** provided literature, while various traveling preachers spread the word. New denominations arose, including the Latter-day Saints and Seventh-day Adventists.

Another movement associated with the Second Great Awakening was the **temperance movement**, focused on ending the production and use of alcohol. One major organization behind the temperance movement was the **Society for the Promotion of Temperance**, formed in 1826 in Boston.

## Early Leaders in the Women's Rights Movement

The women's rights movement began in the 1840s with leaders including Elizabeth Cady Stanton, Sojourner Truth, Ernestine Rose, and Lucretia Mott. In 1869, Elizabeth Cady Stanton and Susan B. Anthony formed the **National Woman Suffrage Association**, fighting for women's right to vote.

In 1848 in Seneca Falls, the first women's rights convention was held, with about three hundred attendees. The two-day **Seneca Falls Convention** discussed the rights of women to vote (suffrage) as well as equal treatment in careers, legal proceedings, etc. The convention produced a "Declaration of Sentiments" which outlined a plan for women to attain the rights they deserved. **Frederick Douglass** supported the women's rights movement, as well as the abolition movement. In fact, women's rights and abolition movements often went hand-in-hand during this time period.

## Effects of the Missouri Compromise on the Tensions Between the North and South

By 1819, the United States had developed a tenuous balance between slave and free states, with exactly twenty-two senators in Congress from each faction. However, Missouri was ready to join the union. As a slave state, it would tip the balance in Congress. To prevent this imbalance, the **Missouri Compromise** brought the northern part of Massachusetts into the union as Maine, establishing it as a free state to balance the admission of Missouri as a slave state. In addition, the remaining portion of the Louisiana Purchase was to remain free north of **latitude 36°30'**. Since cotton did not grow well this far north, this limitation was acceptable to congressmen representing the slave states.

However, the proposed Missouri constitution presented a problem, as it outlawed immigration of free blacks into the state. Another compromise was in order, this time proposed by **Henry Clay**. According to this new compromise, Missouri's would never pass a law that prevented anyone from entering the state. Through this and other work, Clay earned his title of the "**Great Compromiser.**"

> ➤ **Review Video:** Missouri Compromise
> *Visit **mometrix.com/academy** and enter **Code**: **848091**

## Popular Sovereignty and the Compromise of 1850

In addition to the pro-slavery and anti-slavery factions, a third group rose who felt that each individual state should decide whether to allow or permit slavery within its borders. The idea that a state could make its own choices was referred to as **popular sovereignty**.

When California applied to join the union in 1849, the balance of congressional power was again threatened. The **Compromise of 1850** introduced a group of laws meant to bring an end to the conflict:
- California's admittance as a free state
- The outlaw of the slave trade in Washington, D.C
- An increase in efforts to capture escaped slaves
- The right of New Mexico and Utah territories to decide individually whether to allow slavery

In spite of these measures, debate raged each time a new state prepared to enter the union.

## Kansas-Nebraska Act Trigger of Additional Conflict

With the creation of the Kansas and Nebraska territories in 1854, another debate began. Congress allowed popular sovereignty in these territories, but slavery opponents argued that the Missouri Compromise had already made slavery illegal in this region. In Kansas, two separate governments arose, one pro-slavery and one anti-slavery. Conflict between the two factions rose to violence, leading Kansas to gain the nickname of "**Bleeding Kansas.**"

> ➤ **Review Video:** Sectional Crisis: The Kansas-Nebraska Act
> Visit *mometrix.com/academy* and enter *Code*: **982119**

## Dred Scott Decision

Abolitionist factions coalesced around the case of **Dred Scott**, using his case to test the country's laws regarding slavery. Scott, a slave, had been taken by his owner from Missouri, which was a slave state. He then traveled to Illinois, a free state, then on to the Minnesota Territory, also free based on the Missouri Compromise. After several years, he returned to Missouri and his owner subsequently died. Abolitionists took Scott's case to court, stating that Scott was no longer a slave but free, since he had lived in free territory. The case went to the Supreme Court.

The Supreme Court stated that, because Scott, as a slave, was not a US citizen, his time in free states did not change his status. He also did not have the right to sue. In addition, the Court determined that the **Missouri Compromise** was unconstitutional, stating that Congress had overstepped its bounds by outlawing slavery in the territories.

> ➤ **Review Video:** Dred Scott Act
> Visit *mometrix.com/academy* and enter *Code*: **364838**

## Incidents at Harper's Ferry and John Brown's Role

John Brown, an abolitionist, had participated in several anti-slavery activities, including killing five pro-slavery men in retaliation, after the sacking of Lawrence, Kansas, an anti-slavery town. He and other abolitionists also banded together to pool their funds and build a runaway slave colony.

In 1859, Brown seized a federal arsenal in **Harper's Ferry**, located in what is now West Virginia. Brown intended to seize guns and ammunition and lead a slave rebellion. **Robert E. Lee** captured Brown and 21 followers, who were subsequently tried and hanged. While Northerners took the executions as an indication that the government supported slavery, Southerners were of the opinion that most of the North supported Brown and were, in general, anti-slavery.

## Presidential Candidates for the 1860 Election

The 1860 Presidential candidates represented four different parties, each with a different opinion on slavery:
- **John Breckinridge**, representing the Southern Democrats, was pro-slavery but urged compromise to preserve the Union.
- **Abraham Lincoln**, of the Republican Party, was anti-slavery.

- **Stephen Douglas**, of the Northern Democrats, felt that the issue should be determined locally, on a state-by-state basis.
- **John Bell**, of the Constitutional Union Party, focused primarily on keeping the Union intact.

In the end, Abraham Lincoln won both the popular and electoral election. Southern states, who had sworn to secede from the Union if Lincoln was elected did so, led by South Carolina. Shortly thereafter, the Civil War began when Confederate shots were fired on **Fort Sumter** in Charleston.

## North vs. South in the Civil War

The Northern states had significant advantages, including:
- **Larger population**—the North consisted of 24 states while the South had 11.
- **Better transportation and finances**—with railroads primarily in the North, supply chains were much more dependable, as was overseas trade.
- **Raw materials**—the North held the majority of America's gold, as well as iron, copper, and other minerals vital to wartime.

The South's advantages included:
- **Better-trained military officers**—many of the Southern officers were West Point trained and had commanded in the Mexican and Indian wars.
- **Familiarity with weapons**—the climate and lifestyle of the South meant most of the people were experienced with both guns and horses. The industrial North had less extensive experience.
- **Defensive position**—the South felt that victory was guaranteed, since they were protecting their own lands, while the North would be invading.
- **Well-defined goals**—the South fought an ideological war to be allowed to govern themselves and preserve their way of life. The North originally fought to preserve the Union and later to free the slaves.

## Benefit of the Emancipation Proclamation on the Union's Military Strategy

The Emancipation Proclamation, issued by President Lincoln on January 1, 1863, freed all slaves in **Confederate states** that were still in rebellion against the Union. While the original proclamation did not free any slaves in the states actually under Union control, it did set a precedent for the emancipation of slaves as the war progressed.

The **Emancipation Proclamation** worked in the Union's favor as many freed slaves and other black troops joined the **Union Army**. Almost 200,000 blacks fought in the Union army, and over 10,000 served in the navy. By the end of the war, over 4 million slaves had been freed, and in 1865 slavery was abolished in the **13th amendment** to the Constitution.

> ➢ **Review Video:** Emancipation Proclamation
> *Visit* ***mometrix.com/academy*** *and enter **Code**: **181778***

## Major Events of the Civil War

Six major events of the Civil War and their outcomes or significance are:
- The **First Battle of Bull Run** (July 21, 1861)—this was the first major land battle of the war. Observers, expecting to enjoy an entertaining skirmish, set up picnics nearby. Instead, they

found themselves witness to a bloodbath. Union forces were defeated, and the battle set the course of the Civil War as long, bloody and costly.

- The **Capture of Fort Henry** by Ulysses S. Grant—this battle in February of 1862 marked the Union's first major victory.
- The **Battle of Gettysburg** (July 1-3, 1863)—often seen as the turning point of the war, Gettysburg also saw the largest number of casualties of the war, with over 50,000 dead, wounded, or missing. Robert E. Lee was defeated, and the Confederate army, significantly crippled, withdrew.
- The **Overland Campaign** (May and June of 1864)—Grant, now in command of all the Union armies, led this high casualty campaign that eventually positioned the Union for victory.
- **Sherman's March to the Sea**—William Tecumseh Sherman, in May of 1864, conquered Atlanta. He then continued to Savannah, destroying vast amounts of property as he went.
- Following Lee's defeat at the Appomattox Courthouse, General Grant accepted **Lee's surrender** in the home of Wilmer McLean in Appomattox, Virginia on April 9, 1865.

## Circumstances of Lincoln's Assassination

The Civil War ended with the surrender of the South on April 9, 1865. Five days later, Lincoln and his wife, Mary, attended the play *Our American Cousin* at the Ford Theater. **John Wilkes Booth** performed his part in a conspiracy to aid the Confederacy by shooting Lincoln in the back of the head. Booth was tracked down and killed by Union soldiers 12 days later. Lincoln, carried from the theater to a nearby house, died the next morning.

## Goals of Reconstruction and the Freedmen's Bureau

In the aftermath of the Civil War, the South was left in chaos. From 1865 to 1877, government on all levels worked to help restore order to the South, ensure civil rights to the freed slaves, and bring the Confederate states back into the Union. This became known as the **Reconstruction period**. In 1866, Congress passed the **Reconstruction Acts**, placing former Confederate states under military rule and stating the grounds for readmission into the Union.

The **Freedmen's Bureau** was formed to help freedmen both with basic necessities like food and clothing and also with employment and finding of family members who had been separated during the war. Many in the South felt the Freedmen's Bureau worked to set freed slaves against their former owners. The Bureau was intended to help former slaves become self-sufficient, and to keep them from falling prey to those who would take advantage of them. It eventually closed due to lack of funding and to violence from the **Ku Klux Klan**.

## Policies of the Radical and Moderate Republicans

The **Radical Republicans** wished to treat the South quite harshly after the war. **Thaddeus Stevens**, the House Leader, suggested that the Confederate states be treated as if they were territories again, with ten years of military rule and territorial government before they would be readmitted. He also wanted to give all black men the right to vote. Former Confederate soldiers would be required to swear they had never supported the Confederacy (knows as the "Ironclad Oath") in order to be granted full rights as American citizens.

In contrast, the **moderate Republicans** wanted only black men who were literate or who had served as Union troops to be able to vote. All Confederate soldiers except troop leaders would also be able to vote. Before his death, **Lincoln** had favored a more moderate approach to

- 94 -

Reconstruction, hoping this approach might bring some states back into the Union before the end of the war.

## Black Codes and the Civil Rights Bill

The Black Codes were proposed to control freed slaves. They would not be allowed to bear arms, assemble, serve on juries, or testify against whites. Schools would be segregated, and unemployed blacks could be arrested and forced to work. The **Civil Rights Act** countered these codes, providing much wider rights for the freed slaves.

**Andrew Johnson**, who became president after Lincoln's death, supported the Black Codes and vetoed the Civil Rights Act in 1865 and again in 1866. The second time, Congress overrode his veto and it became law.

Two years later, Congress voted to **impeach** Johnson, the culmination of tensions between Congress and the president. He was tried and came within a single vote of being convicted, but ultimately was acquitted and finished his term in office.

## Purpose of the Thirteenth, Fourteenth and Fifteenth Amendments

The Thirteenth, Fourteenth and Fifteenth Amendments were all passed shortly after the end of the Civil War:
- The **Thirteenth Amendment** was ratified by the states on December 6, 1865. This amendment prohibited slavery in the United States.
- The **Fourteenth Amendment** overturned the Dred Scott decision, and was ratified July 9, 1868. American citizenship was redefined: a citizen was any person born or naturalized in the US, with all citizens guaranteed equal legal protection by all states. It also guaranteed citizens of any race the right to file a lawsuit or serve on a jury.
- The **Fifteenth Amendment** was ratified February 3, 1870. It states that no citizen of the United States can be denied the right to vote based on race, color, or previous status as a slave.

> ➤ **Review Video:** The 13th Amendment
> Visit *mometrix.com/academy* and enter *Code*: **800185**

> ➤ **Review Video:** The 14th Amendment
> Visit *mometrix.com/academy* and enter *Code*: **851325**

> ➤ **Review Video:** The 15th Amendment
> Visit *mometrix.com/academy* and enter *Code*: **287199**

## Phases of Reconstruction

The three phases of Reconstruction are:
- **Presidential Reconstruction**—largely driven by President Andrew Johnson's policies, the Presidential phase of Reconstruction was lenient on the South and allowed continued discrimination against and control over blacks.
- **Congressional Reconstruction**—Congress, controlled largely by Radical Republicans, took a different stance, providing a wider range of civil rights for blacks and greater control over

Southern government. Congressional Reconstruction is marked by military control of the former Confederate States.

- **Redemption**—gradually, the Confederate states were readmitted into the union. During this time, white Democrats took over the government of most of the South. In 1877, President Rutherford Hayes withdrew the last federal troops from the South.

## Carpetbaggers and Scalawags

The chaos in the south attracted a number of people seeking to fill the power vacuums and take advantage of the economic disruption. **Scalawags** were southern Whites who aligned with Freedmen to take over local governments. Many in the South who could have filled political offices refused to take the necessary oath required to grant them the right to vote, leaving many opportunities for Scalawags and others. **Carpetbaggers** were northerners who traveled to the South for various reasons. Some provided assistance, while others sought to make money or to acquire political power during this chaotic period.

## Transcontinental Railroad

In 1869, the **Union Pacific Railroad** completed the first section of a planned **transcontinental railroad**. This section went from Omaha, Nebraska to Sacramento, California. Ninety percent of the workers were Chinese, working in very dangerous conditions for very low pay. With the rise of the railroad, products were much more easily transported across the country. While this was positive overall for industry throughout the country, it was often damaging to family farmers, who found themselves paying high shipping costs for smaller supply orders while larger companies received major discounts.

## Measures to Limit Immigration in the 19th Century

In 1870, the **Naturalization Act** put limits on US citizenship, allowing full citizenship only to whites and those of African descent. The **Chinese Exclusion Act of 1882** put limits on Chinese immigration. The **Immigration Act of 1882** taxed immigrants, charging fifty cents per person. These funds helped pay administrative costs for regulating immigration. **Ellis Island** opened in 1892 as a processing center for those arriving in New York. 1921 saw the **Emergency Quota Act** passed, also known as the **Johnson Quota Act**, which severely limited the number of immigrants allowed into the country.

## Agriculture in the 19th Century

Technological Advances in Agricultural Changes
During the mid 1800s, irrigation techniques improved significantly. Advances occurred in cultivation and breeding, as well as fertilizer use and crop rotation. In the Great Plains, also known as the Great American Desert, the dense soil was finally cultivated with steel plows. In 1892, gasoline-powered tractors arrived, and were widely used by 1900. Other advancements in agriculture's toolset included barbed wire fences, combines, silos, deep-water wells, and the cream separator.

Major Actions that Helped Improve Agriculture
Four major government actions that helped improve US agriculture in the nineteenth century are:
- The **Department of Agriculture** came into being in 1862, working for the interests of farmers and ranchers across the country.

- The **Morrill Land-Grant Acts** were a series of acts passed between 1862 and 1890, allowing land-grant colleges.
- In conjunction with land-grant colleges, the **Hatch Act of 1887** brought agriculture experiment stations into the picture, helping discover new farming techniques
- In 1914, the **Smith-Lever Act** provided cooperative programs to help educate people about food, home economics, community development and agriculture. Related agriculture extension programs helped farmers increase crop production to feed the rapidly growing nation.

## Inventors from the 1800s

Major inventors from the 1800s and their inventions are:
- Alexander Graham Bell—the telephone
- Orville and Wilbur Wright—the airplane
- Richard Gatling—the machine gun
- Walter Hunt, Elias Howe and Isaac Singer—the sewing machine
- Nikola Tesla—alternating current
- George Eastman—the Kodak camera
- Thomas Edison—light bulbs, motion pictures, the phonograph
- Samuel Morse—the telegraph
- Charles Goodyear—vulcanized rubber
- Cyrus McCormick—the reaper
- George Westinghouse—the transformer, the air brake

This was an active period for invention, with about 700,000 patents registered between 1860 and 1900.

## Gilded Age

The time period from the end of the Civil War to the beginning of the First World War is often referred to as the **Gilded Age**, or the **Second Industrial Revolution**. The US was changing from an agricultural-based economy to an **industrial economy**, with rapid growth accompanying the shift. In addition, the country itself was expanding, spreading into the seemingly unlimited West.

This time period saw the beginning of banks, department stores, chain stores, and trusts—all familiar features of the modern-day landscape. Cities also grew rapidly, and large numbers of immigrants arrived in the country, swelling the urban ranks.

> ➤ **Review Video:** The Gilded Age: An Overview
> Visit **mometrix.com/academy** and enter **Code**: **684770**

## Factors Leading to the Development of the Populist Party

A major **recession** struck the United States during the 1890s, with crop prices falling dramatically. **Drought** compounded the problems, leaving many American farmers in crippling debt. The **Farmers' Alliance** formed in 1875, drawing the rural poor into a single political entity.

Recession also affected the more industrial parts of the country. The **Knights of Labor**, formed in 1869 by **Uriah Stephens**, was able to unite workers into a union to protect their rights. Dissatisfied by views espoused by industrialists, these two groups, the Farmers Alliance and the Knights of Labor, joined to form the **Populist Party**, also known as the People's Party, in 1892. Some of the elements of the party's platform included:

- National currency
- Graduated income tax
- Government ownership of railroads as well as telegraph and telephone systems
- Secret ballots for voting
- Immigration restriction
- Single-term limits for President and Vice-President

The Populist Party was in favor of decreasing elitism and making the voice of the common man more easily heard in the political process.

### Growth of the Labor Movement Through the Late 19th Century

One of the first large, well-organized strikes occurred in 1892. Called the **Homestead Strike**, it occurred when the Amalgamated Association of Iron and Steel Workers struck against the Carnegie Steel Company. Gunfire ensued, and Carnegie was able to eliminate the plant's union. In 1894, workers in the American Railway Union, led by Eugene Debs, initiated the **Pullman Strike** after the Pullman Palace Car Co. cut their wages by 28 percent. President Grover Cleveland called in troops to break up the strike on the grounds that it interfered with mail delivery. Mary Harris "Mother" Jones organized the **Children's Crusade** to protest child labor. A protest march proceeded to the home of President Theodore Roosevelt in 1903. Jones also worked with the United Mine Workers of America, and helped found the **Industrial Workers of the World**.

> ➤ **Review Video:** The Gilded Age: Labor Strikes
> Visit *mometrix.com/academy* and enter *Code*: **683116**

> ➤ **Review Video:** The Gilded Age: Labor Unions
> Visit *mometrix.com/academy* and enter *Code*: **749692**

### Panic of 1893

Far from a US-centric event, the **Panic of 1893** was an economic crisis that affected most of the globe. As a response, President Grover Cleveland repealed the **Sherman Silver Purchase Act**, afraid it had caused the downturn rather than boosting the economy as intended. The Panic led to bankruptcies, with banks and railroads going under and factory unemployment rising as high as 25 percent. In the end, the **Republican Party** regained power due to the economic crisis.

### Progressive Era

From the 1890s to the end of the First World War, **Progressives** set forth an ideology that drove many levels of society and politics. The Progressives were in favor of workers' rights and safety, and wanted measures taken against waste and corruption. They felt science could help improve society, and that the government could—and should—provide answers to a variety of social problems. Progressives came from a wide variety of backgrounds, but were united in their desire to improve society.

## Muckrakers and the Progressive Movement

"Muckrakers" was a term used to identify aggressive investigative journalists who exposed scandals, corruption, and many other wrongs in late nineteenth century society. Among these intrepid writers were:
- **Ida Tarbell**—she exposed John D. Rockefeller's Standard Oil Trust.
- **Jacob Riis**—a photographer, he brought the living conditions of the poor in New York to the public's attention.
- **Lincoln Steffens**—he worked to expose political corruption in municipal government.
- **Upton Sinclair**—his book *The Jungle* led to reforms in the meat-packing industry.

Through the work of these journalists, many new policies came into being, including workmen's compensation, child labor laws, and trust-busting.

## Provisions of the Sixteenth, Seventeenth, Eighteenth and Nineteenth Amendments

The early twentieth century saw several amendments made to the US Constitution:
- The **Sixteenth Amendment** (1913) established a federal income tax.
- The **Seventeenth Amendment** (1913) allowed popular election of senators.
- The **Eighteenth Amendment** (1919) prohibited the sale, production and transportation of alcohol. This amendment was later repealed by the Twenty-first Amendment.
- The **Nineteenth Amendment** (1920) gave women the right to vote.

These amendments largely grew out of the Progressive Era, as many citizens worked to improve American society.

## Role of the Federal Trade Commission in Eliminating Trusts

**Muckrakers** such as Ida Tarbell and Lincoln Steffens brought to light the damaging trend of trusts—huge corporations working to monopolize areas of commerce so they could control prices and distribution. The **Sherman Antitrust Act** and the **Clayton Antitrust Act** set out guidelines for competition among corporations and set out to eliminate these trusts. The **Federal Trade Commission** was formed in 1914 in order to enforce antitrust measures and ensure that companies were operated fairly and did not create controlling monopolies.

> ➤ **Review Video:** The Progressive Era
> *Visit **mometrix.com/academy** and enter **Code**: 722394*

## Government Dealings with Native Americans Through the End of the 19th Century

America's westward expansion led to conflict and violent confrontations with Native Americans such as the **Battle of Little Bighorn**. In 1876, the American government ordered all Indians to relocate to reservations. Lack of compliance led to the **Dawes Act** in 1887, which ordered assimilation rather than separation: Native Americans were offered American citizenship and a piece of their tribal land if they would accept the lot chosen by the government and live on it separately from the tribe. This act remained in effect until 1934. Reformers also forced Indian children to attend **Indian Boarding Schools**, where they were not allowed to speak their native language and were immersed into a Euro-American culture and religion. Children were often abused in these schools, and were indoctrinated to abandon their identity as Native Americans.

In 1890, the massacre at **Wounded Knee**, accompanied by Geronimo's surrender, led the Native Americans to work to preserve their culture rather than fight for their lands.

## Role of Native Americans in Wartime Through the Beginning of the 20th Century

The **Spanish-American War** (1898) saw a number of Native Americans serving with Teddy Roosevelt in the Rough Riders. Apache scouts accompanied General John J. Pershing to Mexico, hoping to find **Pancho Villa**. More than 17,000 Native Americans were drafted into service for **World War I**, though at the time they were not considered legal citizens. In 1924, Indians were finally granted official citizenship by the **Indian Citizenship Act**.

After decades of relocation, forced assimilation, and genocide, the number of Native Americans in the US has greatly declined. Though many Native Americans have chosen—or have been forced—to assimilate, about 300 reservations exist today, with most of their inhabitants living in abject poverty.

## Events Leading up to the Spanish-American War

Spain had controlled **Cuba** since the fifteenth century. Over the centuries, the Spanish had quashed a variety of revolts. In 1886, slavery ended in Cuba, and another revolt was rising.

In the meantime, the US had expressed interest in Cuba, offering Spain $130 million for the island in 1853, during Franklin Pierce's presidency. In 1898, the Cuban revolt was underway. In spite of various factions supporting the Cubans, the US President, William McKinley, refused to recognize the rebellion, preferring negotiation over involvement in war. Then the *Maine*, a US battleship in Havana Harbor, was blown up, killing 266 crew members. The US declared war two months later, and the war ended with a **Spanish surrender** in less than four months.

## Importance of the Panama Canal

Initial work began on the **Panama Canal** in 1881, though the idea had been discussed since the 1500s. The canal greatly reduces the length and time needed to sail from one ocean to the other by connecting the Atlantic to the Pacific through the Isthmus of Panama, which joins South America to North America. Before the canal was built, travelers had to sail around the entire perimeter of South America to reach the West Coast of the US. The French began the work after successfully completing the **Suez Canal**, which connected the Mediterranean Sea to the Red Sea. However, due to disease and high expense the work moved slowly and after eight years the company went bankrupt, suspending work. The US purchased the holdings, and the first ship sailed through the canal in 1914. The Panama Canal was constructed as a lock-and-lake canal, with ships lifted on locks to travel from one lake to another over the rugged, mountainous terrain. In order to maintain control of the Canal Zone, the US assisted Panama in its battle for independence from **Columbia**.

## Influence of Big Stick Diplomacy on American Foreign Policy in Latin America

Theodore Roosevelt's famous quote, "Speak softly and carry a big stick," is supposedly of African origins, at least according to Roosevelt. He used this proverb to justify expanded involvement in foreign affairs during his tenure as President. The US military was deployed to protect American interests in **Latin America**. Roosevelt also worked to maintain an equal or greater influence in Latin America than those held by European interests. As a result, the US Navy grew larger, and the

US generally became more involved in foreign affairs. Roosevelt felt that if any country was left vulnerable to control by Europe, due to economic issues or political instability, the US had not only a right to intervene, but was **obligated** to do so. This led to US involvement in Cuba, Nicaragua, Haiti and the Dominican Republic over several decades leading into the First and Second World Wars.

## Taft's Dollar Diplomacy vs. Roosevelt's Diplomatic Theories

During William Howard Taft's presidency, Taft instituted "**Dollar Diplomacy**." This approach was America's effort to influence Latin America and East Asia through economic rather than military means. Taft saw past efforts in these areas to be political and warlike, while his efforts focused on peaceful economic goals. His justification of the policy was to protect the **Panama Canal**, which was vital to US trade interests.

In spite of Taft's assurance that Dollar Diplomacy was a peaceful approach, many interventions proved violent. During Latin American revolts, such as those in **Nicaragua**, the US sent troops to settle the revolutions. Afterwards, bankers moved in to help support the new leaders through loans. Dollar Diplomacy continued until 1913, when Woodrow Wilson was elected President.

## Wilson's Approach to International Diplomacy

Turning away from Taft's "Dollar Diplomacy," Wilson instituted a foreign policy he referred to as "**moral diplomacy**." This approach still influences American foreign policy today.

Wilson felt that **representative government and democracy** in all countries would lead to worldwide stability. Democratic governments, he felt, would be less likely to threaten American interests. He also saw the US and Great Britain as the great role models in this area, as well as champions of world peace and self-government. Free trade and international commerce would allow the US to speak out regarding world events.

Main elements of Wilson's policies included:
- Maintaining a strong military
- Promoting democracy throughout the world
- Expanding international trade to boost the American economy

## Major Events of World War I

World War I occurred from 1914 to 1918 and was fought largely in Europe. Triggered by the assassination of Austrian Archduke Franz Ferdinand, the war rapidly escalated. At the beginning of the conflict, Woodrow Wilson declared the US neutral. Major events influencing US involvement included:
- **Sinking of the *Lusitania***—the British passenger liner RMS *Lusitania* was sunk by a German U-boat in 1915. Among the 1,000 civilian victims were over 100 American citizens. Outraged by this act, many Americans began to push for US involvement in the war, using the *Lusitania* as a rallying cry.
- **German U-boat aggression**—Wilson continued to keep the US out of the war, using as his 1916 reelection slogan, "He kept us out of war." While he continued to work toward an end of the war, German U-boats began to indiscriminately attack American and Canadian merchant ships carrying supplies to Germany's enemies in Europe.

- 101 -

- **Zimmerman Telegram** —the final event that brought the US into World War I was the interception of the Zimmerman Telegram (also known as the Zimmerman Note). In this telegram, Germany proposed forming an alliance with the Mexico if the US entered the war.

> ➢ **Review Video:** World War I: An Overview
> *Visit **mometrix.com/academy** and enter **Code: 659767***

## Efforts in the US During World War I Supporting the War Effort

American **railroads** came under government control in December 1917. The widespread system was consolidated into a single system, with each region assigned a director. This greatly increased the efficiency of the railroad system, allowing the railroads to supply both domestic and military needs. Control returned to private ownership in 1920. In 1918, **telegraph, telephone, and cable services** also came under Federal control, to be returned to private management the next year.  The **American Red Cross** supported the war effort by knitting clothes for Army and Navy troops. They also helped supply hospital and refugee clothing and surgical dressings. Over eight million people participated in this effort.  To generate wartime funds, the US government sold **Liberty Bonds**. In four issues, they sold nearly $25 billion—more than one fifth of Americans purchased them. After the war, a fifth bond drive was held, but sold "**Victory Liberty Bonds**."

## Influence of Wilson's Fourteen Points on the Final Peace Treaties that Ended World War I

President Woodrow Wilson proposed **Fourteen Points** as the basis for a peace settlement to end the war. Presented to the US Congress in January 1918, the Fourteen Points included:
- Five points outlining **general ideals**
- Eight points to resolve **immediate problems** of political and territorial nature
- One point proposing an **organization of nations** (the League of Nations) with the intent of maintaining world peace

In November of that same year, Germany agreed to an **armistice**, assuming the final treaty would be based on the Fourteen Points. However, during the peace conference in Paris 1919, there was much disagreement, leading to a final agreement that punished Germany and the other Central Powers much more than originally intended. Henry Cabot Lodge, who had become the Foreign Relations Committee chairman in 1918, wanted an unconditional surrender from Germany and was concerned about the article in the **Treaty of Versailles** that gave the League of Nations power to declare war without a vote from the US Congress. A **League of Nations** was included in the Treaty of Versailles at Wilson's insistence. The Senate rejected the Treaty of Versailles, and in the end Wilson refused to concede to Lodge's demands. As a result, the US did not join the League of Nations.

> ➢ **Review Video:** Woodrow Wilson's Fourteen Points
> *Visit **mometrix.com/academy** and enter **Code: 335789***

## Major Changes and Events that Took Place in America During the 1920s

The post-war 1920s saw many Americans moving from the farm to the city, with growing prosperity in the US. The **Roaring Twenties**, or the **Jazz Age**, was driven largely by growth in the automobile and entertainment industries. Individuals like Charles Lindbergh, the first aviator to make a solo flight cross the Atlantic Ocean, added to the American admiration of individual accomplishment. Telephone lines, distribution of electricity, highways, the radio, and other inventions brought great changes to everyday life.

## Major Cultural Movements of the 1920s Influenced by African Americans

The **Harlem Renaissance** saw a number of African-American artists settling in Harlem in New York. This community produced a number of well-known artists and writers, including Langston Hughes, Nella Larsen, Zora Neale Hurston, Claude McKay, Countee Cullen and Jean Toomer. The growth of jazz, also largely driven by African Americans, defined the **Jazz Age**. Its unconventional, improvisational style matched the growing sense of optimism and exploration of the decade. Originating as an offshoot of the blues, jazz began in New Orleans. Some significant jazz musicians were Duke Ellington, Louis Armstrong and Jelly Roll Morton. **Big Band** and **Swing Jazz** also developed in the 1920s. Well-known musicians of this movement included Bing Crosby, Frank Sinatra, Count Basie, Benny Goodman, Billie Holiday, Ella Fitzgerald and The Dorsey Brothers.

## Provisions and Importance of the National Origins Act of 1924

The National Origins Act (Johnson-Reed Act) placed limitations on **immigration**. The number of immigrants allowed into the US was based on the population of each nationality of immigrants who were living in the country in 1890. Only two percent of each nationality's 1890 population numbers were allowed to immigrate. This led to great disparities between immigrants from various nations, and Asian immigration was not allowed at all. Some of the impetus behind the Johnson-Reed Act came as a result of paranoia following the **Russian Revolution**. Fear of communist influences in the US led to a general fear of immigrants.

## Origins of the Red Scare

World War I created many jobs, but after the war ended these jobs disappeared, leaving many unemployed. In the wake of these employment changes the **International Workers of the World** and the **Socialist Party**, headed by Eugene Debs, became more and more visible. Workers initiated strikes in an attempt to regain the favorable working conditions that had been put into place before the war. Unfortunately, many of these strikes became violent, and the actions were blamed on "Reds," or Communists, for trying to spread their views into America. With the recent Bolshevik Revolution in Russia, many Americans feared a similar revolution might occur in the US. The **Red Scare** ensued, with many individuals jailed for supposedly holding communist, anarchist or socialist beliefs.

## Growth of Civil Rights for African Americans

Marcus Garvey founded the **Universal Negro Improvement Association and African Communities League (UNIA-ACL)**, which became a large and active organization focused on building black nationalism. In 1909, the **National Association for the Advancement of Colored People (NAACP)** came into being, working to defeat Jim Crow laws. The NAACP also helped prevent racial segregation from becoming federal law, fought against lynchings, helped black soldiers in WWI become officers, and helped defend the Scottsboro Boys, who were unjustly accused of rape.

## Ku Klux Klan

In 1866, Confederate Army veterans came together to fight against Reconstruction in the South, forming a group called the **Ku Klux Klan (KKK)**. With white supremacist beliefs, including anti-Semitism, nativism, anti-Catholicism, and overt racism, this organization relied heavily on violence to get its message across. In 1915, they grew again in power, using a film called *The Birth of a Nation*, by D.W. Griffith, to spread their ideas. In the 1920s, the reach of the KKK spread far into the North and Midwest, and members controlled a number of state governments. Its membership and power began to decline during the Great Depression, but experienced a resurgence later.

## American Civil Liberties Union

The American Civil Liberties Union (**ACLU**), founded in 1920, grew from the American Union Against Militarism. The ACLU helped conscientious objectors avoid going to war during WWI, and also helped those being prosecuted under the **Espionage Act** (1917) and the **Sedition Act** (1918), many of whom were immigrants. Their major goals were to protect immigrants and other citizens who were threatened with prosecution for their political beliefs, and to support labor unions, which were also under threat by the government during the Red Scare.

## Goals of the Anti-Defamation League

In 1913, the Anti-Defamation League was formed to prevent anti-Semitic behavior and practices. Its actions also worked to prevent all forms of racism, and to prevent individuals from being discriminated against for any reason involving their race. They spoke against the Ku Klux Klan, as well as other racist or anti-Semitic organizations. This organization still works to fight discrimination against all minorities.

## Roosevelt's New Deal

The **Great Depression**, which began in 1929 with the stock market crash, grew out of several factors that had developed over the previous years including:
- Growing economic disparity between the rich and middle classes, with the rich amassing wealth much more quickly than the lower classes
- Disparity in economic distribution in industries
- Growing use of credit, leading to an inflated demand for some goods
- Government support of new industries rather than agriculture
- Risky stock market investments, leading to the stock market crash

Additional factors contributing to the Depression also included the **Labor Day Hurricane** in the Florida Keys (1935) and the **Great Hurricane of 1938** in New England, along with the **Dust Bowl** in the Great Plains, which destroyed crops and resulted in the displacement of as many as 2.5 million people.

> ➤ **Review Video:** The Great Depression
> *Visit **mometrix.com/academy** and enter* **Code: 635912**

**Franklin D. Roosevelt** was elected president in 1932 with his promise of a "**New Deal**" for Americans. His goals were to provide government work programs to provide jobs, wages and relief to numerous workers throughout the beleaguered US. Congress gave Roosevelt almost free rein to produce relief legislation. The goals of this legislation were:

- **Relief**—creating jobs for the high numbers of unemployed
- **Recovery**—stimulating the economy through the National Recovery Administration
- **Reform**—passing legislation to prevent future, similar economic crashes

The Roosevelt Administration also passed legislation regarding ecological issues, including the Soil Conservation Service, aimed at preventing another Dust Bowl.

## Roosevelt's Alphabet Organizations

So-called "alphabet organizations" set up during Roosevelt's administration included:

- **Civilian Conservation Corps** (CCC)—provided jobs in the forestry service
- **Agricultural Adjustment Administration** (AAA)—increased agricultural income by adjusting both production and prices
- **Tennessee Valley Authority** (TVA)—organized projects to build dams in the Tennessee River for flood control and production of electricity, resulting in increased productivity for industries in the area, and easier navigation of the Tennessee River
- **Public Works Administration** (PWA) and Civil Works Administration (CWA)—provided a multitude of jobs, initiating over 34,000 projects
- **Works Progress Administration** (WPA)—helped unemployed persons to secure employment on government work projects or elsewhere

## Actions Taken During the Roosevelt Administration to Prevent Future Crashes

The Roosevelt administration passed several laws and established several institutions to initiate the "reform" portion of the New Deal, including:

- **Glass-Steagall Act**—separated investment from commercial banking
- **Securities Exchange Commission (SEC)**—helped regulate Wall Street investment practices, making them less dangerous to the overall economy
- **Wagner Act**—provided worker and union rights to improve relations between employees and employers
- **Social Security Act of 1935**—provided pensions as well as unemployment insurance

Other actions focused on insuring bank deposits and adjusting the value of American currency. Most of these regulatory agencies and government policies and programs still exist today.

## Major Regulations Regarding Labor After the Great Depression

Three major regulations regarding labor that were passed after the Great Depression are:

- The **Wagner Act** (1935)—also known as the National Labor Relations Act, it established that unions were legal, protected members of unions, and required collective bargaining. This act was later amended by the Taft-Hartley Act of 1947 and the Landrum-Griffin Act of 1959, which further clarified certain elements.
- **Davis-Bacon Act** (1931)—provided fair compensation for contractors and subcontractors
- **Walsh-Healey Act** (1936)—established a minimum wage, child labor laws, safety standards, and overtime pay

## Accomplishments of the Lyndon B. Johnson Presidency

Kennedy's Vice President, **Lyndon Johnson**, assumed the presidency after Kennedy's **assassination**. He supported civil rights bills, tax cuts, and other wide-reaching legislation that Kennedy had also supported. Johnson saw America as a "**Great Society**," and enacted legislation to fight disease and poverty, renew urban areas, support education and environmental conservation. Medicare and Medicaid were instituted under his administration. He continued Kennedy's support of space exploration and he is also known, although less positively, for his handling of the **Vietnam War**.

## Factors that Led to the Growth of the Civil Rights Movement

In the 1950s, post-war America was experiencing a rapid growth in prosperity. However, African-Americans found themselves left behind. Following the lead of **Mahatma Gandhi**, who led similar class struggles in India, African-Americans began to demand equal rights. Major figures in this struggle included:

- **Rosa Parks**—often called the "mother of the Civil Rights Movement," her refusal to give up her seat on the bus to a white man served as a seed from which the movement grew.
- **Martin Luther King, Jr.**—the best-known leader of the movement, King drew on Gandhi's beliefs and encouraged non-violent opposition. He led a march on Washington in 1963, received the Nobel Peace Prize in 1964, and was assassinated in 1968.
- **Malcolm X**—espousing less peaceful means of change, Malcolm X became a Black Muslim, and supported black nationalism.

## Impact of Stokely Carmichael, Adam Clayton Powell, and Jesse Jackson on the Civil Rights Movement

- **Stokely Carmichael**—Carmichael originated the term "Black Power" and served as head of the *Student Nonviolent Coordinating Committee*. He believed in black pride and black culture, and felt separate political and social institutions should be developed for blacks.
- **Adam Clayton Powell**—chairman of the *Coordinating Committee for Employment*, he led rent strikes and other actions, as well as a bus boycott, to increase the hiring of blacks.
- **Jesse Jackson**—Jackson was selected to head the *Chicago Operation Breadbasket* in 1966, and went on to organize boycotts and other actions. He also had an unsuccessful run for President.

## Events of the Civil Rights Movement

Three major events of the Civil Rights Movement are:
- **Montgomery Bus Boycott**—in 1955, *Rosa Parks* refused to give her seat on the bus to a white man. As a result, she was tried and convicted of disorderly conduct and of violating local ordinances. A 381-day bus boycott ensued, protesting segregation on public buses.
- **Desegregation of Little Rock**—in 1957, after the Supreme Court decision on *Brown v. Board of Education*, which declared "separate but equal" unconstitutional, the Arkansas school board voted to desegregate their schools. Even though Arkansas was considered progressive, its governor brought in the Arkansas National Guard to prevent nine black students from entering Central High School in Little Rock. President Eisenhower responded by federalizing the National Guard and ordering them to stand down.

- **Birmingham Campaign**—protestors organized a variety of actions such as sit-ins and an organized march to launch a voting campaign. When the City of Birmingham declared the protests illegal, the protestors, including *Martin Luther King, Jr.*, persisted and were arrested and jailed.

## Pieces of Legislation Passed as a Result of the Civil Rights Movement

Three major pieces of legislation passed as a result of the Civil Rights movement are:
- **Brown v. Board of Education** (1954)—the Supreme Court declared that "separate but equal" accommodations and services were unconstitutional.
- **Civil Rights Act of 1964**—this declared discrimination illegal in employment, education, or public accommodation.
- **Voting Rights Act of 1965**—this act ended various activities practiced, mostly in the South, to bar blacks from exercising their voting rights. These included poll taxes and literacy tests.

## US Perspective on the Progression of the Vietnam War

After World War II, the US pledged, as part of its foreign policy, to come to the assistance of any country threatened by **communism**. When Vietnam was divided into a communist North and democratic South, much like Korea before it, the eventual attempts by the North to unify the country under Communist rule led to intervention by the US. On the home front, the **Vietnam War** became more and more unpopular politically, with Americans growing increasingly discontent with the inability of the US to achieve the goals it had set for the Asian country. When President **Richard Nixon** took office in 1969, his escalation of the war led to protests at Kent State in Ohio, during which several students were killed by National Guard troops. Protests continued, eventually resulting in the end of the compulsory draft in 1973. In that same year, the US departed Vietnam. In 1975, the south surrendered, and Vietnam became a unified country under communist rule.

## Effects of US Cold War Foreign Policy Acts on the International Relationships

The following are US Cold War foreign policy acts and how they affected international relationships, especially between the US and the Soviet Union:
- **Marshall Plan**—this sent aid to war-torn Europe after WWII, largely focusing on preventing the spread of communism.
- **Containment Policy**—proposed by George F. Kennan, the containment policy focused on containing the spread of Soviet communism.
- **Truman Doctrine**—Harry S. Truman stated that the US would provide both economic and military support to any country threatened by Soviet takeover.
- **National Security Act**—passed in 1947, this act reorganized the government's military departments into the Department of Defense, as well as creating the Central Intelligence Agency and the National Security Council.

The combination of these acts led to the **Cold War**, with Soviet communists attempting to spread their influence and the US and other countries trying to contain or stop this spread.

> ➤ **Review Video:** The Cold War: The United States and Russia
> *Visit **mometrix.com/academy** and enter **Code**: 981433*

**NATO, Warsaw Pact, and the the Berlin Wall**

NATO, the **North Atlantic Treaty Organization**, came into being in 1949. It essentially amounted to an agreement among the US and Western European countries that an attack on any one of these countries was to be considered an attack against the entire group. Under the influence of the Soviet Union, the Eastern European countries of the USSR, Bulgaria, East Germany, Poland, Romania, Albania, Hungary, and Czechoslovakia responded with the **Warsaw Pact**, which created a similar agreement among those nations. In 1961, a wall was built to separate communist East Berlin from democratic West Berlin. This was a literal representation of the "**Iron Curtain**" that separated the democratic and communist countries through the world.

**Effect of the Arms Race on Post WW II International Relations**

After World War II, major nations, particularly the US and USSR, rushed to develop highly advanced weapons systems such as the **atomic bomb** and later the **hydrogen bomb**. These countries seemed determined to outpace each other with the development of numerous, deadly weapons. These weapons were expensive and extremely dangerous, and it is possible that the war between US and Soviet interests remained "cold" due to the fear that one side or the other would use these powerful weapons.

**End of the Cold War and the Dissolution of the Soviet Union**

In the late 1980s, **Mikhail Gorbachev** led the Soviet Union. He introduced a series of reform programs. **Ronald Reagan** famously urged Gorbachev to tear down the **Berlin Wall** as a gesture of growing freedom in the Eastern Bloc, and in 1989 it was demolished, ending the separation of East and West Germany. The Soviet Union relinquished its power over the various republics in Eastern Europe, and they became independent nations with their own individual governments. In 1991, the **USSR** was dissolved and the Cold War also came to an end.

> ➢ **Review Video:** The Cold War: Resolution
> *Visit* ***mometrix.com/academy*** *and enter* ***Code***: 278032

**Technological Advances that Occurred After World War II**

Numerous technological advances after the Second World War led to more effective treatment of diseases, more efficient communication and transportation, and new means of generating power. Advances in **medicine** increased the human lifespan in developed countries, and near-instantaneous **communication** opened up a myriad of possibilities. Some of these advances include:
- Discovery of penicillin (1928)
- Supersonic air travel (1947)
- Nuclear power plants (1951)
- Orbital satellite leading to manned space flight (Sputnik, 1957)
- First man on the moon (1969)

**US Policy Toward Immigrants After World War II**

Prior to WWII, the US had been limiting **immigration** for several decades. After WWII, policy shifted slightly to accommodate political refugees from Europe and elsewhere. So many people were displaced by the war that in 1946, the UN formed the **International Refugee Organization** to deal with the problem. In 1948, the US Congress passed the **Displaced Persons Act**, which allowed over 400,000 European refugees to enter the US, most of them concentration camp survivors and refugees from Eastern Europe.

In 1952, the **United States Escapee Program (USEP)** increased the quotas, allowing refugees from communist Europe to enter the US, as did the **Refugee Relief Act**, passed in 1953. At the same time, however, the **Internal Security Act of 1950** allowed deportation of declared communists, and Asians were subjected to a quota based on race, rather than country of origin. Later changes included:
- **Migration and Refugee Assistance Act** (1962)—provided aid for refugees in need
- **Immigration and Nationality Act** (1965)—ended quotas based on nation of origin
- **Immigration Reform and Control Act** (1986)—prohibited the hiring of illegal immigrants, but also granted amnesty to about three million illegals already in the country

## Policies and Legislation Enacted Expanding Minority Rights

Several major acts have been passed, particularly since WWII, to protect the rights of minorities in America. These include:
- Civil Rights Act (1964)
- Voting Rights Act (1965)
- Age Discrimination Act (1967)
- Americans with Disabilities Act (1990)

Other important movements for civil rights included a prisoner's rights movement, movements for immigrant rights, and the women's rights movement. The National Organization for Women (NOW) was established in 1966 and worked to pass the Equal Rights Amendment. The amendment was passed, but not enough states ratified it for it to become part of the US Constitution.

## Interventionist and Isolationist Approaches in World War II

When war broke out in Europe in 1939, President Roosevelt stated that the US would remain **neutral**. However, his overall approach was considered "**interventionist**," as he was willing to provide aid to the Allies without actually entering the conflict. Thus the US supplied a wide variety of war materials to the Allied nations in the early years of the war.

**Isolationists** believed the US should not provide any aid to the Allies, including supplies. They felt Roosevelt, by assisting the Allies, was leading the US into a war for which it was not prepared. Led by Charles Lindbergh, the Isolationists believed that any involvement in the European conflict endangered the US by weakening its national defense.

> ➤ **Review Video:** World War II: An Overview
> *Visit **mometrix.com/academy** and enter **Code**: 759402*

## Sequence of Events that Led the US to Declare War and Enter World War II

In 1937, Japan invaded China, prompting the US to eventually halt exports to Japan. Roosevelt also did not allow Japanese interests to withdraw money held in US banks. In 1941, **General Tojo** rose to power as the Japanese prime minister. Recognizing America's ability to bring a halt to Japan's expansion, he authorized the bombing of **Pearl Harbor** on December 7. The US responded by declaring war on Japan. Partially because of the **Tripartite Pact** among the Axis Powers, Germany and Italy then declared war on the US, later followed by Bulgaria, Hungary, and other Axis nations.

## Occurrences of World War II that Led to the Surrender of Germany

In 1941, **Hitler** violated the non-aggression pact he had signed with Stalin two years earlier by invading the USSR. **Stalin** then joined the **Allies**. Stalin, Roosevelt and Winston Churchill planned to defeat Germany first, then Japan, bringing the war to an end.

In 1942-1943, the Allies drove **Axis** forces out of Africa. In addition, the Germans were soundly defeated at Stalingrad.

The **Italian Campaign** involved Allied operations in Italy between July 1943 and May 1945, including Italy's liberation. On June 6, 1944, known as **D-Day**, the Allies invaded France at Normandy. Soviet troops moved on the eastern front at the same time, driving German forces back. By April 25, 1945, Berlin was surrounded by Soviet troops. On May 7, Germany surrendered.

> ➤ **Review Video:** World War II: Germany
> *Visit **mometrix.com/academy** and enter **Code**: 951452*

## Major Events of World War II the Led to the Surrender of Japan

War continued with **Japan** after Germany's surrender. Japanese forces had taken a large portion of Southeast Asia and the Western Pacific, all the way to the Aleutian Islands in Alaska. **General Doolittle** bombed several Japanese cities while American troops scored a victory at Midway. Additional fighting in the Battle of the Coral Sea further weakened Japan's position. As a final blow, the US dropped two **atomic bombs** on Japan, one on Hiroshima and the other on Nagasaki. This was the first time atomic bombs had been used in warfare, and the devastation was horrific and demoralizing. Japan surrendered on September 2, 1945, which became **V-J Day** in the US.

> ➤ **Review Video:** World War II: Japan
> *Visit **mometrix.com/academy** and enter **Code**: 313104*

## Significance of the 442nd Regimental Combat Team, the Tuskegee Airmen, and the Navajo Code Talkers during World War II

The 442nd Regimental Combat Team consisted of Japanese-Americans fighting in Europe for the US. The most highly decorated unit per member in US history, they suffered a 93% casualty rate during the war. The **Tuskegee Airmen** were African-American aviators, the first black Americans allowed to fly for the military. In spite of being ineligible to become official navy pilots, they flew over 15,000 missions and were highly decorated. The **Navajo Code Talkers** were native Navajo who used their traditional language to transmit information among Allied forces. Because Navajo is a language and not simply a code, the Axis powers were never able to translate it. Use of Navajo Code Talkers to transmit information was instrumental in the taking of Iwo Jima and other major victories of the war.

## Circumstances and Opportunities for Women During World War II

Women served widely in the military during WWII, working in numerous positions, including the **Flight Nurses Corps**. Women also moved into the workforce while men were overseas, leading to over 19 million women in the US workforce by 1944. **Rosie the Riveter** stood as a symbol of these women and a means of recruiting others to take needed positions. Women, as well as their families left behind during wartime, also grew **Victory Gardens** to help provide food.

## Importance of the Atomic Bomb During World War II

The atomic bomb, developed during WWII, was the most powerful bomb ever invented. A single bomb, carried by a single plane, held enough power to destroy an entire city. This devastating effect was demonstrated with the bombing of **Hiroshima** and **Nagasaki** in 1945 in what later became a controversial move, but ended the war. The bombings resulted in as many as 150,000 immediate deaths and many more as time passed after the bombings, mostly due to **radiation poisoning**.

Whatever the arguments against the use of "The Bomb," the post WWII era saw many countries develop similar weapons to match the newly expanded military power of the US. The impact of those developments and use of nuclear weapons continues to haunt international relations today.

## Importance of the Yalta Conference and the Potsdam Conference

In February 1945, Joseph Stalin, Franklin D. Roosevelt and Winston Churchill met in Yalta to discuss the post-war treatment of the **Axis nations**, particularly Germany. Though Germany had not yet surrendered, its defeat was imminent. After Germany's official surrender, Joseph Stalin, Harry Truman (Roosevelt's successor), and Clement Attlee (replacing Churchill partway through the conference) met to formalize those plans. This meeting was called the **Potsdam Conference**. Basic provisions of these agreements included:
- Dividing Germany and Berlin into four zones of occupation
- Demilitarization of Germany
- Poland remaining under Soviet control
- Outlawing the Nazi Party
- Trials for Nazi leaders
- Relocation of numerous German citizens
- The USSR joining the United Nations, established in 1945
- Establishment of the United Nations Security Council, consisting of the US, the UK, the USSR, China and France

## Agreements Made with Post-War Japan

**General Douglas MacArthur** led the American **military occupation of Japan** after the country surrendered. The goals of the US occupation included removing Japan's military and making the country a democracy. A 1947 constitution removed power from the emperor and gave it to the people, as well as granting voting rights to women. Japan was no longer allowed to declare war, and a group of 28 government officials were tried for war crimes. In 1951, the US finally signed a peace treaty with Japan. This treaty allowed Japan to rearm itself for purposes of self-defense, but stripped the country of the empire it had built overseas.

## US Treatment of Immigrants During and After World War II

In 1940, the US passed the **Alien Registration Act**, which required all aliens older than fourteen to be fingerprinted and registered. They were also required to report changes of address within five days.

Tension between whites and Japanese immigrants in **California**, which had been building since the beginning of the century, came to a head with the bombing of **Pearl Harbor** in 1941. Believing that even those Japanese living in the US were likely to be loyal to their native country, the president ordered numerous Japanese to be arrested on suspicion of subversive action and isolated in exclusion zones known as **War Relocation Camps**. Approximately 120,000 Japanese-Americans, two-thirds of them US citizens, were sent to these camps during the war.

## General State of the US After World War II

Following WWII, the US became the strongest political power in the world, becoming a major player in world affairs and foreign policies. The US determined to stop the spread of **communism**, having named itself the "**arsenal of democracy**" during the war.  In addition, America emerged with a greater sense of itself as a single, integrated nation, with many regional and economic differences diminished. The government worked for greater equality and the growth of communications increased contact among different areas of the country.  Both the aftermath of the Great Depression and the necessities of WWII had given the government greater **control** over various institutions as well as the economy. This also meant that the American government took on greater responsibility for the well-being of its citizens, both in the domestic arena, such as providing basic needs, and in protecting them from foreign threats. This increased role of providing basic necessities for all Americans has been criticized by some as "**the welfare state**."

## Accomplishments of Harry S. Truman

Harry S. Truman took over the presidency from Franklin D. Roosevelt near the end of WWII. He made the final decision to drop atomic bombs on Japan and played a major role in the final decisions regarding treatment of post-war Germany.  On the domestic front, Truman initiated a 21-point plan known as the **Fair Deal**. This plan expanded Social Security, provided public housing, and made the Fair Employment Practice Committee permanent. Truman helped support Greece and Turkey (which were under threat from the USSR), supported South Korea against communist North Korea, and helped with recovery in Western Europe. He also participated in the formation of **NATO**, the North Atlantic Treaty Organization.

## Events and Importance of the Korean War

The Korean War began in 1950 and ended in 1953. For the first time in history, a world organization—the **United Nations**—played a military role in a war. North Korea sent communist troops into South Korea, seeking to bring the entire country under communist control. The UN sent out a call to member nations, asking them to support South Korea. Truman sent troops, as did many other UN member nations. The war ended three years later with a **truce** rather than a peace treaty, and Korea remains divided at the **38th parallel north**, with communist rule remaining in the North and a democratic government ruling the South.

## Accomplishments of Dwight D. Eisenhower

Eisenhower carried out a middle-of-the-road foreign policy and brought the US several steps forward in equal rights. He worked to minimize tensions during the Cold War, and negotiated a peace treaty with Russia after the death of Stalin. He enforced desegregation by sending troops to Little Rock Central High School in Arkansas, as well as ordering the desegregation of the military. Organizations formed during his administration included the Department of Health, Education and Welfare, and the National Aeronautics and Space Administration (NASA).

## Presidency of John F. Kennedy

Although his term was cut short by his assassination, **JFK** instituted economic programs that led to a period of continuous expansion in the US unmatched since before WWII. He formed the Alliance for Progress and the Peace Corps, organizations intended to help developing nations. He also oversaw the passage of new civil rights legislation, and drafted plans to attack poverty and its causes, along with support of the arts. Kennedy's presidency ended when he was assassinated by **Lee Harvey Oswald** in 1963.

## Events of the Cuban Missile Crisis

The Cuban Missile Crisis occurred in 1962, during John F. Kennedy's presidency. Russian Premier **Nikita Khrushchev** decided to place nuclear missiles in **Cuba** to protect the island from invasion by the US. An American U-2 plane flying over the island photographed the missile bases as they were being built. Tensions rose, with the US concerned about nuclear missiles so close to its shores, and the USSR concerned about American missiles that had been placed in **Turkey**. Eventually, the missile sites were removed, and a US naval blockade turned back Soviet ships carrying missiles to Cuba. During negotiations, the US agreed to remove their missiles from Turkey and agreed to sell surplus wheat to the USSR. A telephone hotline between Moscow and Washington was set up to allow instant communication between the two heads of state to prevent similar incidents in the future.

## Events of the Richard Nixon Presidency

Richard Nixon is best known for the **Watergate scandal** during his presidency, but other important events marked his tenure as president, including:
- End of the Vietnam War
- Improved diplomatic relations between the US and China, and the US and the USSR
- National Environmental Policy Act passed, providing for environmental protection
- Compulsory draft ended
- Supreme Court legalized abortion in Roe v. Wade
- Watergate

The Watergate scandal of 1972 ended Nixon's presidency. Rather than face impeachment and removal from office, he **resigned** in 1974.

## Events of the Gerald Ford Presidency

Gerald Ford was appointed to the vice presidency after Nixon's vice president **Spiro Agnew** resigned in 1973 under charges of tax evasion. With Nixon's resignation, Ford became president.

Ford's presidency saw negotiations with Russia to limit nuclear arms, as well as struggles to deal with inflation, economic downturn, and energy shortages. Ford's policies sought to reduce governmental control of various businesses and reduce the role of government overall. He also worked to prevent escalation of conflicts in the Middle East.

## Events of the Jimmy Carter Presidency

Jimmy Carter was elected as president in 1976. Faced with a budget deficit, high unemployment, and continued inflation, Carter also dealt with numerous matters of international diplomacy including:

- **Torrijos-Carter Treaties**—the US gave control of the Panama Canal to Panama.
- **Camp David Accords**—negotiations between Anwar el-Sadat, the president of Egypt, and Menachem Begin, the Israeli Prime Minister, led to a peace treaty between Egypt and Israel.
- **Strategic Arms Limitation Talks (SALT)**—these led to agreements and treaties between the US and the Soviet Union.
- **Iran Hostage Crisis**—after the Shah of Iran was deposed, an Islamic cleric, Ayatollah Khomeini, came to power. The shah came to the US for medical treatment and Iran demanded his return so he could stand trial. In retaliation, a group of Iranian students stormed the US Embassy in Iran. Fifty-two American hostages were held for 444 days.

Jimmy Carter was awarded the **Nobel Peace Prize** in 2002.

## Events of the Ronald Reagan Presidency

Ronald Reagan, at 69, became the oldest American president. The two terms of his administration included notable events such as:

- Reaganomics, also known as supply-side, trickle-down, or free-market economics, involving major tax cuts
- Economic Recovery Tax Act of 1981
- First female justice appointed to the Supreme Court—Sandra Day O'Connor
- Massive increase in the national debt – from $1 trillion to $3 trillion
- Reduction of nuclear weapons via negotiations with Mikhail Gorbachev
- Iran-Contra scandal—cover-up of US involvement in revolutions in El Salvador and Nicaragua
- Deregulation of savings and loan industry
- Loss of the space shuttle *Challenger*

## Events of the George H. W. Bush Presidency

Reagan's presidency was followed by a term under his former Vice President, **George H. W. Bush**. Bush's run for president included the famous "**thousand points of light**" speech, which was instrumental in increasing his standing in the election polls. During Bush's presidency, numerous international events took place, including:

- Fall of the Berlin wall and Germany's unification
- Panamanian dictator Manuel Noriega captured and tried on drug and racketeering charges
- Dissolution of the Soviet Union
- Gulf War, or Operation Desert Storm, triggered by Iraq's invasion of Kuwait

- Tiananmen Square Massacre in Beijing, China
- Ruby Ridge
- The arrival of the World Wide Web

## Events of the William Clinton Presidency

William Jefferson "Bill" Clinton was the second president in US history to be impeached, but he was not convicted, and maintained high approval ratings in spite of the impeachment. Major events during his presidency included:
- Family and Medical Leave Act
- Don't Ask, Don't Tell, a compromise position regarding homosexuals serving in the military
- North American Free Trade Agreement, or NAFTA
- Defense of Marriage Act
- Oslo Accords
- Siege at Waco, Texas, involving the Branch Davidians led by David Koresh
- Bombing of the Murrah Federal Building in Oklahoma City, Oklahoma
- Troops sent to Haiti, Bosnia and Somalia to assist with domestic problems in those areas

## Events of the George W. Bush Presidency

George W. Bush, son of George Herbert Walker Bush, became president after Clinton. Major events during his presidency included:
- September 11, 2001, al-Qaeda terrorists hijack commercial airliners and fly into the World Trade Center towers and the Pentagon, killing nearly 3000 Americans
- US troops sent to Afghanistan to hunt down al-Qaeda leaders, including the head of the organization, Osama Bin Laden; beginning of the War on Terror
- US troops sent to Iraq, along with a multinational coalition, to depose Saddam Hussein and prevent his deployment of suspected weapons of mass destruction
- Subprime mortgage crisis and near collapse of the financial industry, leading to the Great Recession; first of multiple government bailouts of the financial industry

## Events of the Barack Obama Presidency

Barack Obama, a first-term senator from Illinois, became the first African-American president. Major events included:
- Multiple bailout packages and spending efforts, in an attempt to inject more money into a stagnant economy
- Massive increase in the national debt – from $10 trillion to $18 trillion
- Reinforcement of the War on Terror in Afghanistan and Iraq; additional deployment of troops in Libya and Syria
- Capture and execution of Osama Bin Laden
- Passage of the Affordable Care Act, legislation that greatly increased government involvement in the healthcare industry, and required every person living in the US to maintain health insurance coverage
- Moves to broaden gay rights, including the repeal of Clinton's Don't Ask, Don't Tell policy for homosexuals serving in the military

## Election of Donald Trump to the Presidency

Donald Trump, a billionaire real estate tycoon with no prior political experience, was elected to the presidency in a surprise victory over former First Lady and Secretary of State (under Obama) Hillary Clinton amidst a groundswell of **populist** sentiment. His platform focused on increasing immigration enforcement to curb illegal immigration, restricting foreign trade to improve the dwindling American manufacturing industry, and repealing the Affordable Care Act passed during the prior administration.

## Political Changes in Illinois Due to and Following Civil War

Illinois historically voted with the **Democratic party** before the Civil War, during the times of Stephen Douglas. After the election of Lincoln, a moderate Republican, and the Civil War, a majority of the citizens of Illinois switched their allegiance to the party of the Union, the **Republican party**. Lincoln's assassination only strengthened their loyalty. In addition, the Civil War stimulated the formation of a number of new organizations. In wartime, the **Union League Club** had supported the Republican Party in disputes with the "copperheads," who were against unification and for the southern Confederacy. After the war, members of this and other groups used their influence to support Republican elections. The **Grand Army of the Republic**, composed of Union war veterans, was another such group. The war also made Illinois' economy more industrial, so the state then supported the promotion of railroads and the high tariffs favored by the Republican Party.

## Conflicts Within Republican Party During Administration of Andrew Johnson

Abraham Lincoln made **Andrew Johnson** his running mate in 1864 to balance the ticket by appealing to pro-Union Southerners. Johnson succeeded to the presidency upon Lincoln's assassination, inheriting the tasks of Reconstruction. Johnson agreed to emancipation of slaves by the 13th Amendment and to some civil rights for Blacks. However, he also responded to advances of southern White supremacists wanting re-acceptance to the Union while also wanting to control Black citizens. Johnson's lenient attitude toward the South alienated his **Republican constituents**. Radical Republicans wanted a Federal Reconstruction program; moderates wanted state legal rights without federal funding. Illinois Senator **Trumbull** disagreed with those wanting to oust Johnson. However, Johnson's veto of Trumbull's bills for Black civil rights caused moderate and radical Republicans in Illinois and the North to unite in rejecting him. The House of Representatives voted to impeach him in 1868; the Senate came one vote short of approving it.

## Formation of the Liberal Republican Party

During the Reconstruction, **political corruption** was common in the Republican Party, damaging its reputation both in Illinois and throughout the country. The Illinois State Constitution was amended to eliminate a number of legal loopholes of which corrupt officials had taken advantage. Nonetheless, the state government continued to give valuable state contracts to political cronies and to appoint political "hacks" to civil service jobs. In some places, Democrats took the place of Republicans whose reputations were damaged by being involved in scandals. In local Illinois elections in 1869, members of **both parties** often joined to run "citizen tickets" to oppose the "ring tickets" furthered by the Republican system. Political corruption became an issue that divided the Republican Party nationwide. Many Republicans, disenchanted with Ulysses S. Grant's presidency and administration, became political reformers, starting a movement that formed the **Liberal Republican Party** in 1872, a challenge to the traditional American two-party system.

**Influences and Actions of Liberal Republican Party in Illinois and Results of the 1872 Presidential Election**

Once the Liberal Republican Party had formed as a reaction of Republican political reformers against Republican political corruption, a number of Illinois Republicans campaigned for the Liberal Republican Party's candidacy for **President**. These included Illinois Senator Lyman Trumbull; Illinois Governor John Palmer; Supreme Court Justice David Davis; and Gustave Koerner, a German-American politician. However, at the Liberal Republican convention in Cincinnati, Ohio, party members could not agree to the strongest candidate. They settled on **Horace Greeley**, the newspaper editor from New York. Democrats, also unable to select anyone else, endorsed Greeley as their candidate as well. The Liberal Republican Party represented a new middle class of many Republican and some northern Democratic professionals. They wanted competent governmental administration, but they did not seek support from Democrats, farmers, or others disenchanted with the two-party system. The North, including Illinois, voted to re-elect **Ulysses S. Grant** for another corruption-riddled term (1872-1876).

**Challenges to Chicago Politics in Late 1800s**

The devastation caused by the Great Fire of Chicago in 1871, the economic Panic of 1873 and the ensuing depression, a huge influx of immigrants, and the new development of violent incidents over labor disputes, all presented **political challenges** in Chicago, Illinois. The Populist Movement formed the People's Party as part of movements against corruption for political reform. Chicago voters responded to conditions in 1873 by electing a candidate from the **People's Party** to be their mayor, and People's Party members to run their city council. Recent German immigrants to Chicago also formed a **Socialist Party** at this time. The Socialists had many disputes with the People's Party city leadership during the depression of the 1870s. The Chicago administration's response to unemployment was to recommend that individuals should use their own initiative and self-help, while the Socialists wanted the city government to provide jobs and/or relief funds to unemployed citizens.

**Influence of Farmers on American Politics and Economy in Late 1800s**

Following the Civil War, the United States Federal government had taken the wartime inflationary "greenbacks" out of circulation and had returned to adhering to the gold standard. This **deflated** American currency's value. The deflation caused great pressure to debtors, especially farmers, by making it impossible for them to make payments. During the 1870s, many farmers formed **Granges and Farmers' Alliances** for the purposes of political lobbies and helping themselves. This was concurrent with the Populist Movement. The Farmers' Alliances contributed to the Populists until, by 1892, the Populists became a national political organization for the Farmers' Alliances. Its platform advocated national government subtreasuries/warehouses to help farmers with crop storage pending better prices; and coining silver for economic expansion. This appealed to southern and western Democrats, dividing the party and defeating conservative President Grover Cleveland. Nationally, the Populist Party garnered over a million votes, carrying three states in the 1872 election.

**Changes Made to Illinois State Law by Its New Constitution of 1870**

Illinois law had been governed by the same state constitution since 1848 when, in 1869, a **state constitutional convention** was held to rewrite it. This was largely in response to widespread political corruption. This corruption was characterized by state legislation that was passed annually to favor local special interests and/or certain individuals. Political rings of insiders raided state treasury funds via contracts that they had created with the new Illinois State Industrial University at Champaign, and with the Illinois State Penitentiary, to give two examples. Illinois voters insisted that the state constitution be **rewritten** to address these dealings. The new state constitution prohibited most legislation favoring special interests, as well as the legislature's power to override the governor's vetoes. Consistent with the Fifteenth Amendment, the new Illinois State Constitution granted **suffrage** to black citizens of Illinois, although many people in Illinois still resisted civil rights and social equality for black people.

### Illinois State Constitution of 1870, Interests of Illinois Farmers, and Munn v. Illinois

Political graft had long existed in the city of Chicago, the state of Illinois, and within the Republican Party on a national level. Corrupt political deals giving benefits of money and power to politicians at the expense of the public seemed to increase exponentially during the late 1860s after the Civil War. Voters in Illinois finally demanded that their **state constitution**, ratified in 1848, should be rewritten to rein in these damaging and unethical practices, and the state legislature responded by convening a state constitutional convention in 1869 to **amend** the existing document. The new constitution was ratified in 1870 and regulated businesses that held state franchises or licenses to further public interest. When a merchant violated and then challenged these new laws, it culminated in the U.S. Supreme Court's ruling in Munn v. Illinois (1877), which affirmed the regulation of businesses enacted in the Illinois State Constitution.

### Economic Developments in Illinois as Result of Civil War

During the Civil War, Illinois **agriculture** became very important to the Union armies. The corn and grains that Illinois farmers grew supplied troops with rations. Illinois **industry** also supplied the Union armies, as its factories manufactured soldiers' uniforms, wagons, weapons, and other needed items. Because Chicago was located at the center of Northwest America's network of railroads, which was rapidly expanding, it became a main distribution point for goods manufactured in the East to be transported to troops fighting in the West. After the war, the first **Transcontinental Railroad** was finished, running from Omaha to San Francisco, in 1869. Since Chicago already had a railroad connection with Omaha, Chicago also became the center of the Western railroad system. But the war's end also lowered crop prices and European demand for crops, so farmers who had borrowed money to raise production for booming wartime markets could not repay them.

### Effects of Great Chicago Fire of 1871 upon Economic and Business Development

Although the Great Fire destroyed almost 40 percent of Chicago, the city was rebuilt very quickly because of Chicago's strategic geographical position and capital contributions from eastern commerce. Instead of devastation, the opportunities for new construction created by the fire made Chicago a mecca for innovative architecture. **Frank Lloyd Wright** and **Louis Sullivan** became prominent architectural designers in Chicago, gaining nationwide and worldwide fame. Chicago was the site of America's first **skyscrapers**. These were enabled by cement caissons sunk in bedrock deep underground and supporting steel frames. As Chicago also became the nexus of America's Western rail system, Chicago merchants collected lumber, corn, grain, et cetera, from Western and Midwestern farms, and then distributed products manufactured from these crops, such as tools, clothes, and pre-fabricated housing units. Also because of the railroad system, **Sears Roebuck** and **Montgomery Ward** in Chicago both became prominent mail-order businesses when trains enabled widespread delivery of orders.

## Major Manufacturing Industries in Chicago in Mid/Late 1800s

A number of manufacturing companies developed to support the agrarian commerce of the Western United States after the Civil War. Many of these companies began in Chicago or relocated there. The **McCormick Harvester Company** began in Virginia, but in 1848 it moved to Chicago to avail itself of the city's closeness to the West's Grain Belt. This company built an enormous factory on Chicago's West Side, which provided jobs for thousands of employees in the city. On the southwest side of Chicago, the Cudahy, Swift, and Armour companies all built huge slaughterhouses and meat processing and packing plants; collectively, these were known as **Packingtown**. Before the Civil War, St. Louis and New Orleans had become significant to commerce via the Mississippi River steamboats' transportation. With the growth of the railroads, which took the place of steamboats, Chicago superseded St. Louis as the major **commercial center** of the Mississippi Valley region.

## Illinois Women's Involvement in Labor, Social Reform, and Politics Prior to 1900

During the Gilded Age, many women in Illinois had to work, especially immigrants. In 1878, **The Knights of Labor**, a powerful labor union at the time, was notable as the only union accepting African-Americans and women, giving women an unusual chance to participate in a labor organization. The Chicago chapter also afforded immigrant women and families opportunities for social activities by organizing social groups hosting festivals, rallies, and picnics. Affluent middle-class women formed many women's clubs in the 1880s, such as the **Chicago Women's Club**, which worked to prevent juvenile offenders from becoming career criminals. Clubwomen pushed for and got seats on boards of schools and other state and private institutions for women and children. In 1891, the state legislature passed a bill letting women vote in elections of school officials. In 1894, **Lucy Flower** was the first woman elected by Illinois voters as Trustee of the University of Illinois.

## Illinois Politics and Economy in Late 1890s

Republicans swept the 1894 election, defeating Democrats and damaging the administration of conservative Democratic President **Grover Cleveland**. Cleveland's promotion of the gold standard, high tariffs, and laissez-faire economics lost him the support of southern and western Democrats, who preferred the Populist Party's promotion of government support for farmers and others in debt. Illinois politics reflected the growing divisiveness in the party. **Altgeld**, the first non-American-born Illinois Governor, pardoned activists in the Haymarket Riot and refused to deploy State troops against striking Pullman workers. Altgeld's labor/union-friendly policies were overridden by Cleveland's support of management with U.S. Army troops and a court injunction. Illinois' **William Jennings Bryan** spoke in support of coining silver, appealing to many: Chicago was among cities where unemployment approached 20 percent and many women and children went to work for half of men's wages. Bryan's "Cross of Gold" speech advocating free silver won him the nomination at the Chicago Democratic Convention.

## Political Reform in Chicago at End of 19th Century

In the election of 1896, **William McKinley** and the Republican Party overwhelmingly defeated the Populist Party. Regardless, the emphasis of industrialists on efficiency, technology, and expertise provided a new criticism of the graft inherent in party politics. In 1896, the **Municipal Voters' League** was established by citizens of Chicago. This group investigated the city's aldermen for corruption and wrongdoing and was successful in ousting many of the guilty from office. Social movements begun during the Gilded Age had given rise to such developments as the formation of women's clubs for social reform; the election of German-American John Altgeld as the first non-native-born Governor of Illinois; and the success of Jane Addams' Hull House, the first settlement house in the country, to organize immigrants and other poor people to help themselves, and promote Americans' learning about other cultures from immigrants. These movements continued on to become part of the **Progressive Era**.

## Native American Tribes of Illinois

The largest portion of what is now the state of Illinois was once populated by the **Illini**, their original name; this tribe was referred to in English as the Illinois Tribe. In fact, the name Illinois itself is derived from the Algonquian Indian language. In the Miami-Illinois tribal language, **Illiniwek** was a word thought to mean "the people/the men." More Miami Indians lived in Indiana and in Oklahoma than in Illinois. However, the Miami and Illinois tribes each spoke a dialect of the Algonquian language. Much smaller parts of what is now the state of Illinois were once populated by the Chickasaw Tribe; the Dakota Sioux Tribe; the Ho-Chunk Tribe, also referred to as the Winnebago tribe; the Miami Tribe; and the Shawnee Tribe. All of these Native American tribes were living in the territory which became Illinois before the Europeans came to America to settle and colonize its land.

### After Arrival of Europeans

The Illinois, Chickasaw, Dakota Sioux, Winnebago (Ho-Chunk), Miami, and Shawnee tribes were all living in the territory that is now the state of Illinois before Europeans came to America to settle. After European settlers had arrived in the Illinois area, additional Native American tribes migrated from other areas of the American continent. These tribes included the Delaware Tribe, the Kickapoo Tribe, the Ottawa Tribe, the Potawatomi Tribe, the Sac Tribe, the Fox Tribe, and the Wyandot Tribe. Today, there are no Native American tribes living in the state of Illinois officially **recognized** by the United States Federal Government. These tribes have not become extinct; rather, the United States government forced them to move to reservations, mostly in Oklahoma, though some also settled elsewhere; for example, while other groups of the Delaware tribe moved to Oklahoma, the Citizen Delaware Indians stayed in Kansas and are also known as the Kansas Delaware.

## Peoria Indian Tribe

Historically, the Illinois, or Illini, Indians, founded the great **"mound" civilizations** in the central region of the American continent 2,000 to 3,000 years in the past. A number of separate tribes first lived in the areas of the continent that border on the Great Lakes, and which drain into the Mississippi River. These tribes included the Peoria Tribe, the Kaskaskia Tribe, the Piankeshaw Tribe, and the Wea Tribe. In 1854, these tribes merged to form a single tribe. They were then called the **Confederated Peorias**. Peoria Indian tribes lived in Illinois, Michigan, Ohio, and Missouri. When the United States government relocated them, they were first consolidated in Missouri; then they were moved to Kansas; and ultimately, they were resettled in the northeastern region of Oklahoma. Miami, in Ottawa County of Oklahoma, is now the Peorias' tribal headquarters. The United States Federal government now recognizes the Peoria tribe in Oklahoma (1997).

## Theories of Linguistic Origin of the Name Illinois

In the 17th century, the Jesuit missionary **Father Jacques Marquette** explored the northern Mississippi Valley with Louis Jolliet and founded **Sault Ste. Marie**, the first European settlement in Michigan. He claimed that the word Illinois was a tribal word meaning "the men." However, later research by linguists suggests that this word may have been derived instead from the Illinois Indian word **irenweewa**, which in translation means "he speaks in the ordinary way." Scholars believe that the Ojibwa Indians living in the eastern region of the Great Lakes area took this Illinois Indian word and used it as a name for these people; in the Ojibwa tribal language, irenweewa was changed to ilinwe, which French explorers then used, spelling it as "Illinois." The word **Illiniwek**, sometimes translated as "the people," is thought to have developed from the Ojibwa word ilinwek, or the plural of ilinwe.

## Structure of Illinois Indian Tribes' Society

Before European exploration of the Americas began, the society of the Illinois Indian tribes was **egalitarian**. The tribes had chiefs; however, the chiefs were not regarded as rulers. They did influence the members of their tribes, and they were chosen based on their capacity to preserve the well-being of the Illinois society. However, they did not exert significant authority or power over the people. The Illinois used consensual agreement for tribal decisions. Power and resources were distributed relatively equally among members of the tribe. In the late 1600s, French authorities who had been colonizing the land and governing the Illinois Indians exerted the influence of European traditions, requiring chiefs to be responsible for tribal members' activities. They reinforced this by awarding chiefs with medals. By the 1760s, the role of chief had become an office holding the primary political power and requiring the approval of the colonial officials.

## History of Illinois Indian Tribes in Context of European Colonization

In the 1650s, **Iroquois** attacked the Illinois, forcing them west of the Mississippi River until the 1670s. In 1671, **France** claimed the Illinois country. Around 1680, the Iroquois again attacked the Illinois at Starved Rock, driving them out of the Illinois Valley for a time. By 1712, they had returned: their population was around 6,730, and they were living in villages at Starved Rock, Kaskaskia, Cahokia, and Pimetoui. The Illinois country was incorporated into the French colony of **Louisiana** in 1717. In 1756, when the French and Indian War began, the Illinois allied with the **French** against the English and other Indian tribes. To escape British rule, many moved west of the Mississippi. Illinois gained statehood in 1818 and Peoria tribes ceded their Illinois land to the USA. Indians had been moved to reservations by 1832. The Peoria Tribe (a part of the Illinois) was incorporated in Oklahoma in 1940.

## Illinois Indian Tribes' Deterioration

In 1673, the Illinois tribes were powerful, over 10,000 strong, occupying much land. Then by 1832, 159 years later, only one village of 300 people was left in Illinois. European **colonization**, attacks by other **tribes**, and **disease** decimated their population. Their conversion to European customs caused their loss of native traditions. The Illinois' historical enemies were Pawnee, Osage, and Arikara to their west; Sioux to their northwest; and Quapaw to their south. The Iroquois, who had gotten guns from Europeans, raided them from the 1650s to 1700s. Then hostilities broke out with northern tribes Kickapoo, Sauk, Fox, Potawatomi, and Dakota Sioux, as well as southern tribes Quapaw, Shawnee, and Chickasaw. French, British, and American armies using Indian allies caused some of these wars. Europeans also exposed the Indians to foreign diseases, especially smallpox, for which they had no immunity. Epidemics in 1704, 1732, and 1756 caused massive depopulation of Illinois tribes.

## Economy of Illinois Indian Tribes Before and After European Settlement

As noted by the explorer and Jesuit missionary Father Jacques Marquette from his visit in 1669, the Illinois Indians grew corn, squash, beans, and watermelon. Hunting available in the area included bear, wild cattle, deer, turkey, ducks, cranes, pigeons, and buzzards. Before European settlement, the Illinois Indians were mostly **self-sufficient** in their economy. In addition to growing their own produce and hunting, they traded with Indian tribes of the Great Lakes commodities such as animal furs, hides, and human slaves acquired from tribes west and south of them. When French settlers began to colonize the region, the Illinois also traded these goods with them in return for firearms and other European commodities. Over time, more and more French missionaries and traders settled on the Illinois land and lived among the Illinois Indians. The Illinois Indians gradually became more economically **dependent** on French commerce, and thus they became less self-sufficient.

## Illinois Indian Settlements in 17th Century

Historians and anthropologists refer to the Illinois tribes as **semi-sedentary**; they were not nomadic, but did not always stay in one place. Their settlements were **seasonal**, based on available food sources. They established summer villages near rivers for water, living there in April and May to plant maize (corn), and returning from mid-July to mid-October to harvest it. Some villages held 350 longhouses roofed with mats. On the prairies, the Illinois established summer hunting camps for communal bison hunts, staying there in shorter-term, bark-roofed lodges during June and July. The Illinois built winter villages in the river bottoms, where animals could be hunted. They lived in these winter villages from mid-October through March. To facilitate better hunting, they kept winter villages smaller with fewer people than summer villages, usually having 5-20 wigwams with mat roofs. They sometimes built larger winter villages when under the threat of being attacked.

## Settlement of Illinois After Civil War

Illinois had been the frontier of young America, but by the end of the Civil War, westward expansion changed this. Instead of frontier, Illinois became part of America's **heartland**. Settlers had moved into Iowa, Nebraska, and Kansas looking for new land to cultivate. Gold prospectors had used Panama as a route to get to California. As Illinois became central to the United States, Chicago developed into the West's main **staging area**. New York City and Illinois were connected by the Erie Canal, facilitating transportation and commerce. Chicago's position, where the Mississippi Valley and the Great Lakes met, made it the perfect location as a railway hub, and railroad construction expanded swiftly after the war. Even as Chicago flourished and became wealthy, towns such as Alton, Cairo, and Quincy, Illinois suffered economically when commercial traffic on the Mississippi River declined, while the Illinois Central Railroad serviced ports on the Gulf of Mexico.

## Illinois Urbanization in "Gilded Age" Following Civil War

As crop prices fell following the Civil War, European demand for American crops fell, and American currency was deflated, **farmers** suffered economically. Young people looking for work moved from rural areas to **urban** ones, especially Chicago, where industry created more jobs. Westward expansion beyond the Mississippi River also prompted this movement. Employment opportunities afforded by Chicago's growing wealth attracted many immigrants from other countries. Even Chicago's Great Fire in 1871 was not such a great setback: New York provided funds to rebuild the city and more construction jobs were created, attracting more **immigrants**. Most immigrated from

Southern and Eastern Europe and Ireland. Many had family or friends who had arrived earlier and they followed them to the same cities, facilitating the establishment of new communities. However, immigrants also were met with segregation in housing, jobs, and unions. Many found solutions by establishing themselves in economic sectors neglected by native White Americans.

## Ethnic Composition of Chicago in 1870s and 1880s and Disagreements over Alcohol

Due to a massive influx of **immigration** in the 1870s-1880s, the majority of Chicago's population became new arrivals who outnumbered the native-born elite society who had settled before the Civil War. During this time period, **Frances Willard**, founder of the Women's Christian Temperance Union, and other reformers from the northern United States advocated for the regulation or even the prohibition of **liquor**. They blamed the abuse of alcohol for poverty, starvation, the disruption of families, and men committing violent acts against women. However, many of the new immigrants from Germany came from social traditions in their country wherein drinking beer and wine were commonplace and important, causing major disagreements with reformers who were against alcohol. German-American members of the Republican Party were angered by the party's inclinations to align with these anti-alcohol reformers, and as a result, many German-American Republicans in Chicago converted to the Democratic Party during this time.

## Contributions of Immigrants in Illinois to Radical Movements in Chicago

Before the Civil War, many Irish people had immigrated to Illinois for decades to work on the construction of the **Illinois and Michigan Canal**. After the war, they established community organizations, often associated with the Catholic Church; these groups gained significant power. Many also supported the cause of Ireland's independence from England. Irish-Americans contributed substantially to the establishment of labor unions. One of the biggest of these unions was the **Knights of Labor**. The Irish brought their strategy of the boycott from Ireland to America. Powerful labor unions such as the Knights of Labor employed boycotting against management's financial, legal, and political power. Eastern European and German immigrants brought radical ideas and politics, forming the Socialist and Anarchist movements, highlighted by the **Great Strike of 1877** and the **Haymarket Riot of 1886**. As a result, many middle-class White native-born Americans associated immigrants with labor violence and radical ideas and actions.

## Assimilation of Immigrants into Chicago Political and Social Life in 1880's

By the 1880s, Chicago's population contained more immigrants than native-born Americans due to large waves of **immigration**. Job seekers came mostly from Eastern Europe, Germany, and Ireland for employment opportunities created in Chicago by rebuilding efforts following the 1871 Great Fire and by Chicago's rapidly growing wealth as the new hub of the railroad systems and as an industrial center. In 1892, the first non-American-born Chicago governor, **John Peter Altgeld**, was elected. By this time, many other immigrants had achieved positions of political leadership in Chicago. However, immigrants also encountered discrimination and fewer opportunities, relying on their ethnic communities socially and in business. **Jane Addams** wanted to learn about other cultures. While many reformers wanted to teach immigrants "Yankee virtues" of self-control and thriftiness, Addams formed **Hull House**, the first settlement house in America, partly for assisting immigrants in self-help and organizing themselves, as well as uplifting the poor.

## Religion in Chicago and Illinois During Gilded Age

The Northern United States had been largely **Protestant** since its beginnings. In the 1850s, many **Catholics** immigrated to America from Eastern and Southern Europe and Ireland. Native American-born Protestants often disagreed religiously and culturally with these Catholic immigrants. American Protestants developed such an aversion to both Catholicism and immigration that some of them reacted by founding the **Know-Nothings**, also called the American Party. In 1870 **Dwight L. Moody**, a Chicago minister, recruited **Ira Sankey**, a gospel singer, and they toured America and Europe promoting Moody's new fundamentalist, ecumenical Christianity, which opposed Calvinist doctrine such as original sin and preached about the love of God. Though he had critics, Moody became the most popular evangelist of the Gilded Age. In 1880, in lower Illinois, **Augustine Tolton** was ordained as America's first Black priest. His first all-Black parish in Quincy met such opposition from local Whites that he relocated to a parish in Chicago.

## Role of Chicago in American Realist Literary Movement in 1890s and 1900s

Chicago played a major part in the development of the **American Realist** school of literature during the 1890s. **Hamlin Garland** was a newspaper reporter in Chicago who had grown up on a farm in rural Wisconsin. In addition to his journalism, Garland wrote novels that depicted the grim realities of life on a farm, which disabused many American readers of their idealized notions about farm life. **Theodore Dreiser** also worked in Chicago as a journalist and wrote short stories and novels. He compiled research notes on the city, informing his famous work *Sister Carrie* about the ascent and decline of a young woman in Chicago. Pulitzer Prize-winning author **Upton Sinclair** worked undercover for seven weeks in Chicago's meat-packing plants as research for his best-selling, muckraking novel *The Jungle*. Its 1906 exposure of conditions prompted the passage of the Pure Food and Drug Act and the Meat Inspection Act that year.

## World's Columbian Exposition of 1893 in Chicago

The World's Columbian Exposition was held in Chicago in 1893 to commemorate the 400th anniversary of Columbus' New World landing and celebrate American culture, business, and society. More than 27 million people came to Chicago to attend this fair. The fairgrounds included fourteen main buildings and spanned 633 acres. The consistently neo-classical style and similar construction materials of all of the buildings caused people to nickname them the **White City**. The fair had a centrally located classical statue, a large reflecting pool, and a fountain. The many exhibits included agriculture, machinery, manufacturing, transportation, electricity, and the liberal arts; a Palace of Fine Arts building with over 8,000 works of art; and a women's building devoted to women's accomplishments. Other, smaller buildings also displayed goods from the American states, the American territories, and from more than twenty other nations as well.

Presage of Leisure and Recreational Activities of 20th Century American Lifestyles

In 1893, Chicago was host to the World's Columbian Exposition, a giant fair to celebrate Columbus' landing in America 400 years before, and the cultural, social, industrial, and business accomplishments of America. This fair featured many exhibits of an educational and informational nature. In addition, it featured many sources of entertainment. On the midway of the fair, the first Ferris Wheel in the world was constructed. In addition, the exposition included a fun house, a swimming pool, and even a zoo. Official exhibitions from other countries were contributed to the exposition. Business entrepreneurs set up exhibits depicting life in less affluent villages of other nations. Just outside of the fair grounds, Buffalo Bill's Wild West Show had been established, and many attendees went to see it when they visited the fair. The exposition thus pioneered the mass amusements and cultural accomplishments and activities characteristic of **20ᵗʰ century American leisure and recreation**.

Turner's "The Significance of the Frontier in American History"
The World's Columbian Exposition was a huge 1893 fair in Chicago to celebrate cultural and social achievements as well as Columbus' American landing 400 years earlier. One way that it was related to historian **Frederick Jackson Turner's** paper, "The Significance of the Frontier in American History," was that Turner presented this piece in connection with the Exposition. Another way it was related was that Turner's argument both contradicted the social achievements highlighted in the Exposition by casting doubt on their future, and struck a chord among listeners. Turner argued that according to the 1890 census, there was no more frontier to conquer on the American continent. He found that the American frontier experience had forged the national character and democracy, asking what would happen in a future without this experience. He voiced a concern of many Americans about their modern society's future. Thus, while controversial, Turner's thesis was also influential.

## Louis Sullivan

Louis Sullivan was an architect who was known for creating innovative building designs. **Sullivan** emerged in the later 1800s as the leader of the new **Chicago School of Architects**. When the "White City" buildings of the 1893 World's Columbian Exposition fair were constructed in Chicago, all using similar building materials and conforming to a neo-classical style, Sullivan protested that these buildings would set back architectural progress by fifty years. Rebuilding much of Chicago after the Great Fire of 1871 presented increased opportunities for architects. New designers invented a construction method enabling skyscrapers to be erected. Two landmarks in Chicago designed by Sullivan near the end of his career were the **Auditorium Theater** in 1889 and the **Chicago Stock Exchange Building** in 1893. He influenced generations of younger architects, including Frank Lloyd Wright, who after working for Sullivan started his own practice in Chicago and pioneered the Prairie School of Architecture.

## John Dewey

John Dewey was a philosopher from Vermont who taught at the University of Michigan in the 1890s. At the end of the World's Columbian Exposition, which was held in Chicago in 1893, the Midway Plaisance which had hosted the fair remained, and the University of Chicago built a new campus on those grounds. **John D. Rockefeller**, founder of the Standard Oil Company and millionaire, donated funds to recruit faculty members from the Northeast to teach at the new campus, including **John Dewey**. Dewey was a major proponent of the new **Pragmatist philosophy**. In Chicago he was inspired by Jane Addams' Hull House to develop a new instrumentalist philosophy for living. He believed our experiences are problem-solving instruments. He endorsed the **Scientific Method** and felt students should learn by experimenting and interacting with their environments. Dewey founded the University of Chicago's Laboratory School, which became a national center for educational reform.

## Employment Conditions in Illinois Following Passage of Civil Rights Laws

The **Fourteenth Amendment** and the Reconstruction's **Civil Rights acts** allowed Black people to vote and serve as jurors. Illinois was required to change its state laws to conform to the federal legislation. During this time, Chicago schools became **integrated**, and state-funded colleges also admitted Black students. However, in the northern United States, less than 2 percent of the population was African-American. Because many northern Whites resisted integration or were unsure about it, social progress for Blacks in the North, including Illinois, was slow. Many White Illinois employees wanted to limit Black workers to unskilled labor to prevent competition. The Knights of Labor admitted Black members, but it was the exception among labor unions. In central and southern Illinois, many Blacks were recruited from the South to work in **coal mines**, often because White miners were on strike. The United Mine Workers organized integrated local unions, gaining over 20,000 Black members by 1900.

## Activists for Racial Equality in Chicago

In Illinois as in the rest of the North, many African-American people worked as unskilled laborers or servants during this time. They received lower pay than White workers for the same work. Housing in the North at this time was also strictly **segregated**, so Blacks were forced to live only in certain neighborhoods. As Chicago became a big city, it became a mecca for African-American political and intellectual activity. **Lucy Parsons**, a prominent African-American speaker, organized the **Chicago Working Women's Union** and began publishing her own newspaper, "Freedom," in 1891. Her husband, **Albert Parsons**, was White. Together the Parsons came to be among the most famous organizers and radical social critics in Chicago. **Ferdinand Barnett**, a graduate of City of Chicago Law School, became the first African-American Assistant State's Attorney in Illinois. Barnett was also founder and editor of the **Chicago Conservator**, a newspaper devoted to Black civil rights.

## Ida B. Wells

Ida B. Wells was the daughter of slaves in Mississippi. She managed to obtain an education and started teaching school while still in her teens. She challenged segregation of facilities while teaching in Memphis by suing a railroad company. She became a journalist focusing on **social injustices against African-Americans**, writing exposés of lynch mobs after three of her friends were lynched. These pieces garnered national fame. She confronted Frances Willard's Women's Christian Temperance Union for supporting Southern reformers' acceptance of lynching. Wells published a piece entitled Why the Colored American Is Not in the World's Columbian Exposition in 1894 to call attention to the exclusion by White fair organizers of Black people and exhibits. She became a touring lecturer to further her political activism and to escape threats against her in Memphis. She then married **Ferdinand Barnett**, Illinois' first Black Assistant State's Attorney and Chicago Conservator founder/editor, moving to Chicago.

## Women's Suffrage Movement

Women's suffrage got national attention from an 1848 Seneca Falls, New York convention, but thereafter it was eclipsed by the issue of abolition of slavery before, during, and after the Civil War. When the **Fifteenth Amendment** gave Black men the vote, overlooking women, the movement became divided by disagreement whether women's suffrage should/should not be attached to this amendment. Reformers founded the **Illinois Woman Suffrage Association** in 1869, but women did not get the vote under the 1870 Illinois State Constitution. Reformers **Alta Hulett, Judge James**, and **Myra Colby Bradwell** got laws passed from 1860-1890 giving women rights to equal post-divorce child guardianship, to control their own earnings, control and maintain their own property, pursue any profession or occupation, and benefit from the estates of deceased husbands. Bradwell helped pass an 1873 law allowing qualified women to hold school offices; in 1874, ten women were elected to be county school superintendents.

## Women's Christian Temperance Union

**Frances Willard**, of Chicago suburb Evanston, Illinois, founded the **Women's Christian Temperance Union** in 1874. This organization based its concept of "home protection," or defense of the family unit, upon the natural role of women as mothers. Willard and the WCTU united the women's rights movement with the philosophy that only women's morality could reform corrupt male political practices. Many pursued women's right to vote for this purpose. The WCTU's motto was "Agitate – Educate – Legislate." In 1877, Frances Willard was the first woman in history to speak before an official session of the Illinois General Assembly. In addition to working for women's suffrage and for temperance, the WCTU also advocated for social reform. For example, in 1889, the Chicago chapter of the organization ran a mission shelter accommodating 4,000 homeless women annually, a men's lodging house, an industrial school, two Sunday schools, a free medical dispensary, and a low-priced restaurant.

# ILTS Practice Test

1. Where was the first great human civilization located?
   a. Egypt
   b. Greece
   c. Mesopotamia
   d. Samaria

2. Which of the following was not an ancient Egyptian ruler?
   a. Anubis
   b. Hatshepsut
   c. Ramses' II
   d. Tutankhamen

3. How did the Crusader army that went on the First Crusade differ from the Crusader armies that Pope Urban II envisioned?
   a. There was no difference. The people of Europe were accustomed to obeying clerical direction and eagerly joined the cause creating an army that was primarily made up of faithful Christians from all social classes led by a select group of knights who were responsible for leading and training their armies.
   b. There was no difference. The people of Europe obeyed clerical direction and stayed home to pray for the success of an army composed entirely of knights and professional other military personnel.
   c. Pope Urban II had envisioned an army of skilled knights and professional soldiers; instead, men and women from all classes joined together to retake the Holy Land.
   d. Pope Urban II had envisioned an army composed of faithful Christians of from all social classes led by a group of select knights; instead the army was primarily made up of knights and other professional military personnel.

4. Which western European monastic order developed an early form of banking that helped make pilgrimages to the Holy Land safer for the pilgrims?
   a. The Knights Templar
   b. The Knights Hospitaller
   c. The Knights of Malta
   d. The Barbary Corsairs

5. Which early feminist work was written by Mary Wollstonecraft?
   a. A Vindication of the Rights of Woman
   b. The Declaration of Sentiments
   c. Frankenstein
   d. The Awakening

6. What is the historical significance of the Dome on the Rock's site to Jews?
   a. It is the traditional site of Jesus Christ's crucifixion and resurrection
   b. It is located on Temple Mount, where the Second Temple previously stood and the traditional site of Solomon's Temple
   c. It is the traditional site of Mohammed's ascent into heaven
   d. It is the site of the founding of the Islamic religion.

7. How did the Nile shape the Ancient Egyptian Empire?
    a. It provided a nonnavigable boundary for the Egyptian Empire.
    b. It eroded land, creating natural harbors for Egyptian fishermen.
    c. It routinely flooded, eroding the limited desert farmland.
    d. It routinely flooded, leaving behind fertile silt that helped make large scale agriculture possible.

8. In which country does a large part of the native, traditionally nomadic people currently live in large tents known as yurts or gers?
    a. Indonesia
    b. Mongolia
    c. Thailand
    d. India

9. Which of the following was not a tax levied on the American colonies by the British government in the 1760's and 70's?
    a. The Sugar Act of 1764
    b. The Stamp Act of 1765
    c. The Lead Act of 1772
    d. The Tea Act of 1773

10. To whom was the Declaration of Independence addressed and why?
    a. To the British Parliament, because the colonists were opposed to being ruled by a king who had only inherited his throne and only considered the popularly elected Parliament to hold any authority over them
    b. To the King of England because the colonists were upset that Parliament was passing laws for them even though they did not have the right to elect members of Parliament to represent their interests.
    c. To the Governors of the rebelling colonies so that they would know that they had 30 days to either announce their support of the Revolution or to return to England.
    d. To the colonial people as a whole. The Declaration of Independence was intended to outline the wrongs that had been inflicted on them by the British military and inspire them to rise up in protest.

11. How did the ruling in Marbury v. Madison alter the Supreme Court's power in the federal government?
    a. It lessened it. The Supreme Court was concerned about the possibility of judges overturning laws enacted by voters through referendums and took away that power.
    b. It increased it. The decision in Marbury v. Madison gave the Supreme Court it's now traditional right to overturn legislation.
    c. It increased it. The decision in Marbury v. Madison strengthened the Supreme Court's Constitutional right to overturn legislation.
    d. There was no change. Marbury v. Madison was a case involving a president who was unwilling to obey laws enacted by his predecessor; there was nothing about the case or decision that would have more than a cursory connection to federal powers of government

12. Which President of the United States changed the date of Thanksgiving from the last Thursday of November to the fourth Thursday of November?
    a. George Washington
    b. Andrew Jackson
    c. Abraham Lincoln
    d. Franklin D. Roosevelt

13. Which of the following is an example of historiography?
    a. An explanation of past treatments of an historical event.
    b. A geographer using physical geography to explain historical events.
    c. A historical treatise on a single aspect of a larger historical event.
    d. Historiography is not a valid historical term

14. Which of the following questions would most likely be asked by a historian concerned with the philosophy of history?
    a. What issues shaped the writing of Plato's Republic?
    b. Should history be measured by changes in individual lives or by larger political trends?
    c. Why were the religions of Shinto and Buddhism able to merge in Japan?
    d. Should historians study modern primitive cultures as a means of learning about past civilizations?

15. You are researching the Battle of the Bulge's Malmedy Massacre. Four potential sources offer conflicting accounts of one aspect of the event. Based on the principles of historical research, which source is most likely to be accurate?
    a. Wikipedia
    b. A newspaper article written by a reporter who interviewed several surviving soldiers over the weeks following the massacre.
    c. The account of a wounded survivor written immediately following the massacre.
    d. One of your teaching colleague's lecture notes.

16. Which of the following is considered to be the largest cause of death among Native Americans following the arrival of European colonists in North America?
    a. Wounds from wars with the European settlers
    b. Wounds from wars with the other Native American tribes
    c. European diseases
    d. Exposure during the wintry, forced marches on which the European settlers forced them

17. What is the historical significance of the Dome on the Rock's site to Muslims?
    a. It is the traditional site of Jesus Christ's crucifixion and resurrection
    b. It is located on Temple Mount, where the Second Temple previously stood and the traditional site of Solomon's Temple
    c. It is the traditional site of Mohammed's ascent into heaven
    d. It is the site of the founding of the Islamic religion.

18. What method did Johannes Gutenberg use to create printing plates for his printing press?
    a. Woodcuts – he had a team of apprentices carve each page out of wood plates.
    b. Metal etchings – the letters were etched into specially treated metal plates which were then placed in special acid baths to create printing plates.
    c. Moveable clay type – Gutenberg carved moveable type out of clay and would press the letters into hot wax tablets to create printing plates.
    d. Moveable type – Gutenberg cast metal type through the use of molds in order to achieve the individual letters which were then loaded into composing sticks, which were then used to form printing plates.

19. Which group(s) of people were originally responsible for selecting the members of the U.S. Senate?
    a. State legislatures
    b. State governors
    c. State electors
    d. State residents, subject to voting eligibility

20. The Erie Canal is 363 miles long and connects which body of water to Lake Erie?
    a. The Mississippi River
    b. The Hudson River
    c. The Susquehanna River
    d. The Lehigh River

21. The telephone was a solution to which of the following problems with the telegraph?
    a. Telegraph lines were thick and difficult to maintain.
    b. Telegraph messages could only be received by people who had specialized equipment.
    c. Telegraphs could only relay one message at a time.
    d. Telegraphs frequently broke down if subject to extended use.

22. Why did each Incan ruler have to earn his own fortune?
    a. A tradition that all the wealth an Incan king accumulated during his reign would be used to house and care for the king's mummified remains.
    b. A tradition that all of a deceased king's wealth would be added to the main Incan temple's treasury.
    c. A tradition that all of a deceased king's wealth would be used to create a large public work in the king's memory.
    d. A belief that the new king needed to prove his worth through conquest and adding to the royal treasury.

23. How would this picture be most appropriately used?
    a. As an example of a Suffragist picket sign.
    b. As an example of American response to Versailles Treaty.
    c. As an example of early American use of Biblical allusions.
    d. As an example of an early American response to the German Nazi movement.

Credit: National Archives and Records Administration. http://teachpol.tcnj.edu/amer_pol_hist/thumbnail297.html

24. What was the ancient Agora of Athens?
   a. It was the main temple to Athena, where scholars would go to give lectures and pray for wisdom.
   b. It was the Athenian ruling body.
   c. It was the city of Athens's main source of drinking water and a place where Athenian women traditionally gathered.
   d. It was the name of the primary marketplace and also an important gathering center for Athenians.

25. Who was Genghis Khan?
   a. The founder of the Mongol Empire
   b. The leader of the Hunnic Empire in the 5th Century who led his people to attack into Western Europe.
   c. The leader of the 19th Century Taiping Rebellion
   d. None of the above

26. Which of the following is not necessarily an example of an educator introducing his own bias into the educational process?
   a. A teacher only using materials and sources that he knows are reputable and declining to use unverified material in his lessons.
   b. A textbook author choosing to only use sources that place his favorite U.S. president in a good light and his least favorite U.S. president in a bad light.
   c. A teacher only using primary sources that he agrees with and ridiculing a student who provides a verifiable primary source that offers a conflicting opinion.
   d. All of the above are examples of bias

27. Which of the following words can be defined as "a list events organized in order of their occurrence?"
   a. Anachronism
   b. Anno Domini
   c. Chroma
   d. Chronology

28. Who was Lewis and Clark's guide?
   a. Pocahontas
   b. Sacagawea
   c. Squanto
   d. Wauwatosa

29. What was the standard government economic principle in the late nineteenth and early twentieth centuries?
   a. Laissez faire
   b. Social Darwinism
   c. Keynesian Economics
   d. Monetarism

30. What was the purpose of Lyndon Johnson's Great Society?
    a. To eliminate poverty and racial injustice in America
    b. To erase the last vestiges of the Great Depression from the American economic landscape.
    c. To encourage economic prosperity through trickledown economics.
    d. To increase educational standards in the United States.

31. What were Woodrow Wilson's Fourteen Points?
    a. A list of reasons why women should not be given the right to vote.
    b. A list of conditions to which France and Great Britain had to agree before the United States would enter World War I.
    c. His plan for the rehabilitation of Germany after World War I
    d. His plan for stimulating the economy and turning the United States into a major economic power.

32. Which of the following American cities was not founded by people fleeing religious persecution?
    a. Plymouth, Massachusetts
    b. Jamestown, Virginia
    c. Boston, Massachusetts
    d. Providence, Rhode Island

33. Which of the following is not a skill that a student should have learned by the beginning of eighth grade?
    a. Identifying important events in the European exploration and colonization of North America.
    b. Evaluating the relationships between past and present conflicts.
    c. Identifying the reasons that the U.S. entered World War I.
    d. Creating a timeline.

34. Which of the following is an example of providing a connection between history and economics?
    a. Using maps showing post-World War II migration patterns.
    b. Using charts and maps to illustrate the growth of U.S. cities.
    c. Discussing the effects of weather on world history.
    d. Discussing the role of food shortages and inflation in the Russian Revolution.

35. Which economic crisis led to the creation of the SEC?
    a. The Panic of 1907
    b. The Post World War I Recession
    c. The Great Depression
    d. The Recession of 1953

36. What was the purpose of the Mayflower Compact?
    a. To create and enact a series of laws for the Pilgrims.
    b. To create a temporary government for the Pilgrims.
    c. To memorialize the Pilgrims' promises to raise their children according to their religious ideals.
    d. To memorialize the laws under which the Pilgrims had previously been living

37. What was Manifest Destiny?
    a. The idea that the United States was intended by God to expand to fill North America.
    b. The idea that England was intended by God to expand its empire to fill the world.
    c. The idea that England was intended by God to colonize the non-European world.
    d. The idea that the United States was intended by God to spread democracy throughout the world.

38. What was the purpose of the Marshall Plan?
    a. To rebuild Europe after World War I and strengthen the United States' Western allies.
    b. To rebuild Europe after World War II and prevent the spread of Communism in post-war Europe.
    c. To create jobs for U.S. servicemen following World War II.
    d. To build hospitals for wounded war veterans following World War I.

39. Most of the earliest civilizations flourished in or near what sort of geographic feature?
    a. Mountains
    b. Valleys
    c. Oceans
    d. Rivers

40. Which of the following is a true statement concerning the Magna Carta?
    a. It's main purpose was to prevent the Church from increasing its holdings.
    b. It created a system of majority rule in England.
    c. It was meant to protect the rights and property of the few powerful families that topped the feudal system.
    d. It was concerned with the rights of all Britons and frequently mentions the common people.

41. Which statement is an accurate reflection of Mayan urban life?
    a. The Mayas were a sophisticated urbanized culture, whose people predominately lived in large cities.
    b. The Mayas lived in urban communities, supported by a small number of highly productive farms.
    c. Mayan cities were primarily used as religious centers.
    d. Mayan cities were primarily used as government centers.

42. What were Martin Luther's 95 theses?
    a. His charter for the Lutheran Church
    b. Criticisms of practices in the Catholic Church
    c. A document explaining his differences with other Protestant churches
    d. Reasons why the Bible should be translated into popular languages.

43. Which U.S. Founding Father is credited with founding the Federalist Party?
    a. John Adams
    b. Thomas Jefferson
    c. Alexander Hamilton
    d. George Washington

44. Who were the Shoguns?
    a. Chinese military leaders
    b. Japanese military leaders
    c. Chinese religious leaders
    d. Japanese religious leaders

45. Which of the following is a true statement concerning the Iroquois Confederacy?
    a. It was a Confederacy of French fur trappers and settlers and members of the Iroquois tribes during the French and Indian War.
    b. It was a group of seven Native American tribes who joined together to protect themselves against European incursions into their territories.
    c. Its members were also known as the Five Civilized Tribes.
    d. It made decisions through a democratic process.

46. Which of the following was one of reasons that James Oglethorpe wished to found the colony of Georgia?
    a. To create an escape-proof penal colony in North America.
    b. To create a refuge for England's "worthy poor."
    c. To increase the Virginia Company's profitability
    d. To build a new port city to aid in the existing colonists' plans for westward expansion.

47. Which of the following is not a true statement concerning the beginnings of slavery in the Virginia colony?
    a. Slavery was established quickly as a means of securing a cheap source of labor.
    b. Initially slaves could become free through converting to Christianity.
    c. The number of slaves in Virginia increased as tobacco planters required a steady supply of labor.
    d. Early Virginian slaves included both Africans and Native Americans.

48. Why were the "Five Civilized Tribes" given that name?
    a. They had advanced military systems.
    b. In recognition of the assistance they gave early European settlers.
    c. They had advanced social and government systems.
    d. They had formed a complex Confederacy dedicated to preserving peace amongst themselves.

49. Who famously crossed the Rubicon in 49 BC?
    a. Julius Caesar
    b. Cleopatra
    c. Mark Antony
    d. Marcus Brutus

50. What was the basis of Edward Jenner's original smallpox vaccine?
    a. Liquid from chickenpox sores
    b. Liquid from cowpox sores
    c. Liquid from smallpox sores
    d. Liquid from acne sores

51. Which Japanese city was the first to be attacked with an atomic bomb?
    a. Hiroshima
    b. Nagasaki
    c. Nagoya
    d. Tokyo

52. Which of the following peoples did not practice a form of feudalism?
    a. The Norsemen (Vikings)
    b. The Germans
    c. The Persians
    d. The Byzantines

*Use the following passage to answer questions 53-55:*

> The United States' Constitution is the longest-lived written constitution in world history and has served as the model for the constitutions of other nations. Several factors contribute to its survival into the twenty-first century, the most important being the Constitution's simplicity and the built-in permission to amend it as necessary.

> Simplicity gives the Constitution flexibility. In it, basic rules do not change but within these rules, laws and practices can and are modified to meet the needs of the people and the state. If the Constitution had specific rules and laws concerning dynamic forces such as the economy, it would have quickly become outmoded or obsolete as the United States came to face challenges and situations that the original framers could not have predicted. The Constitution's framers realized that they could not anticipate the future and so created a document that provided a basic framework of government that could be amended without being cast aside as new situations and needs arose. This ability to amend the Constitution aided the pro-Constitution Federalists in the fight to ratify it as they gained support with the promise of the Bill of Rights which soothed early concerns regarding the rights of man.

53. Assuming that the above passage was from a student's essay, which of the following questions would it best answer?
    a. How is the U.S. Constitution a simple document?
    b. Why was the United States' Constitution used as a model for other countries' constitutions?
    c. Which attributes have contributed to the U.S. Constitution's longevity?
    d. What was the Federalist Party's earliest public action?

54. Which of the following is the best explanation of how the information in the above passage could be used in a class focused on a subject other than History?
    a. To describe the formation of the U.S. Constitution in a government class.
    b. To explain the basis of U.S. law in a government class.
    c. To explain why the U.S. Constitution can be amended in a current events class
    d. To describe attributes of the U.S. Constitution in a government class.

55. How could the information in the above passage be used to form a connection between history and modern government?

    a. To explain how Enlightenment ideas shaped American legal theory.

    b. To explain why the Constitution's framers chose to create a basic framework for government rather than create a strict, unchangeable model.

    c. To explain how the American two-party political system began.

    d. To explain why it was necessary to have a written Constitution.

56. Which of the following was a contemporary argument against The Bill of Rights?

    a. The concern that it didn't apply to the states.

    b. The belief that a bill of rights would infringe upon states' rights.

    c. The concern that specifically stating one right would create an argument against an unstated right.

    d. The belief that the Bill of Rights would be too great a check on government's ability to function.

57. What were the Federalist Papers meant to accomplish?

    a. To encourage people to join the Federalist Party

    b. To explain the necessity of the federalist system

    c. To assist in the ratification of the Constitution

    d. To expose a series of scandals relating to the Federalist Party

58. What was Franklin D. Roosevelt's "court packing" plan?

    a. A plan to influence court outcomes by packing the observation gallery with his own supporters.

    b. A plan to prevent cases from coming to trial by filing a large number of other cases in order to create judicial gridlock.

    c. A plan to keep Roosevelt surrounded by his own supporters to give him a greater impression of popularity.

    d. A plan to appoint a second justice for every federal justice over the age of seventy.

59. How did the invention of the cotton gin change the cotton industry in the United States?

    a. It decreased the amount of labor needed to grow cotton, thereby decreasing the demand for slaves.

    b. It had no overall effect on the cotton industry.

    c. It made Southern cotton plantations dependant on Northern textile factories who could use the gins to efficiently clean cotton.

    d. It turned cotton into a viable cash crop resulting in cotton becoming a major Southern export.

60. What was the purpose of the Sherman Anti-Trust Act?

    a. To prevent unions from striking

    b. To prevent restraints on free trade

    c. To encourage international trade

    d. To prevent corporate tax evasion

61. How were the Mexican-American War and the U.S. annexation of Texas connected?
    a. Mexico had informed Texas that an agreement to join the United States was the same as a declaration of war.
    b. The Mexican War began as Texas's war of independence.
    c. Mexico wanted Texas to remain independent as a buffer between itself and the U.S. and declared war in hopes of halting the annexation.
    d. There was no relation.  Mexico did not care what Texas did.

62. What did the landmark Supreme Court case, *Brown v. The Board of Education of Topeka* decide?
    a. That school busing was inherently Constitutional.
    b. That the doctrine of separate but equal was Unconstitutional.
    c. That racially separate educational facilities deprive people of equal protection under the laws.
    d. That Plessy v. Ferguson was appropriately decided.

63. Which of the following did not occur during or because of the French Revolution?
    a. The Reign of Terror
    b. Economic crisis
    c. The ending of feudal practices and slavery in France
    d. The calling together of the Estates General

64. Before 1854, which of the following countries had regular trading relations with Japan?
    a. The Netherlands
    b. Great Britain
    c. France
    d. Italy

65. Which of the following was a power granted to the U.S. Congress under the Articles of Confederation?
    a. The power to collect taxes
    b. The power to enter into treaties with foreign governments
    c. The power to enforce laws
    d. The power to regulate interstate commerce

66. According to Plato's *Republic*, which sort of person would make the best head of state?
    a. A philosopher
    b. A great general
    c. An elderly farmer
    d. A young noble, trained for rule from birth

67. Which of the following was not an effect of the Neolithic agricultural revolution?
    a. The establishment of social classes
    b. The building of permanent settlements
    c. An overall increase in leisure time
    d. All of the above were effects of the Neolithic agricultural revolution

68. Which of the following U.S. Constitutional Amendments lowered the voting age to eighteen?
    a. The 24th
    b. The 25th
    c. The 26th
    d. The 27th

69. Which of the following is an effect that mountains can have on a society?
   a. Acting as a source of food
   b. Protecting the society from invasion
   c. Providing a means of cultural diffusion
   d. Providing a source of transportation

70. Which statement is the best summary of the Monroe Doctrine?
   a. That European powers were not to interfere with the affairs of North America
   b. That no European power could forbid the United States from trading with another sovereign state
   c. That European powers were to not to interfere with affairs in the Western Hemisphere and that the United States would stay out of affairs in Europe.
   d. None of the Above

71. Who was the first President of South Africa to be elected in a fully representative South African election?
   a. Mahatma Gandhi
   b. Thabo Mbeki
   c. Kgalema Motlanthe
   d. None of the above

72. Which of the following events was a proximate cause of World War I?
   a. The Japanese bombing of Pearl Harbor
   b. The assassination of the Austrian-Hungarian Empire's Archduke Ferdinand
   c. The sinking of the RMS Lusitania
   d. The British interception of the Zimmerman telegram

73. Who was Boris Yeltsin?
   a. A Russian politician credited with breaking up the USSR
   b. A Russian politician who was instrumental in the Russian Revolution
   c. A Ukrainian politician who encouraged his country to break away from the Eastern bloc countries
   d. A Scandinavian politician who successfully prevented his country from joining the Warsaw Pact

74. Which of the following best describes The Truman Doctrine?
   a. The United States has the sole authority to assist other democracies located in North and South America.
   b. The United States must not interfere with the internal struggles of countries outside the Western Hemisphere.
   c. The United States must support free peoples who are resisting attempted subjugation by armed minorities or by outside pressures.
   d. None of the above

75. In 1955 the Soviet Union formed the Warsaw Treaty Organization to counterbalance which of the following?
  a. NAFTA
  b. NATO
  c. The U.N. Security Counsel
  d. The Four Power Pact

76. Which of the following was an advantage that the South held over the North at the beginning of the Civil War?
  a. Greater industry and capability to produce war materials
  b. Larger population/more available manpower
  c. Better railroad system
  d. Better military commanders

77. Which of the following was not one of the ways that the Mormon migration was unique among the American pioneers?
  a. They transported an entire culture across the American West.
  b. They traveled as highly organized companies.
  c. They improved the trail, built ferries and, planted crops as a means of assisting those who would follow them
  d. All of the above

78. Which of the following was a long term effect of the New Deal?
  a. The end of the Great Depression
  b. An increase in the role the federal government played in the U.S. economy.
  c. Decreased price supports for U.S. farmers
  d. All of the above

79. Who was César Chávez?
  a. The leader of a movement to improve working conditions for migrant laborers.
  b. A civil rights leader who worked to improve inner city conditions.
  c. A civil rights leader who dedicated his life to immigration reform
  d. None of the above

80. Which of the following is not a result of the Civil Rights Movement's work in the 1950s and 60s?
  a. The government enacted legislation prohibiting racial discrimination in employment.
  b. Disenfranchisement of African Americans was declared illegal.
  c. Court rulings that segregation in schools violated the Constitution led to a near instantaneous desegregation of public educational facilities.
  d. The government enacted legislation prohibiting racial discrimination in the housing market.

81. Which of the following was an effect of industrialization in the United States?
  a. Large growth in city populations
  b. A general shift from self-employment to being employed by others
  c. Increased economic/employment opportunities for women
  d. All of the above

82. Which of the following were causes of The Dust Bowl?
  I.     Wind erosion
  II.    Too many cultivated fields being left fallow at once
  III.   Severe droughts
    a. I, II, & III
    b. I & II
    c. I & III
    d. II & III

83. Enlightenment principles signaled a departure from which of the following types of government rule?
    a. Monarchy
    b. Democracy
    c. Anarchy
    d. Republicanism

84. What was the first well-known American school of painting?
    a. The Boston Revolutionaries
    b. The Savannah Art School
    c. The New York Artists' Guild
    d. The Hudson River School

85. What does the Communist Manifesto claim makes up all of history?
    a. Battles between political ideas
    b. Class struggles
    c. Battles to control the means of production
    d. None of the above

86. In a market economy, what is the theoretical basis for the price of an individual good?
    a. Central Control
    b. Supply and Demand
    c. Cost Gouging
    d. Income and Industry

87. Which of the following is a way that the Internet affected world wide economies?
    a. It made near instantaneous communication possible.
    b. It caused an overall increase in the cost of transactions.
    c. It increased consumer access to goods.
    d. It increased the barriers to entry in retail situations.

88. Which of the following was a method that the government in Nazi Germany used gain control of German children?
    a. Mandating membership in government sponsored youth organizations
    b. Including propaganda in textbooks
    c. Mandating activities scheduled to conflict with church services and interfere with family life
    d. All of the above

89. What was the purpose of John Locke's Two Treatises on Government?
    a. To support the results of the Glorious Revolution
    b. To provide support for the American Revolution
    c. To provide support for the French Revolution
    d. To provide support for the Irish Revolution

*Use the following statistical table to answer Question 90*

Median U.S. income by amount of schooling, in dollars
Source: U.S. Census Bureau, Current Population Survey, Annual Social and Economic Supplements.

| Year | 9-12th grade, no diploma | High School graduate | Some College, no degree | Associates Degree | Bachelors Degree or higher |
|------|------|------|------|------|------|
| 2007 | 24,492 | 40,456 | 50,419 | 60,132 | 84,508 |
| 2002 | 23,267 | 35,646 | 45,333 | 51,058 | 73,600 |
| 1997 | 19,851 | 33,779 | 40,015 | 45,258 | 63,292 |

90. Which of the following could you infer from the data presented above?
    a. Persons without a high school diploma receive smaller monetary increases in their income than persons with a high school diploma.
    b. Increased education increases a person's earning potential
    c. Income generally increases over time.
    d. All of the above

91. Which of the following is the most appropriate reason to use audio-visual materials in the classroom?
    a. To fill time when the teacher is not prepared for a class
    b. To give students additional insight into the forces that shaped the historical event you are studying.
    c. To fill time when a substitute will be teaching your class
    d. None of the above

92. Why did the United States originally get involved with Vietnam?
    a. To prevent the spread of Communism in Southeast Asia
    b. To aid France in its attempt to maintain its colonial presence in Vietnam.
    c. To prevent the overthrow of a pro-Western regime
    d. None of the above

93. Researching the history of levee building in the United States is most likely to also touch upon which of the following disciplines?
    I.    Economics
    II.   Geography
    III.  Sociology
    a. I only
    b. II only
    c. I and II
    d. I and III

94. Which of the following is a purpose of a research question?
    a. To determine if one's topic can be researched
    b. To focus a broad research topic
    c. To evaluate your research topic
    d. None of the above

95. After reading the journals of several citizens of your home town, you find that several of them share the same opinions on a topic. In your paper, you infer that most of the population shared this opinion. What is this an example of?
    a. Using your sources to create a generalization
    b. Using your sources to identify a cause and effect relationship
    c. Finding a main idea
    d. All of the above

96. A historian is researching daily life in your home town in the 1840s. What might he do to locate sources?
    a. Contact descendants of people who lived in your town to see if they have any records
    b. Go to your home town's court house to see if land or court records are available.
    c. Go to your home town's library to see if they have information about the town's history
    d. All of the above

97. In which of the following circumstances would it be appropriate to use a chronological view to understand history?
    a. When discussing the role of religion in ancient civilizations
    b. When discussing cultural differences between civilizations in different climates
    c. When discussing the U.S.-Soviet race to the moon
    d. When looking at the role of families in various civilizations

98. In studying the causes of the crusades, which other academic discipline would be the least beneficial?
    a. Sociology
    b. Economics
    c. Literature
    d. Geography

99. Which of the following documents would be most appropriate to determine a historical figure's personal opinion on an event in which he was involved?
    a. A biography written by a close friend of him or her.
    b. The historical figure's personal journal
    c. A biography written by a noted historian with a related specialty
    d. Letters written by the historical figure's aide or assistant.

100. Which of the following are topics that should be covered in a high school (grades 9-12) U.S. history class?

I.   The Great Depression
II.  The Jacksonian Era Indian removal
III. Cold War foreign policy
IV.  Progressive era reforms

   a. I, II, & III
   b. II & IV
   c. I, III & IV
   d. I & III

# Answer Key and Explanations

1. C: The first great human civilization was the Sumerian civilization which was located in Mesopotamia. Mesopotamia encompasses the area between the Tigris and Euphrates Rivers in modern-day Iraq and is also referred to as "the Cradle of Civilization," and includes part of the Fertile Crescent. The Sumerian civilization is credited with being the first to practice serious, year round agriculture. There is question over whether Sumeria or Ancient Egypt was the first to have a written language. Sumeria's writing began hieroglyphically and then developed into a form of writing known as cuneiform.

2. A: Anubis was the Egyptian god of the dead, typically depicted as being half human and half jackal. Hatshepsut was an Egyptian queen who declared herself king while acting as regent for her stepson (who was also her son-in-law). She was the fifth pharaoh of Egypt's 18th dynasty Ramesses (or Ramses) II was the third pharaoh of Egypt's 19th Dynasty, and Egypt's greatest, most powerful and most celebrated pharaoh. He is also traditionally considered to be the pharaoh of the Bible's Book of Exodus. His tomb in the Valley of the Kings was discovered in 1881. Tutankhamen was the boy pharaoh whose tomb was found in 1922, intact and untouched by tomb raiders, leading to a surge of popular interest in ancient Egypt.

3. C: Pope Urban II's plan for an army made up of previously trained military personnel was thwarted by the popular excitement concerning the First Crusade. This led to the creation of large armies primarily made up of untrained, unskilled, undisciplined, and ill- or unequipped soldiers, most of whom were recruited from the poorest levels of society. These armies were the first to set forth on the Crusade, which became known as the People's Crusade. Even though some of these armies contained knights, they were ultimately ineffective as fighting forces. These armies were prone to rioting and raiding surrounding areas for food and supplies and were viewed as a destabilizing influence by local leaders. They were defeated in battle and many converted to Islam to avoid being killed.

4. A: Knights Templar is the name by which the Poor Fellow-Soldiers of Christ and of the Temple of Solomon is more commonly called. The Knights Templar began as a small and impoverished order intended to serve as a fighting force in the Holy Land, but soon grew into a large organization and a favorite charity. As the Templars' resources grew, their operations did and their activities included the management of an early form of banking that permitted travelers to carry less money with them, making the travelers a less tempting target for thieves and increasing their safety.

5. A: Mary Wollstonecraft wrote *A Vindication of the Rights of Woman* in the late eighteenth century in response to contemporary events and practices. Wollstonecraft called for equality in education at a time when many people believed that women only required domestic education that would enable them to run households. *The Declaration of Sentiments* was a document addressing the rights of women; it was primarily written by Elizabeth Cady Stanton and then read to and signed by the delegates to the Seneca Falls Convention. *Frankenstein* was written by Mary Wollstonecraft's daughter, Mary Wollstonecraft Shelley. *The Awakening* was written by Kate Chopin and published in 1899.

6. B: The Dome of the Rock is the oldest existing Muslim structure and was built on the traditional site of Mohammed's ascent into heaven on Temple Mount. Before this, however, the Temple Mount was the site of the Jewish Second Temple which stood from the 6th Century BC until AD 70 when it was destroyed by Romans in response to a Jewish uprising in Jerusalem. The Temple Mount is also

the traditional site of Solomon's Temple (also known as the First Temple) and its one remaining wall, known as the Western Wall or the Wailing Wall is an important Jewish shrine.

7. D: The Nile River was the lifeblood of the Ancient Egyptian Empire and is sometimes credited with being the reason this empire was able to become one of history's most stable societies. Its yearly floods replenished the soil by leaving fertile silt that made large scale agriculture possible in the land immediately surrounding the river. The agriculture provided Egypt with goods to trade, further enriching the empire. The Nile was also the center of Egyptian cultural and spiritual life. The ancient Egyptians believed that the pharaoh was responsible for providing the yearly floods as part of his role as the divinely appointed ruler.

8. B: The Mongol people have traditionally been nomads living in large white felt tents that are commonly known as "yurts" or "gers" and in Mongolia, many of these people still live in this traditional housing. The term yurt is of Turkish and Russian origins, while ger is the Mongolian term. The Mongol ger is designed, decorated and positioned based on a strict formula determined by religion, tradition, and superstition. Today the Mongol people are spread over the Asian steppe region including Mongolia, and parts of Russia, China Afghanistan and Pakistan.

9. C: The Sugar Act of 1764 raised import duties on goods which were not of British origin, including sugar, while reducing the import tax on molasses. The Stamp Act of 1765 was a tax of paper and printed products, intended to help the British government recoup some of the costs of the French and Indian War. It was extremely unpopular with the colonists and was repealed in 1766. Lead was one of the goods taxed under the Townshend Acts, enacted in 1767, but it did not receive its own specific tax act. The Tea Act of 1773 was another unpopular tax and led to tea boycotts and was the catalyst for the Boston Tea Party.

10. B: The Founding Fathers decided that because the colonies did not have the right to elect representatives to the British Parliament they could not be justly ruled by Parliament. They envisioned the British Empire's government as being headed by the King of England, under whom the various local parliaments and legislative bodies served to enact laws for the peoples whom they represented. By addressing their ills to the king, the Founding Fathers sought to prevent the appearance that they acknowledged the British Parliament in London as having any authority over the American colonies.

11. B: Marbury v. Madison started with the election of Thomas Jefferson as third President of the United States. The lame-duck Congress responded by issuing a large number of judicial patents, which the incoming president and Secretary of State refused to deliver to their holders. Marbury, who was to receive a patent as Justice of the Peace, sued to demand delivery. What makes this case important is the decision which declared the judiciary's ability to overturn legislation that conflicted with the Constitution. The case states:

"It is emphatically the province and duty of the judicial department to say what the law is. Those who apply the rule to particular cases must, of necessity, expound and interpret that rule. If two laws conflict with each other, the courts must decide on the operation of each.

"So if a law be in opposition to the Constitution; if both the law and the constitution apply to a particular case, so that the court must either decide that case conformably to the law, disregarding the Constitution; or conformably to the Constitution, disregarding the law; the court must determine which of these conflicting rules governs the case. This is of the very essence of judicial duty.

"If, then, the courts are to regard the Constitution, and the Constitution is superior to any ordinary act of the legislature, the Constitution, and not such ordinary act, must govern the case to which they both apply."

Later the ruling states: "The judicial power of the United States is extended to all cases arising under the Constitution." It was in this way that the Supreme Court achieved its now traditional ability to strike down laws and to act as the final arbitrator of what is and is not allowed under the U.S. Constitution.

12. D: Abraham Lincoln issued the Thanksgiving Proclamation on October 3, 1863, in which he specified the last Thursday of November as a day of thanksgiving. The last Thursday in November was the traditional date for the Thanksgiving holiday for the next 76 years. In 1939, President Roosevelt tried to change the holiday's date from the last Thursday in November to the second to last Thursday in November in order to stimulate the economy by creating a longer Christmas shopping season. This action met with resistance in some parts of the country, and a compromise was reached in 1941, setting the date of Thanksgiving as the fourth Thursday in November.

13. A: Historiography can be described as the study of the study of history. It is a term used to describe the entire body of historical literature, the writing of history and the critical examination of past historical writings and historical sources. A typical historiographic essay will be a critical look at the past historical research whether it is a broad look at the study of history as a whole or of a specific subject that is being analyzed.

14. B: The philosophy of history is concerned with the ultimate significance of history as a field of study and asks questions concerning how history should be studied, including what social unit is correct to use when studying history—whether it is more important to look at the individual lives of ordinary people or to concentrate on the so-called big picture, looking at the overall trends in a society or culture; only giving personal treatment to people, such as George Washington, who had particular significance to the events surrounding them. The philosophy of history also looks for broad historical trends and progress.

15. C: When researching historical events, the best sources are typically the earliest sources, particularly if they are primary sources written by witnesses soon after the event. While Wikipedia and your colleague's notes might be accurate, they are removed from the actual event and to you, their sources are thus in question. The newspaper article and the wounded survivor's account are both good sources. Without knowing anything about the personal reliability of the authors, it is best to accept the survivor's account as it is both a personal, primary account and the earliest record available to you.

16. C: While wounds from war most certainly killed more than a few, European disease laid waste to vast swaths of Native American people who has no immunity to the foreign diseases which the Europeans carried. The forced marches took place in the mid-19th century under Andrew Jackson's presidency and are thus removed from the time frame in question.

17. C: The Dome of the Rock is the oldest existing Muslim structure, the shrine having been completed in AD 691. The rock in question is the traditional site for Mohammed's ascent into heaven accompanied by the angel Gabriel and documented in the Koran. The Dome of the Rock is a shrine for Muslim pilgrims and non-Muslims have commonly been barred from visiting the monument. The most recent ban lasted from 2000 to 2006. The religion of Islam was founded in Mecca, which is located in present-day Saudi Arabia.

18. D: Gutenberg's press used moveable metal type which he formed casting a metal alloy into molds made for each character. These individual pieces were then organized by letter. The letters were loaded into composing sticks that were then loaded into a metal form to create printing plates. As the printing press spread across Europe, printers began using woodcut prints to include illustrations in their products. While Gutenberg is generally given credit for the invention of moveable type, in the 1040s Pi Sheng, a Chinese inventor and alchemist, created moveable type using clay characters which were then pressed into wax-coated plates for printing.

19. A: The U.S. Constitution, Article I, Section 3 states that: "The Senate of the United States shall be composed of two Senators from each state, chosen by the legislature thereof, for six years; and each Senator shall have one vote." This was the practice until the Seventeenth Amendment was ratified on April 8, 1913. The Seventeenth Amendment states that U.S. Senators are to be elected by the people of the states which they serve and that the state executive branches may appoint replacement Senators if a Senate seat becomes vacant mid-term, until the state legislature can arrange for a popular election.

20. B: The Erie Canal opened in 1825 and created a water route between the Hudson River and Lake Erie. Water routes have historically been cheaper and easier than overland ones and the Erie Canal was originally proposed in the 1700s as a means of providing a shipping route to assist in settling the areas west of the Appalachian Mountains. The Mississippi River is to the west of the Great Lakes, its source is in Minnesota and it discharges into the Gulf of Mexico approximately 100 miles downstream of New Orleans, Louisiana. The Susquehanna River runs through New York, Pennsylvania and Maryland and is the home of Three Mile Island, the site of the United States' largest nuclear disaster. The Lehigh River is located in eastern Pennsylvania.

21. C: The telegraph was a gigantic leap forward in the realm of communications. Before the telegraph, messages could take days, weeks or months to reach their intended recipient, based upon the distance that they had to travel. The telegraph allowed people to send methods through use of electric signals transmitted over telegraph wires, allowing for instantaneous communications. The main drawbacks to the telegraph included the need to "translate" the message into and out of the appropriate telegraphic code and that the telegraph could only relay one message at a time. In contrast, the telephone allowed for spoken communication between people at different locations, increasing the efficiency and speed as the people on each end of the conversation could communicate multiple messages quickly and in one telephone conversation.

22. A: The Incan civilization was very wealthy and the Incan rulers' individual wealth was used to care for their mummified remains following their deaths in order to emphasize the king's divinity as descendants of the Incan sun god Inti. When an Incan king died not only would his wealth be used to care for his remains, there would also be human sacrifices as the king's servants and favorite wives would be sacrificed so that they could continue serving him in the afterlife.

23. A: This picture was taken outside of the White House in 1918 and could be used to show students an example of a woman picketing as part of the fight to win the right to vote. In 1917, Alice Paul had begun organizing her followers into groups in order to picket the White House with signs intended to embarrass President Woodrow Wilson into supporting women's right to vote. These picketers did so at their own peril as many were arrested on charges of obstructing traffic. Those who were convicted served sentences at a local workhouse where they were subject to harsh conditions, including force-feedings.

24. D: Besides being Athens' primary marketplace, the Agora also served as a central point where ancient Athenians would go to meet friends, conduct business, discuss ideas and participate in local government. While most ancient Greek cities contained agorés, the Athenian Agora was particularly known for its intellectual opportunities. Socrates, Plato and Aristotle were all known to frequent the Athenian agora. The Athenian Agora is also credited with being the birthplace of democracy. The ancient Athenian democracy allowed all citizens the opportunity to vote on civic matters and serve on juries.

25. A: Genghis Khan, also spelled Chinggis Khan, was the son of a minor Mongol chieftain, born circa 1162 AD. His birth name was Temujin and he grew up in poverty, but gradually built his own power base to include a confederacy of Mongol clans. He was named Genghis Khan, or universal ruler, in 1206. Attila the Hun was the 5th Century Hunnic leader who led his people to attack into Western Europe, going as far as Gaul (modern day France). The leader of China's 19th Century Taiping Rebellion was Hong Xiuquan, also known as Hong Houxiu.

26. A: Bias is a form of prejudice, and a historical work is considered biased when it is unreasonably shaped by the author's personal or institutional prejudices. It is wise for a teacher to choose material that comes from reputable sources and to verify that all material used in classroom presentations is reliable and appropriate. As long as the teacher is willing to do these things and show a variety of historical opinions, this is not an example of bias.

27. D: Chronology can be defined as a list of events organized in order of their occurrence. An anachronism is a chronological error; something or someone who appears out of order chronologically. Anachronisms are frequently seen in popular entertainment dramatizations of historical events. Anno Domini is a Latin term meaning "in the year of [Our] Lord," more frequently seen as the abbreviation A.D. (e.g., "the Battle of Hastings was fought in A.D. 1066."). Chroma is a word used to describe color.

28. B: Sacagawea acted as Lewis and Clark's guide during their exploration of the Louisiana Purchase. She had been separated from her family at a young age and was reunited with her brother on the course of the expedition. Pocahontas was the daughter of Powhatan, the leader of the Algonquian tribes at the beginning of the 17th Century when the colony of Jamestown was founded in modern-day Virginia. Squanto's actual name was Tisquantum. He was the Native American who helped the Pilgrims after their first winter in Massachusetts. Wauwatosa is a suburb of Milwaukee, Wisconsin.

29. A: The idea behind Laissez faire was to leave the market alone and let it take care of itself with minimal government intervention. Opponents of this policy often blame it for causing the situation which led to the Great Depression while supporters claim that it was an increase of government interference in the market that led to the Great Depression. Social Darwinism is the idea that the fittest members of society will rise to the top and flourish. Keynesian Economics advocates that the government should use its powers to stabilize the economy through raising and lowering interest rates and creating demand through government spending, frequently leading to deficit spending. Keynesian economic theory is chiefly concerned with microeconomic trends and short-term solutions. It's founder, John Maynard Keynes, was quoted saying, "[i]n the long run, we are all dead." Monetarism is an economic school of thought that concentrates on macroeconomic principles and long-term solutions to economic problems. An economist supporting this policy would be in favor of policies that are monetarily neutral in the long term but are not neutral in the short term.

30. A: Lyndon Johnson became president following the assassination of John F. Kennedy on November 22, 1963. The Great Society was a series of social programs implemented under the direction of Lyndon Johnson. The Great Society's goal was to eliminate poverty and racial injustice in America. The Great Society began with economic reforms including a tax cut and the creation of the Office of Economic Opportunity. From there, it grew to include the enaction of laws creating the Medicare and Medicaid systems to assist the elderly and poor with their health care costs, respectively. Educational and Housing reforms followed.

31. C: Woodrow Wilson's Fourteen Points were set forth in a speech which he gave to a joint session of Congress on January 8, 1918, approximately 10 months before the end of World War I on November 11, 1918. These points set forth his plan for the rehabilitation of Germany and the creation of a lasting peace in Europe. They included adjustments of European borders, including the creation of an independent Polish state and allowing the peoples of Europe the benefits of self-determination.

32. B: Jamestown, Virginia was originally founded and settled by members of the Virginia Company of London, chartered by King James I of England. The Virginia Company was a profit-making venture and the first settlers of Jamestown were instructed to search for gold and a water route to Asia. Plymouth, Massachusetts was founded by the Pilgrims in 1620. Boston, Massachusetts was founded by the Puritans in 1630. The Pilgrims and Puritans were fleeing religious persecution in England. Providence, Rhode Island was founded in 1638 by followers of Roger Williams, a former Puritan leader, and his followers who had been exiled from Massachusetts due to their break with the Puritans.

33. C: Identifying the reasons that the U.S. entered World War I is most appropriate for high school students studying U.S. History. Important events in the European exploration and colonization of North America, evaluating the relationship between past and present conflicts, and creating and interpreting timelines are all lower level skills.

34. D: Using maps to show post-World War II migration patterns or using charts and maps to illustrate the growth of U.S. cities would be examples of using appropriate visual aids in teaching history. Discussing the effects of weather on world history would be an example of connecting history with geography. Food shortages and inflation are both connected to economic conditions and discussing their destabilizing influence as a contributing factor to the Russian Revolution in 1917 would be an example of connecting history and economics.

35. C: The Great Depression began with the 1929 Stock Market Crash on Thursday, October 24, also known as Black Thursday. This crash was the beginning of a market collapse that continued as investors began panicking and banks began to fail. The crash was due to rampant stock speculation and fraud. Many people had invested in the belief that the Stock Market could only go up, and unscrupulous people had taken advantage of this by creating sham companies or artificially pumping up stock shares. The SEC, or Securities and Exchange Commission, was created in 1934 to regulate stock exchanges.

36. B: The Pilgrims' initial intention had been to settle in Northern Virginia where England had already established a presence. As there was no government in place in New England, some Pilgrims believed that they had no legal or moral duty to remain with the Pilgrims' new colony which needed their labor and support. Because of this, the Mayflower Compact created a government in New England and was signed on board the Mayflower on November 11, 1620 by each of the adult men who made the journey. The Compact's life was relatively short, due to its

being superceded by the Pierce Patent in 1621 which had been signed by the king of England and had granted the Pilgrims the right of self-government in Plymouth. In spite of its short lifespan, the Mayflower Compact is credited with being North America's first constitution.

37. A: Manifest Destiny was the idea that the United States was intended by God to expand to fill North America. There were various ideas on what this meant, yet at minimum it was the belief that the United States should expand to the Pacific Ocean. At maximum, it was the belief that the United States should expand to fill North America and South America. The idea behind why the United States should expand through greater territorial acquisitions was to expand the American ideals of freedom, democracy and self-government.

38. B: The Marshall Plan was the popular name for the European Recovery Program, named after Secretary of State George C. Marshall. Marshall had originally proposed the Plan as a solution to the widespread inflation, unemployment, food shortages and general lack of resources following World War II in a commencement speech at Harvard University in 1947. As enacted, it was intended to provide a solution to these problems and to prevent the spread of communism by decreasing Soviet influence.

39. D: Early civilizations flourished alongside rivers such as the Nile in Egypt, the Euphrates in Mesopotamia, and the Yellow River in China. Besides providing the ancient settlers with a water source, these rivers also provided the land with the rich and fertile silt that the rivers deposited during their regular flooding cycles, making large scale agriculture possible for the ancient peoples.

40. C: The original Magna Carta, signed by King John on June 15, 1215, was meant to protect the rights and property of the few powerful families that topped the feudal system. Its primary purpose was to force King John to recognize the supremacy of ancient liberties, to limit his ability to raise funds and to reassert the principle of due process. The majority of the English population at that time was mentioned only once, in a clause concerning the use of court-set fines to punish minor offences. The last clause, which created an enforcement council of tenants-in-chief and clergymen would have severely limited the king's power and introduced the policy of 'majority rule.' However, the time was not yet right for the introduction of majority rule. In September 1215, three months after the signing of the Magna Carta, Pope Innocent III, at John's urging, annulled the "shameful and demeaning agreement, forced upon the king by violence and fear." A civil war broke out over this, which ended when John died the following year, in October 1216.

41. C: Even though the Maya were one of the two cultures to develop an urban civilization in a rain forest, their culture was predominately based upon rural life. Cities were primarily used as religious centers while day-to-day life usually centered around farming in the surrounding rainforest. Due to the rainforest land's relative infertility, Mayans used slash and burn agriculture methods that required them to move to new farming plots every two to seven years. Under these conditions it took a large amount of land to support even one family.

42. B: The 95 Theses were part of a letter of protest that Martin Luther wrote to his archbishop in 1517, when Luther was a monk in the Catholic Church. These theses criticized church practices, particularly the practice of selling indulgences. Some sources claim Luther nailed this document to the door of the All Saint's Church in Wittenberg (located in modern-day Germany). Luther's intention was to reform the Catholic Church from within, but his letter soon placed him at the center of a religious and civil revolt. He was excommunicated in 1520.

43. C: Alexander Hamilton was the Founding Father who is credited with founding the Federalist Party. Hamilton was a proponent of the idea that the young country required the support of the rich and powerful in order to survive. This party grew out of Hamilton's political connections in Washington and was particularly popular in the northeastern United States. John Adams was a member of this party. George Washington's personal beliefs were most closely aligned with the Federalist Party, but he disliked political parties and refused to become a member of one. Thomas Jefferson was the founder of the Democratic-Republican Party.

44. B: The Shoguns were Japanese military leaders. During the Tokuwaga shogunate, which began in 1603, the shogun held the actual power in the Japanese government even though Japan was technically ruled by an emperor. In actuality, the emperor was primarily a ceremonial leader and access to him was restricted to members of the shogun's family.

45. D: The Iroquois Confederacy was a participatory democracy made up of Native American tribes in what is now the Northeastern United States. Each of the member tribes were permitted to send male representatives selected by the tribe's female members to the Confederacy's main counsel where each representative was permitted to vote on matters affecting the tribes. The beginnings of the Iroquois Confederacy are disputed, but it is accepted that the Confederacy was originally made up of the Mohawk, Seneca, Onondaga, Cayuga, and Oneida tribes; the Tuscaroras joined the Confederacy in 1722. The Confederacy was formed with the intention of decreasing intertribal violence and encouraging peaceful resolution of differences between the tribes.

46. B: James Oglethorpe was a philanthropist who wanted to give England's "worthy poor" the opportunity to prosper away from the highly stratified class structure in England. The original idea was to include people released from debtors' prison among the colonists, though none of the original 114 colonists were debtors just released. Oglethorpe's intention was to create a classless society so that Georgia would not develop the same problems that had plagued England. Oglethorpe was one of the original colonists, even though the colonial charter prohibited him from profiting from the colony and was frequently referred to as the colony's "resident trustee."

47. A: The historical evidence shows that the initial workers on tobacco plantations in Virginia were primarily indentured servants who would eventually receive their freedom. The path to slavery in its later forms was gradual, beginning with slavery as a form of punishment for legal infractions. Massachusetts became the first colony to legalize slavery in 1641, followed by other states, including Virginia. This was followed by laws declaring that any children born to a slave mother would be slaves themselves in 1662 and a later decision that all persons who were not Christians in their "native country" would be slaves in 1705.

48. C: The term Five Civilized Tribes came into use during the middle of the 19th Century as a means of referring to the Creek, Cherokee, Choctaw, Chickasaw, and Seminole tribes, each of whom had developed complex social and government systems including written constitutions, judicial, legislative and executive systems, complex agriculture practices and the establishment of public schools.

49. A: In 50 BC, Julius Caesar was called back to Rome by the Roman Senate in order to stand trial for treason and corruption. When he reached the Rubicon, he decided to ignore Roman Law and the Mos Maiorum (uncodified tradition with nearly the force of law), and instead took one legion to Rome with him, famously uttering the words "the die is cast." This was the beginning of a chain of events that led to the creation of the first Roman triumvirate and the transition of Rome from a Republic to an Empire, with Julius Caesar as "Perpetual Dictator," until his murder in the Senate. His

adopted son Octavius (later taking the regnal name "Augustus") eventually became the first emperor.

50. B: Edward Jenner's initial smallpox vaccine was comprised of liquid from a young milkmaid's cowpox sores. Jenner was a country doctor who had noticed that persons who had suffered from the relatively mild disease of cowpox did not later catch the much more serious and deadly smallpox. At this time, the main preventative measure against smallpox was to inoculate healthy people with the liquid from smallpox sores from those who had mild cases of smallpox. Unfortunately, this practice often lead to healthy people having full blown cases of smallpox that resulted in death. Jenner's belief was that if he could inoculate someone with the liquid from cowpox pustules, they would then be immune from smallpox without the risk of contracting a full case of smallpox. In May 1796, Jenner diagnosed a patient, a milkmaid named Sarah Nelmes, with cowpox and received permission from a local farmer to inoculate the farmer's son James with cowpox, and then expose him to smallpox. Jenner made two cuts on James's arms and poured liquid from Sarah Nelmes's sores on them before binding the wound. James came down with a mild case of cowpox six weeks later, after James was well again, Jenner exposed him to smallpox, which the young boy did not contract. Jenner conducted further tests and in 1798 he published his findings in a report which introduced the words vaccination (adapted from the Latin word for cow).

51. A: Hiroshima had an atom bomb detonated over it on August 6, 1945, officially beginning the atomic age; Nagasaki was bombed three days later. Both cities were selected for atomic bombing because they had not been previously bombed during the war.

52. A: Feudalism was a common practice during the Middle Ages, popular as a means of providing social structure and for maintaining the established government and social order. It was most widespread and systemic in Europe but also practiced in other parts of the world including Persia and the Byzantine Empire. The Norsemen of what is now known as Scandinavia, however, were an exception to European feudalism and lived in a fairly egalitarian society where rank was strongly based on personal merit. This is not to say that the Norsemen were entirely opposed to the class delineations of feudalism; when the French King Charles the Simple ceded to them the land that became the province of Normandy, the Norsemen who settled there settled into a feudalistic structure that their descendants took with them to England during the Norman Conquest, where the feudal system was used to assist with subduing the newly-conquered English people.

53. C: The passage describes the reasons why the Constitution has managed to last for over two hundred years and would be an appropriate part of an essay answering question C. It might also be an appropriate part of an essay answering questions A or B, but because this passage directly deals with the Constitution's longevity C is the best answer. The Federalist Party was a distinct group from the Federalists who supported the ratification of the Constitution.

54. D: The passage could be best used to describe the attributes of the U.S. Constitution in a government class. The passage does not go in-depth into the formation of the Constitution, the basis of U.S. law or why the U.S. Constitution can be amended.

55. B: The passage describes the reasons the U.S. Constitution has survived for so long, including the fact that it provides a set of basic rules but allows amendment so that it can be altered as new situations arise.

56. C: The people who were opposed to the idea of having a bill of rights in the Constitution were primarily concerned that by specifically enumerating a set of rights, that there would be an

argument that the rights not listed did not exist or were not important. The Bill of Rights did not initially apply to the states even though there was some concern that the states were more likely to infringe upon individual liberties than the federal government.

57. C: The Federalist Papers were written and published anonymously by John Jay, Alexander Hamilton, and James Madison as part of their effort to ratify the Constitution. There are 85 letters in total and they were meant to convince normal Americans that they should support the Constitution by explaining what it meant and what it was intended to accomplish.

58. D: The New Deal met with conservative opposition, especially in the Supreme Court, whose conservative justices frequently blocked New Deal legislation. The plan that was dubbed the "court packing" plan was to appoint a second justice for every justice over the age of seventy. Because all of the conservative justices on the Supreme Court were over seventy, this would have given Roosevelt the ability to appoint enough justices to swing the Court to his favor. However, this plan was met with extreme popular disapproval which led to its eventual abandonment.

59. D: Eli Whitney's cotton engine (or gin) was designed to aid in the cleaning of American cotton. Before this invention, cleaning American short-staple cotton was a long and tedious process as all the cotton seeds had to be removed from the cotton by hand, usually by slaves. Whitney's invention could clean more cotton than an individual person could, thereby increasing cotton's profitability and turning it into a cash crop. As cotton became a viable cash crop, the amount of land dedicated to its cultivation increased, as well as the number of laborers needed to work in the cotton fields, which resulted in an overall increase in the number of slaves held in the southern United States. As cotton production increased, cotton also became a major Southern export as textile mills in both the northern United States and Europe became dependant on Southern cotton.

60. B: The Sherman Anti-Trust Act of 1890 was enacted in response to the growth of large monopolies in the period following the end of the Civil War. While its purpose was to prevent restraints on free trade, it was not strictly enforced. Additionally, the wording was vague enough that it was also used to break up labor unions. It was replaced by the Clayton Antitrust Act in 1914.

61. A: The Texas Rebellion began in 1835 when a group of Texan leaders declared independence from Mexico. Texas won independence in 1836, but the U.S. initially held back on plans for annexation due to concerns that such an act would lead to war with Mexico. In 1845, however, the U.S. Senate ratified the treaty and Texas became the country's 28th state on December 29 of that year. The war with Mexico, which had broken off diplomatic relations with the U.S. in 1844 when the treaty was agreed upon, began in 1846 following news of skirmishes between American and Mexican forces along the Rio Grande.

62. C: The U.S. Supreme Court justices had decided that *Brown* would have a unanimous holding (the legal term for a court's rulings or decisions) before they determined what that holding would be, which resulted in a fairly narrow holding that "the plaintiffs and others similarly situated for whom the actions have been brought are, by reason of the segregation complained of, deprived of the equal protection of the laws guaranteed by the Fourteenth Amendment." This decision was used in later Civil Rights cases as a legal precedent for the idea that the doctrine of "separate but equal" was inherently unconstitutional, reversing the precedent set by *Plessy v. Ferguson.*

63. D: The French Revolution began in 1789, but its end date has been difficult to define. The Reign of Terror was intended as a means of fighting the revolutionaries' enemies and began with the execution of the Queen Marie Antoinette on October 17, 1793. While there was an economic crisis

leading up to the French Revolution, there was also a severe economic crisis during/following the Revolution (depending on one's preferred end date). One of the effects of the Revolution was the ending of feudalism and slavery in France. With regard to the Estates-General, King Louis XVI had called together the Estates-General on August 8, 1788, stated that the Estates General would convene in May 1789.

64. A: Under the rule of the shoguns, Japan was primarily a closed country; contact with outsiders was severely limited. As a general rule, outsiders who attempted to go to Japan were killed, as were Japanese people who attempted to leave. The primarily exceptions to this rule were Chinese and Dutch traders who were granted permission to trade with the Japanese people. This situation changed in 1854 when the United States and Japan entered into a treaty of permanent friendship following U.S. Commodore Matthew Perry's entry into what is now Tokyo Bay Harbor in 1853 (albeit with an armed fleet).

65. B: The Articles of Confederation granted the federal Congress the power to enter into treaties. It did not grant Congress the abilities to collect taxes, enforce laws or to regulate interstate commerce (it could impose some regulations on commerce with foreign entities), these shortcomings led to the eventual abandonment of the Articles of Confederation in favor of the Constitution, which is still in force today.

66. A: In *The Republic*, Plato calls for a philosopher king, selected from the ranks of philosophers who are at least fifty years old and given the power of absolute rule for life. Plato's belief was that in this society there should be no laws as they would interfere with the king's ability to use his judgment.

67. C: The Neolithic agricultural revolution resulted in an overall decrease in leisure time, in comparison with people living in hunter-gatherer societies, due to such factors as sustaining an increased standard of living and caring for the increased number of children born to families living in permanent settlements.

68. C: The 26th Amendment states: "The right of citizens of the United States, who are 18 years of age or older, to vote, shall not be denied or abridged by the United States or any state on account of age. " The 24th Amendment invalidates poll taxes as a requirement to vote. The 25th Amendment deals with presidential succession. The 27th Amendment deals with Congress members' compensation.

69. B: Mountains provide societies with a natural protective barrier, making it difficult for an outside force to invade them. The Swiss Alps are frequently credited with being a reason that Switzerland has managed to maintain its independence and neutrality. The barrier created by the mountains can also discourage trade and prevent cultural diffusion.

70. C: The principles held in the Monroe Doctrine were not new when President James Monroe issued it in a speech before Congress on December 2, 1823, however that did not stop them from becoming his namesake and shaping American foreign policy, even through the World Wars to which the U.S. remained aloof until threatened with attack in the Western Hemisphere. Germany's attempt to convince Mexico to attack the United States, promising Mexico that it would receive several U.S. states as a reward, was one of the issues that convinced the U.S. to intervene in what had hitherto been seen as a European war. In World War II, the United States remained officially neutral until attacked at Pearl Harbor. The Monroe Doctrine was largely ignored by European

powers, but underscored the American belief that the United States was the appropriate dominant power in the Western Hemisphere.

71. D: Nelson Mandela was the first President of South Africa to be elected in a fully representative South African election. He was succeeded by Thabo Mbeki, who was succeeded by Kgalema Motlanthe. Mahatma Gandhi was an Indian who lived in South Africa for a time and greatly influenced Nelson Mandela. He was also the leader of India's independence movement.

72. B: On June 28, 1914, Archduke Franz Ferdinand and his wife the Duchess Sophia von Chotkova were assassinated by Gavrilo Princip, a member of The Black Hand, a secret society whose intention was to create an independent Serbian country. This act was the first of a series of events that resulted in the beginning of World War later that summer. The Japanese bombed Pearl Harbor on December 7, 1941, bringing the United States into World War II. The sinking of the RMS *Lusitania* and the British interception of the Zimmerman telegram, in which Germany attempted to encourage Mexico to attack the United States, led to the United States entering World War I in 1917.

73. A: Boris Yeltsin was a Russian politician who was instrumental in the breaking up of the USSR and the end of Communism in Russia. In 1991, he was elected President of the Russian Federation in Russia's first democratic election.

74. C: This was almost a direct quote from President Truman's 1947 address before Congress which later became known The Truman Doctrine. The address explained his reasoning as to why the United States needed to offer assistance to Greece and Turkey.

75. B: The Warsaw Treaty Organization was meant to counterbalance NATO, or the North Atlantic Treaty Organization. Members of NATO included the United States, Great Britain, France and West Germany and pledged to consider an attack on one of them as an attack on all of them. NAFTA (the North American Free Trade Agreement) was signed by President Clinton in 1994 and lifted most trade barriers between the United States, Mexico and, Canada. The Soviet Union was a member of the U.N. Security Counsel which is charged with maintaining international Peace and Security. The Four Power Pact was a pre-World War II treaty in which the United States, Great Britain, Japan and France agreed to respect each other's Pacific territories.

76. D: At the beginning of the Civil War, the Confederacy drew many skilled officers such as Robert E. Lee out of the Union army and used them as the backbone of its military leadership. The Union Army, meanwhile, went through a series of unsatisfactory generals before Lincoln found Ulysses S. Grant. The other options were advantages that the North held over the South.

77. D: The Mormon pioneers were members of The Church of Jesus Christ of Latter-day Saints and their trek west was intended to transport their entire culture across the plains to a place where they would be safe from the persecutions they had suffered in their previous settlements, including Missouri's Extermination Order (1838) and the assassination of the church's leader, Joseph Smith, on June 27, 1844 in Carthage, Illinois, while under the protection of Illinois' governor. In moving their culture across the Plains, the Mormons not only moved the people but took care to bring religious and secular books and musical instruments on their thousand mile journey. One of the first buildings in Salt Lake City was a theater. On the trek west, the Mormons divided themselves into highly organized companies and worked to improve the trail and provide resources for those coming after them, including the building of way stations, ferries and the planting of crops. They also kept detailed records of their experiences for the use of future pioneers, and an early Mormon

pioneer invented the odometer as a means of calculating how far his company had traveled each day. Their migration is the most highly organized mass migration in U.S. history.

78. B: The New Deal did not end the Depression. The Depression only ended after the beginning of World War II when there was a huge increase in demand for goods and manpower. The New Deal increased the agricultural price supports offered to farmers and increased the role that the federal government played in the U.S. economy.

79. A: Cesar Chavez was a migrant farm worker who founded the United Farm Workers Organizing Committee. He was instrumental in bringing about several reforms that improved living and working conditions for migrant workers including the banning of certain grape pesticides and of the short handled hoe used in lettuce harvesting.

80. C: While Civil Rights Era Supreme Court decisions did declare that segregation in schools violated the equal protection clause of the Constitution, these decisions did not lead to instantaneous desegregation of schools, as people in many locations resisted desegregation even going to the length of closing public schools to prevent it. In other areas the National Guard had to be called in to enforce orders to integrate the schools.

81. D: The industrialization of the United States led to an overall decrease in the number of farmers as people moved from the country to the city in search of the new jobs created by industrialization. This move also resulted in fewer Americans being self-employed, as they instead became wage earners working for other people. Industrialization also led to an overall increase in economic and employment opportunities for women. Many of these opportunities took the form of what we now sometimes think of as "pink collar" jobs such as typing and stenography.

82. A: The Dust Bowl was a period of time, largely coinciding with the Great Depression, in which severe droughts, poor farming techniques, wind erosion and several other factors led to the collapse of farming in the southern Plains states. High grain prices had encouraged farmers to over-cultivate their fields and to bring previously uncultivated land under cultivation, leading to soil depletion and an overall loss in soil moisture as farmers would frequently burn their wheat stubble. This was a problem because the long grasses in the Plains states had previously been instrumental in keeping the soil in place. This loss meant that windstorms now began picking up soil, eroding fields and destroying crops. The Dust Bowl resulted in thousands of farmers losing their farms. Many of them traveled to California where they worked as migrant farm workers. John Steinbeck's *The Grapes of Wrath* tells the story of one family who lost their farm in Oklahoma due to the Dust Bowl.

83. A: The Enlightenment, also known as The Age of Enlightenment and The Age of Reason, occurred in the eighteenth century and centered on a belief in reason. The Enlightenment encouraged the ideals of liberty, self-governance, natural rights and natural law. Both the American Revolution and the French Revolution had their genesis in Enlightenment ideals which encouraged the idea that the common man should have a say in government. This was a departure from the most common types of governance, including monarchy and the belief in the divine right of kings. Enlightenment leaders tended to prefer representative republics as a form of government.

84. D: The Hudson River School was the first well-known American school of painting. Its members intended to break away from the European art schools and develop a distinct American art school of thought through their celebration of the American landscape.

85. B: The Communist Manifesto claims that history has been a series of class struggles; that the rise of Communism will eliminate class boundaries and end the struggle. Karl Marx, the Manifesto's primary author, ended with a call for the working class of the world to start a revolution against the order of things, forcibly taking over the means of production. The final lines read:

"The Communists disdain to conceal their views and aims. They openly declare that their ends can be attained only by the forcible overthrow of all existing social conditions. Let the ruling classes tremble at a Communist revolution. The proletarians have nothing to lose but their chains. They have a world to win. Workingmen of all countries, unite!"

86. B: In a pure market economy, price is typically seen as a reflection of supply and demand. A larger supply will result in a lower price and a greater demand will result in a lower price.

87. C: The Internet has increased the number of methods in which near-instantaneous communication is possible, but this is not necessarily an economic spur. The internet has also generally caused a decrease in transaction costs and barriers to entry in retail situations (e.g., it is much less expensive to start a website to sell your goods than it is to open a brick and mortar store. Ones website has the potential to reach out to a much larger group of potential consumers). The Internet has also increased consumer access to goods by making it easier for consumers to locate what they want.

88. D: All of the answers are ways in which the Nazi government attempted to gain control of German children.

89. A: John Locke was an English philosopher aligned with the Whig party. He wrote his Two Treatises on Government in support of the Glorious Revolution which occurred when William of Orange took over the throne from James II in 1688-89.

90. D: The information in this table shows the median incomes of persons who have achieved various educational levels. Looking at the table, one can see that from 1997 to 2007, persons without a high school degree had their median income increase by less than $5,000 while persons with a high school degree had their median income increase by more than $6,000. One can also see that as a general matter, the more education a person has, the higher their income will be and that income typically increases over time.

91. B: The most appropriate reason listed in the question is to give students additional insight into the forces that shaped the historical event they are studying. Audio-visual materials can be used to give students additional perspective; for example, a documentary about the Battle of Gettysburg could be used to provide them with visual representations of historical locations or as a means of illustrating the differences in perspective.

92. B: Following World War II, European powers found themselves in a position where they faced resistance to their colonial rule at a time when they lacked the resources to maintain their presence by force. After France was defeated in Vietnam, the United States remained for reasons that included the two listed in A and C.

93. B: Levees are built to prevent flooding in areas along rivers. They consist of large embankments along the side of a river and typically have a flat top atop which sandbags can be piled to increase the levees' height when necessary. The Mississippi River has one of the world's largest levee systems.

94. B: A research question can be used to focus a research topic that is too broad to be appropriately handled in the format for which one is researching.

95. A: In this situation, you are using the information you have to create a generalization about the opinions of the population.

96. D: All of the listed methods are ways that a historian might locate sources, depending on his actual research question.

97. C: The U.S.-Soviet race to the moon is an example of a circumstance where a chronological point of view would be appropriate as each nation's advances fuelled the other nation's desire to surpass its Cold War rival.

98. C: Literature, while it may have described the crusades after the fact, would not be useful in determining the causes of them. Pope Urban II called the First Crusade at the Council of Clermont in November of 1095. This was primarily in response to three stimuli:

1) Constantinople, the centre of late-Roman, post-Roman and dark-age culture—and a major trading city—was being pressured militarily by the Muslim Seljuk Turks.
2) Christian feudal Europe was teeming with young men, desperate to prove their honor and valor according to the newly-developing code of honor that would shape the middle ages. A move to war would allay the inter- and intra-national squabbling, which was currently taking place throughout Europe, amongst Christians.
3) A new and dangerous religion had come to control Jerusalem, which the Church and Christian Europe saw as their own right.

Therefore, sociology would describe reason 2), a decision based upon sociological factors, such as unemployed youth, ready for war. Geography, combined with economics, would help explain the critical nature of the city of Constantinople, in that it controlled the Bosporus, the waterway between the Mediterranean and Black seas, and thus was the primary non-sea route to the Middle-East). For the crusaders, were it to fall, Muslims would control trade with the East even further, and the heart of Eastern Christianity would be lost.

99. B: The personal journal is the best source in this case because it is the only primary source listed. While a close friend's biography or an aide's letters might include information on the historical figure's personal opinion, the information will be filtered through the other person's memory and personal opinions.

100. C: High school U.S. History classes are intended to cover the history of the United States since Reconstruction. The Great Depression, The Cold War, and the Progressive Era all occurred following reconstruction. The Jacksonian era took place during Andrew Jackson's presidency which lasted from 1829 to 1837.

# Secret Key #1 - Time is Your Greatest Enemy

## Pace Yourself

Wear a watch. At the beginning of the test, check the time (or start a chronometer on your watch to count the minutes), and check the time after every few questions to make sure you are "on schedule."

If you are forced to speed up, do it efficiently. Usually one or more answer choices can be eliminated without too much difficulty. Above all, don't panic. Don't speed up and just begin guessing at random choices. By pacing yourself, and continually monitoring your progress against your watch, you will always know exactly how far ahead or behind you are with your available time. If you find that you are one minute behind on the test, don't skip one question without spending any time on it, just to catch back up. Take 15 fewer seconds on the next four questions, and after four questions you'll have caught back up. Once you catch back up, you can continue working each problem at your normal pace.

Furthermore, don't dwell on the problems that you were rushed on. If a problem was taking up too much time and you made a hurried guess, it must be difficult. The difficult questions are the ones you are most likely to miss anyway, so it isn't a big loss. It is better to end with more time than you need than to run out of time.

Lastly, sometimes it is beneficial to slow down if you are constantly getting ahead of time. You are always more likely to catch a careless mistake by working more slowly than quickly, and among very high-scoring test takers (those who are likely to have lots of time left over), careless errors affect the score more than mastery of material.

# Secret Key #2 - Guessing is not Guesswork

You probably know that guessing is a good idea. Unlike other standardized tests, there is no penalty for getting a wrong answer. Even if you have no idea about a question, you still have a 20-25% chance of getting it right.

Most test takers do not understand the impact that proper guessing can have on their score. Unless you score extremely high, guessing will significantly contribute to your final score.

## Monkeys Take the Test

What most test takers don't realize is that to insure that 20-25% chance, you have to guess randomly. If you put 20 monkeys in a room to take this test, assuming they answered once per question and behaved themselves, on average they would get 20-25% of the questions correct. Put 20 test takers in the room, and the average will be much lower among guessed questions. Why?

1. The test writers intentionally write deceptive answer choices that "look" right. A test taker has no idea about a question, so he picks the "best looking" answer, which is often wrong.

The monkey has no idea what looks good and what doesn't, so it will consistently be right about 20-25% of the time.

2. Test takers will eliminate answer choices from the guessing pool based on a hunch or intuition. Simple but correct answers often get excluded, leaving a 0% chance of being correct. The monkey has no clue, and often gets lucky with the best choice.

This is why the process of elimination endorsed by most test courses is flawed and detrimental to your performance. Test takers don't guess; they make an ignorant stab in the dark that is usually worse than random.

## $5 Challenge

Let me introduce one of the most valuable ideas of this course—the $5 challenge:

- *You only mark your "best guess" if you are willing to bet $5 on it.*
- *You only eliminate choices from guessing if you are willing to bet $5 on it.*

Why $5? Five dollars is an amount of money that is small yet not insignificant, and can really add up fast (20 questions could cost you $100). Likewise, each answer choice on one question of the test will have a small impact on your overall score, but it can really add up to a lot of points in the end.

The process of elimination IS valuable. The following shows your chance of guessing it right:

| If you eliminate wrong answer choices until only this many remain: | Chance of getting it correct: |
|---|---|
| 1 | 100% |
| 2 | 50% |
| 3 | 33% |

However, if you accidentally eliminate the right answer or go on a hunch for an incorrect answer, your chances drop dramatically—to 0%. By guessing among all the answer choices, you are GUARANTEED to have a shot at the right answer.

That's why the $5 test is so valuable. If you give up the advantage and safety of a pure guess, it had better be worth the risk.

What we still haven't covered is how to be sure that whatever guess you make is truly random. Here's the easiest way:

- *Always pick the first answer choice among those remaining.*

Such a technique means that you have decided, **before you see a single test question**, exactly how you are going to guess, and since the order of choices tells you nothing about which one is correct, this guessing technique is perfectly random.

This section is not meant to scare you away from making educated guesses or eliminating choices; you just need to define when a choice is worth eliminating. The $5 test, along with a pre-defined random guessing strategy, is the best way to make sure you reap all of the benefits of guessing.

# Secret Key #3 - Practice Smarter, Not Harder

Many test takers delay the test preparation process because they dread the awful amounts of practice time they think necessary to succeed on the test. We have refined an effective method that will take you only a fraction of the time.

There are a number of "obstacles" in the path to success. Among these are answering questions, finishing in time, and mastering test-taking strategies. All must be executed on the day of the test at peak performance, or your score will suffer. The test is a mental marathon that has a large impact on your future.

Just like a marathon runner, it is important to work your way up to the full challenge. So first you just worry about questions, and then time, and finally strategy:

## Success Strategy

1. Find a good source for practice tests.
2. If you are willing to make a larger time investment, consider using more than one study guide. Often the different approaches of multiple authors will help you "get" difficult concepts.
3. Take a practice test with no time constraints, with all study helps, "open book." Take your time with questions and focus on applying strategies.
4. Take a practice test with time constraints, with all guides, "open book."
5. Take a final practice test without open material and with time limits.

If you have time to take more practice tests, just repeat step 5. By gradually exposing yourself to the full rigors of the test environment, you will condition your mind to the stress of test day and maximize your success.

# Secret Key #4 - Prepare, Don't Procrastinate

Let me state an obvious fact: if you take the test three times, you will probably get three different scores. This is due to the way you feel on test day, the level of preparedness you have, and the version of the test you see. Despite the test writers' claims to the contrary, some versions of the test WILL be easier for you than others.

Since your future depends so much on your score, you should maximize your chances of success. In order to maximize the likelihood of success, you've got to prepare in advance. This means taking practice tests and spending time learning the information and test taking strategies you will need to succeed.

Never go take the actual test as a "practice" test, expecting that you can just take it again if you need to. Take all the practice tests you can on your own, but when you go to take the official test, be prepared, be focused, and do your best the first time!

# Secret Key #5 - Test Yourself

Everyone knows that time is money. There is no need to spend too much of your time or too little of your time preparing for the test. You should only spend as much of your precious time preparing as is necessary for you to get the score you need.

Once you have taken a practice test under real conditions of time constraints, then you will know if you are ready for the test or not.

If you have scored extremely high the first time that you take the practice test, then there is not much point in spending countless hours studying. You are already there.

Benchmark your abilities by retaking practice tests and seeing how much you have improved. Once you consistently score high enough to guarantee success, then you are ready.

If you have scored well below where you need, then knuckle down and begin studying in earnest. Check your improvement regularly through the use of practice tests under real conditions. Above all, don't worry, panic, or give up. The key is perseverance!

Then, when you go to take the test, remain confident and remember how well you did on the practice tests. If you can score high enough on a practice test, then you can do the same on the real thing.

# General Strategies

The most important thing you can do is to ignore your fears and jump into the test immediately. Do not be overwhelmed by any strange-sounding terms. You have to jump into the test like jumping into a pool—all at once is the easiest way.

## Make Predictions

As you read and understand the question, try to guess what the answer will be. Remember that several of the answer choices are wrong, and once you begin reading them, your mind will immediately become cluttered with answer choices designed to throw you off. Your mind is typically the most focused immediately after you have read the question and digested its contents. If you can, try to predict what the correct answer will be. You may be surprised at what you can predict.

Quickly scan the choices and see if your prediction is in the listed answer choices. If it is, then you can be quite confident that you have the right answer. It still won't hurt to check the other answer choices, but most of the time, you've got it!

## Answer the Question

It may seem obvious to only pick answer choices that answer the question, but the test writers can create some excellent answer choices that are wrong. Don't pick an answer just because it sounds right, or you believe it to be true. It MUST answer the question. Once you've made your selection, always go back and check it against the question and make sure that you didn't misread the question and that the answer choice does answer the question posed.

## Benchmark

After you read the first answer choice, decide if you think it sounds correct or not. If it doesn't, move on to the next answer choice. If it does, mentally mark that answer choice. This doesn't mean that you've definitely selected it as your answer choice, it just means that it's the best you've seen thus far. Go ahead and read the next choice. If the next choice is worse than the one you've already selected, keep going to the next answer choice. If the next choice is better than the choice you've already selected, mentally mark the new answer choice as your best guess.

The first answer choice that you select becomes your standard. Every other answer choice must be benchmarked against that standard. That choice is correct until proven otherwise by another answer choice beating it out. Once you've decided that no other answer choice seems as good, do one final check to ensure that your answer choice answers the question posed.

## Valid Information

Don't discount any of the information provided in the question. Every piece of information may be necessary to determine the correct answer. None of the information in the question is there to throw you off (while the answer choices will certainly have information to throw you off). If two seemingly unrelated topics are discussed, don't ignore either. You can be confident there is a relationship, or it wouldn't be included in the question, and you are probably going to have to determine what is that relationship to find the answer.

## Avoid "Fact Traps"

Don't get distracted by a choice that is factually true. Your search is for the answer that answers the question. Stay focused and don't fall for an answer that is true but irrelevant. Always go back to the question and make sure you're choosing an answer that actually answers the question and is not just a true statement. An answer can be factually correct, but it MUST answer the question asked. Additionally, two answers can both be seemingly correct, so be sure to read all of the answer choices, and make sure that you get the one that BEST answers the question.

## Milk the Question

Some of the questions may throw you completely off. They might deal with a subject you have not been exposed to, or one that you haven't reviewed in years. While your lack of knowledge about the subject will be a hindrance, the question itself can give you many clues that will help you find the correct answer. Read the question carefully and look for clues. Watch particularly for adjectives and nouns describing difficult terms or words that you don't recognize. Regardless of whether you completely understand a word or not, replacing it with a synonym, either provided or one you more familiar with, may help you to understand what the questions are asking. Rather than wracking your mind about specific detailed information concerning a difficult term or word, try to use mental substitutes that are easier to understand.

## The Trap of Familiarity

Don't just choose a word because you recognize it. On difficult questions, you may not recognize a number of words in the answer choices. The test writers don't put "make-believe" words on the test, so don't think that just because you only recognize all the words in one answer choice that that answer choice must be correct. If you only recognize words in one answer choice, then focus on that one. Is it correct? Try your best to determine if it is correct. If it is, that's great. If not, eliminate it. Each word and answer choice you eliminate increases your chances of getting the question correct, even if you then have to guess among the unfamiliar choices.

## Eliminate Answers

Eliminate choices as soon as you realize they are wrong. But be careful! Make sure you consider all of the possible answer choices. Just because one appears right, doesn't mean that the next one won't be even better! The test writers will usually put more than one good answer choice for every question, so read all of them. Don't worry if you are stuck between two that seem right. By getting down to just two remaining possible choices, your odds are now 50/50. Rather than wasting too much time, play the odds. You are guessing, but guessing wisely because you've been able to knock out some of the answer choices that you know are wrong. If you are eliminating choices and realize that the last answer choice you are left with is also obviously wrong, don't panic. Start over and consider each choice again. There may easily be something that you missed the first time and will realize on the second pass.

## Tough Questions

If you are stumped on a problem or it appears too hard or too difficult, don't waste time. Move on! Remember though, if you can quickly check for obviously incorrect answer choices, your chances of guessing correctly are greatly improved. Before you completely give up, at least try to knock out a couple of possible answers. Eliminate what you can and then guess at the remaining answer choices before moving on.

## Brainstorm

If you get stuck on a difficult question, spend a few seconds quickly brainstorming. Run through the complete list of possible answer choices. Look at each choice and ask yourself, "Could this answer the question satisfactorily?" Go through each answer choice and consider it independently of the others. By systematically going through all possibilities, you may find something that you would otherwise overlook. Remember though that when you get stuck, it's important to try to keep moving.

## Read Carefully

Understand the problem. Read the question and answer choices carefully. Don't miss the question because you misread the terms. You have plenty of time to read each question thoroughly and make sure you understand what is being asked. Yet a happy medium must be attained, so don't waste too much time. You must read carefully, but efficiently.

## Face Value

When in doubt, use common sense. Always accept the situation in the problem at face value. Don't read too much into it. These problems will not require you to make huge leaps of logic. The test writers aren't trying to throw you off with a cheap trick. If you have to go beyond creativity and make a leap of logic in order to have an answer choice answer the question, then you should look at the other answer choices. Don't overcomplicate the problem by creating theoretical relationships or explanations that will warp time or space. These are normal problems rooted in reality. It's just that the applicable relationship or explanation may not be readily apparent and you have to figure things out. Use your common sense to interpret anything that isn't clear.

## Prefixes

If you're having trouble with a word in the question or answer choices, try dissecting it. Take advantage of every clue that the word might include. Prefixes and suffixes can be a huge help. Usually they allow you to determine a basic meaning. Pre- means before, post- means after, pro - is positive, de- is negative. From these prefixes and suffixes, you can get an idea of the general meaning of the word and try to put it into context. Beware though of any traps. Just because con- is the opposite of pro-, doesn't necessarily mean congress is the opposite of progress!

## Hedge Phrases

Watch out for critical hedge phrases, led off with words such as "likely," "may," "can," "sometimes," "often," "almost," "mostly," "usually," "generally," "rarely," and "sometimes." Question writers insert these hedge phrases to cover every possibility. Often an answer choice will be wrong simply because it leaves no room for exception. Unless the situation calls for them, avoid answer choices that have definitive words like "exactly," and "always."

## Switchback Words

Stay alert for "switchbacks." These are the words and phrases frequently used to alert you to shifts in thought. The most common switchback word is "but." Others include "although," "however," "nevertheless," "on the other hand," "even though," "while," "in spite of," "despite," and "regardless of."

## New Information

Correct answer choices will rarely have completely new information included. Answer choices typically are straightforward reflections of the material asked about and will directly relate to the question. If a new piece of information is included in an answer choice that doesn't even seem to relate to the topic being asked about, then that answer choice is likely incorrect. All of the information needed to answer the question is usually provided for you in the question. You should not have to make guesses that are unsupported or choose answer choices that require unknown information that cannot be reasoned from what is given.

## Time Management

On technical questions, don't get lost on the technical terms. Don't spend too much time on any one question. If you don't know what a term means, then odds are you aren't going to get much further since you don't have a dictionary. You should be able to immediately recognize whether or not you know a term. If you don't, work with the other clues that you have—the other answer choices and terms provided—but don't waste too much time trying to figure out a difficult term that you don't know.

## Contextual Clues

Look for contextual clues. An answer can be right but not the correct answer. The contextual clues will help you find the answer that is most right and is correct. Understand the context in which a phrase or statement is made. This will help you make important distinctions.

## Don't Panic

Panicking will not answer any questions for you; therefore, it isn't helpful. When you first see the question, if your mind goes blank, take a deep breath. Force yourself to mechanically go through the steps of solving the problem using the strategies you've learned.

## Pace Yourself

Don't get clock fever. It's easy to be overwhelmed when you're looking at a page full of questions, your mind is full of random thoughts and feeling confused, and the clock is ticking down faster than you would like. Calm down and maintain the pace that you have set for yourself. As long as you are on track by monitoring your pace, you are guaranteed to have enough time for yourself. When you get to the last few minutes of the test, it may seem like you won't have enough time left, but if you only have as many questions as you should have left at that point, then you're right on track!

## Answer Selection

The best way to pick an answer choice is to eliminate all of those that are wrong, until only one is left and confirm that is the correct answer. Sometimes though, an answer choice may immediately look right. Be careful! Take a second to make sure that the other choices are not equally obvious. Don't make a hasty mistake. There are only two times that you should stop before checking other answers. First is when you are positive that the answer choice you have selected is correct. Second is when time is almost out and you have to make a quick guess!

## Check Your Work

Since you will probably not know every term listed and the answer to every question, it is important that you get credit for the ones that you do know. Don't miss any questions through careless mistakes. If at all possible, try to take a second to look back over your answer selection and make sure you've selected the correct answer choice and haven't made a costly careless mistake (such as marking an answer choice that you didn't mean to mark). The time it takes for this quick double check should more than pay for itself in caught mistakes.

## Beware of Directly Quoted Answers

Sometimes an answer choice will repeat word for word a portion of the question or reference section. However, beware of such exact duplication. It may be a trap! More than likely, the correct choice will paraphrase or summarize a point, rather than being exactly the same wording.

## Slang

Scientific sounding answers are better than slang ones. An answer choice that begins "To compare the outcomes..." is much more likely to be correct than one that begins "Because some people insisted..."

## Extreme Statements

Avoid wild answers that throw out highly controversial ideas that are proclaimed as established fact. An answer choice that states the "process should used in certain situations, if..." is much more likely to be correct than one that states the "process should be discontinued completely." The first is a calm rational statement and doesn't even make a definitive, uncompromising stance, using a hedge word "if" to provide wiggle room, whereas the second choice is a radical idea and far more extreme.

## Answer Choice Families

When you have two or more answer choices that are direct opposites or parallels, one of them is usually the correct answer. For instance, if one answer choice states "x increases" and another answer choice states "x decreases" or "y increases," then those two or three answer choices are very similar in construction and fall into the same family of answer choices. A family of answer choices consists of two or three answer choices, very similar in construction, but often with directly opposite meanings. Usually the correct answer choice will be in that family of answer choices. The "odd man out" or answer choice that doesn't seem to fit the parallel construction of the other answer choices is more likely to be incorrect.

# Special Report: How to Overcome Test Anxiety

The very nature of tests caters to some level of anxiety, nervousness, or tension, just as we feel for any important event that occurs in our lives. A little bit of anxiety or nervousness can be a good thing. It helps us with motivation, and makes achievement just that much sweeter. However, too much anxiety can be a problem, especially if it hinders our ability to function and perform.

"Test anxiety," is the term that refers to the emotional reactions that some test-takers experience when faced with a test or exam. Having a fear of testing and exams is based upon a rational fear, since the test-taker's performance can shape the course of an academic career. Nevertheless, experiencing excessive fear of examinations will only interfere with the test-taker's ability to perform and chance to be successful.

There are a large variety of causes that can contribute to the development and sensation of test anxiety. These include, but are not limited to, lack of preparation and worrying about issues surrounding the test.

## Lack of Preparation

Lack of preparation can be identified by the following behaviors or situations:
- Not scheduling enough time to study, and therefore cramming the night before the test or exam
- Managing time poorly, to create the sensation that there is not enough time to do everything
- Failing to organize the text information in advance, so that the study material consists of the entire text and not simply the pertinent information
- Poor overall studying habits

Worrying, on the other hand, can be related to both the test taker, or many other factors around him/her that will be affected by the results of the test. These include worrying about:
- Previous performances on similar exams, or exams in general
- How friends and other students are achieving
- The negative consequences that will result from a poor grade or failure

There are three primary elements to test anxiety. Physical components, which involve the same typical bodily reactions as those to acute anxiety (to be discussed below). Emotional factors have to do with fear or panic. Mental or cognitive issues concerning attention spans and memory abilities.

## Physical Signals

There are many different symptoms of test anxiety, and these are not limited to mental and emotional strain. Frequently there are a range of physical signals that will let a test taker know that he/she is suffering from test anxiety. These bodily changes can include the following:
- Perspiring
- Sweaty palms

- Wet, trembling hands
- Nausea
- Dry mouth
- A knot in the stomach
- Headache
- Faintness
- Muscle tension
- Aching shoulders, back and neck
- Rapid heart beat
- Feeling too hot/cold

To recognize the sensation of test anxiety, a test-taker should monitor him/herself for the following sensations:
- The physical distress symptoms as listed above
- Emotional sensitivity, expressing emotional feelings such as the need to cry or laugh too much, or a sensation of anger or helplessness
- A decreased ability to think, causing the test-taker to blank out or have racing thoughts that are hard to organize or control.

Though most students will feel some level of anxiety when faced with a test or exam, the majority can cope with that anxiety and maintain it at a manageable level. However, those who cannot are faced with a very real and very serious condition, which can and should be controlled for the immeasurable benefit of this sufferer.

Naturally, these sensations lead to negative results for the testing experience. The most common effects of test anxiety have to do with nervousness and mental blocking.

## Nervousness

Nervousness can appear in several different levels:
- The test-taker's difficulty, or even inability to read and understand the questions on the test
- The difficulty or inability to organize thoughts to a coherent form
- The difficulty or inability to recall key words and concepts relating to the testing questions (especially essays)
- The receipt of poor grades on a test, though the test material was well known by the test taker

Conversely, a person may also experience mental blocking, which involves:
- Blanking out on test questions
- Only remembering the correct answers to the questions when the test has already finished.
Fortunately for test anxiety sufferers, beating these feelings, to a large degree, has to do with proper preparation. When a test taker has a feeling of preparedness, then anxiety will be dramatically lessened.

The first step to resolving anxiety issues is to distinguish which of the two types of anxiety are being suffered. If the anxiety is a direct result of a lack of preparation, this should be considered a normal reaction, and the anxiety level (as opposed to the test results) shouldn't be anything to worry about. However, if, when adequately prepared, the test-taker still panics, blanks out, or seems to overreact, this is not a fully rational reaction. While this can be considered normal too, there are many ways to combat and overcome these effects.

Remember that anxiety cannot be entirely eliminated, however, there are ways to minimize it, to make the anxiety easier to manage. Preparation is one of the best ways to minimize test anxiety. Therefore the following techniques are wise in order to best fight off any anxiety that may want to build.

To begin with, try to avoid cramming before a test, whenever it is possible. By trying to memorize an entire term's worth of information in one day, you'll be shocking your system, and not giving yourself a very good chance to absorb the information. This is an easy path to anxiety, so for those who suffer from test anxiety, cramming should not even be considered an option.

Instead of cramming, work throughout the semester to combine all of the material which is presented throughout the semester, and work on it gradually as the course goes by, making sure to master the main concepts first, leaving minor details for a week or so before the test.

To study for the upcoming exam, be sure to pose questions that may be on the examination, to gauge the ability to answer them by integrating the ideas from your texts, notes and lectures, as well as any supplementary readings.

If it is truly impossible to cover all of the information that was covered in that particular term, concentrate on the most important portions, that can be covered very well. Learn these concepts as best as possible, so that when the test comes, a goal can be made to use these concepts as presentations of your knowledge.

In addition to study habits, changes in attitude are critical to beating a struggle with test anxiety. In fact, an improvement of the perspective over the entire test-taking experience can actually help a test taker to enjoy studying and therefore improve the overall experience. Be certain not to overemphasize the significance of the grade - know that the result of the test is neither a reflection of self worth, nor is it a measure of intelligence; one grade will not predict a person's future success.

To improve an overall testing outlook, the following steps should be tried:
- Keeping in mind that the most reasonable expectation for taking a test is to expect to try to demonstrate as much of what you know as you possibly can.
- Reminding ourselves that a test is only one test; this is not the only one, and there will be others.
- The thought of thinking of oneself in an irrational, all-or-nothing term should be avoided at all costs.

A reward should be designated for after the test, so there's something to look forward to. Whether it be going to a movie, going out to eat, or simply visiting friends, schedule it in advance, and do it no matter what result is expected on the exam.

Test-takers should also keep in mind that the basics are some of the most important things, even beyond anti-anxiety techniques and studying. Never neglect the basic social, emotional and biological needs, in order to try to absorb information. In order to best achieve, these three factors must be held as just as important as the studying itself.

# Study Steps

Remember the following important steps for studying:

- Maintain healthy nutrition and exercise habits. Continue both your recreational activities and social pass times. These both contribute to your physical and emotional well being.
- Be certain to get a good amount of sleep, especially the night before the test, because when you're overtired you are not able to perform to the best of your best ability.
- Keep the studying pace to a moderate level by taking breaks when they are needed, and varying the work whenever possible, to keep the mind fresh instead of getting bored.
- When enough studying has been done that all the material that can be learned has been learned, and the test taker is prepared for the test, stop studying and do something relaxing such as listening to music, watching a movie, or taking a warm bubble bath.

There are also many other techniques to minimize the uneasiness or apprehension that is experienced along with test anxiety before, during, or even after the examination. In fact, there are a great deal of things that can be done to stop anxiety from interfering with lifestyle and performance. Again, remember that anxiety will not be eliminated entirely, and it shouldn't be. Otherwise that "up" feeling for exams would not exist, and most of us depend on that sensation to perform better than usual. However, this anxiety has to be at a level that is manageable.

Of course, as we have just discussed, being prepared for the exam is half the battle right away. Attending all classes, finding out what knowledge will be expected on the exam, and knowing the exam schedules are easy steps to lowering anxiety. Keeping up with work will remove the need to cram, and efficient study habits will eliminate wasted time. Studying should be done in an ideal location for concentration, so that it is simple to become interested in the material and give it complete attention. A method such as SQ3R (Survey, Question, Read, Recite, Review) is a wonderful key to follow to make sure that the study habits are as effective as possible, especially in the case of learning from a textbook. Flashcards are great techniques for memorization. Learning to take good notes will mean that notes will be full of useful information, so that less sifting will need to be done to seek out what is pertinent for studying. Reviewing notes after class and then again on occasion will keep the information fresh in the mind. From notes that have been taken summary sheets and outlines can be made for simpler reviewing.

A study group can also be a very motivational and helpful place to study, as there will be a sharing of ideas, all of the minds can work together, to make sure that everyone understands, and the studying will be made more interesting because it will be a social occasion.

Basically, though, as long as the test-taker remains organized and self confident, with efficient study habits, less time will need to be spent studying, and higher grades will be achieved.
To become self confident, there are many useful steps. The first of these is "self talk." It has been shown through extensive research, that self-talk for students who suffer from test anxiety, should be well monitored, in order to make sure that it contributes to self confidence as opposed to sinking the student. Frequently the self talk of test-anxious students is negative or self-defeating, thinking that everyone else is smarter and faster, that they always mess up, and that if they don't do well, they'll fail the entire course. It is important to decreasing anxiety that awareness is made of self talk. Try writing any negative self thoughts and then disputing them with a positive statement instead. Begin self-encouragement as though it was a friend speaking. Repeat positive statements to help reprogram the mind to believing in successes instead of failures.

# Helpful Techniques

Other extremely helpful techniques include:
- Self-visualization of doing well and reaching goals
- While aiming for an "A" level of understanding, don't try to "overprotect" by setting your expectations lower. This will only convince the mind to stop studying in order to meet the lower expectations.
- Don't make comparisons with the results or habits of other students. These are individual factors, and different things work for different people, causing different results.
- Strive to become an expert in learning what works well, and what can be done in order to improve. Consider collecting this data in a journal.
- Create rewards for after studying instead of doing things before studying that will only turn into avoidance behaviors.
- Make a practice of relaxing - by using methods such as progressive relaxation, self-hypnosis, guided imagery, etc - in order to make relaxation an automatic sensation.
- Work on creating a state of relaxed concentration so that concentrating will take on the focus of the mind, so that none will be wasted on worrying.
- Take good care of the physical self by eating well and getting enough sleep.
- Plan in time for exercise and stick to this plan.

Beyond these techniques, there are other methods to be used before, during and after the test that will help the test-taker perform well in addition to overcoming anxiety.

Before the exam comes the academic preparation. This involves establishing a study schedule and beginning at least one week before the actual date of the test. By doing this, the anxiety of not having enough time to study for the test will be automatically eliminated. Moreover, this will make the studying a much more effective experience, ensuring that the learning will be an easier process. This relieves much undue pressure on the test-taker.

Summary sheets, note cards, and flash cards with the main concepts and examples of these main concepts should be prepared in advance of the actual studying time. A topic should never be eliminated from this process. By omitting a topic because it isn't expected to be on the test is only setting up the test-taker for anxiety should it actually appear on the exam. Utilize the course syllabus for laying out the topics that should be studied. Carefully go over the notes that were made in class, paying special attention to any of the issues that the professor took special care to emphasize while lecturing in class. In the textbooks, use the chapter review, or if possible, the chapter tests, to begin your review.

It may even be possible to ask the instructor what information will be covered on the exam, or what the format of the exam will be (for example, multiple choice, essay, free form, true-false). Additionally, see if it is possible to find out how many questions will be on the test. If a review sheet or sample test has been offered by the professor, make good use of it, above anything else, for the preparation for the test. Another great resource for getting to know the examination is reviewing tests from previous semesters. Use these tests to review, and aim to achieve a 100% score on each of the possible topics. With a few exceptions, the goal that you set for yourself is the highest one that you will reach.

Take all of the questions that were assigned as homework, and rework them to any other possible course material. The more problems reworked, the more skill and confidence will form as a result.

When forming the solution to a problem, write out each of the steps. Don't simply do head work. By doing as many steps on paper as possible, much clarification and therefore confidence will be formed. Do this with as many homework problems as possible, before checking the answers. By checking the answer after each problem, a reinforcement will exist, that will not be on the exam. Study situations should be as exam-like as possible, to prime the test-taker's system for the experience. By waiting to check the answers at the end, a psychological advantage will be formed, to decrease the stress factor.

Another fantastic reason for not cramming is the avoidance of confusion in concepts, especially when it comes to mathematics. 8-10 hours of study will become one hundred percent more effective if it is spread out over a week or at least several days, instead of doing it all in one sitting. Recognize that the human brain requires time in order to assimilate new material, so frequent breaks and a span of study time over several days will be much more beneficial.

Additionally, don't study right up until the point of the exam. Studying should stop a minimum of one hour before the exam begins. This allows the brain to rest and put things in their proper order. This will also provide the time to become as relaxed as possible when going into the examination room. The test-taker will also have time to eat well and eat sensibly. Know that the brain needs food as much as the rest of the body. With enough food and enough sleep, as well as a relaxed attitude, the body and the mind are primed for success.

Avoid any anxious classmates who are talking about the exam. These students only spread anxiety, and are not worth sharing the anxious sentimentalities.

Before the test also involves creating a positive attitude, so mental preparation should also be a point of concentration. There are many keys to creating a positive attitude. Should fears become rushing in, make a visualization of taking the exam, doing well, and seeing an A written on the paper. Write out a list of affirmations that will bring a feeling of confidence, such as "I am doing well in my English class," "I studied well and know my material," "I enjoy this class." Even if the affirmations aren't believed at first, it sends a positive message to the subconscious which will result in an alteration of the overall belief system, which is the system that creates reality.

If a sensation of panic begins, work with the fear and imagine the very worst! Work through the entire scenario of not passing the test, failing the entire course, and dropping out of school, followed by not getting a job, and pushing a shopping cart through the dark alley where you'll live. This will place things into perspective! Then, practice deep breathing and create a visualization of the opposite situation - achieving an "A" on the exam, passing the entire course, receiving the degree at a graduation ceremony.

On the day of the test, there are many things to be done to ensure the best results, as well as the most calm outlook. The following stages are suggested in order to maximize test-taking potential:

- Begin the examination day with a moderate breakfast, and avoid any coffee or beverages with caffeine if the test taker is prone to jitters. Even people who are used to managing caffeine can feel jittery or light-headed when it is taken on a test day.
- Attempt to do something that is relaxing before the examination begins. As last minute cramming clouds the mastering of overall concepts, it is better to use this time to create a calming outlook.
- Be certain to arrive at the test location well in advance, in order to provide time to select a location that is away from doors, windows and other distractions, as well as giving enough time to relax before the test begins.

- Keep away from anxiety generating classmates who will upset the sensation of stability and relaxation that is being attempted before the exam.
- Should the waiting period before the exam begins cause anxiety, create a self-distraction by reading a light magazine or something else that is relaxing and simple.

During the exam itself, read the entire exam from beginning to end, and find out how much time should be allotted to each individual problem. Once writing the exam, should more time be taken for a problem, it should be abandoned, in order to begin another problem. If there is time at the end, the unfinished problem can always be returned to and completed.

Read the instructions very carefully - twice - so that unpleasant surprises won't follow during or after the exam has ended.

When writing the exam, pretend that the situation is actually simply the completion of homework within a library, or at home. This will assist in forming a relaxed atmosphere, and will allow the brain extra focus for the complex thinking function.

Begin the exam with all of the questions with which the most confidence is felt. This will build the confidence level regarding the entire exam and will begin a quality momentum. This will also create encouragement for trying the problems where uncertainty resides.

Going with the "gut instinct" is always the way to go when solving a problem. Second guessing should be avoided at all costs. Have confidence in the ability to do well.

For essay questions, create an outline in advance that will keep the mind organized and make certain that all of the points are remembered. For multiple choice, read every answer, even if the correct one has been spotted - a better one may exist.

Continue at a pace that is reasonable and not rushed, in order to be able to work carefully. Provide enough time to go over the answers at the end, to check for small errors that can be corrected.

Should a feeling of panic begin, breathe deeply, and think of the feeling of the body releasing sand through its pores. Visualize a calm, peaceful place, and include all of the sights, sounds and sensations of this image. Continue the deep breathing, and take a few minutes to continue this with closed eyes. When all is well again, return to the test.

If a "blanking" occurs for a certain question, skip it and move on to the next question. There will be time to return to the other question later. Get everything done that can be done, first, to guarantee all the grades that can be compiled, and to build all of the confidence possible. Then return to the weaker questions to build the marks from there.

Remember, one's own reality can be created, so as long as the belief is there, success will follow. And remember: anxiety can happen later, right now, there's an exam to be written!

After the examination is complete, whether there is a feeling for a good grade or a bad grade, don't dwell on the exam, and be certain to follow through on the reward that was promised...and enjoy it! Don't dwell on any mistakes that have been made, as there is nothing that can be done at this point anyway.

Additionally, don't begin to study for the next test right away. Do something relaxing for a while, and let the mind relax and prepare itself to begin absorbing information again.

From the results of the exam - both the grade and the entire experience, be certain to learn from what has gone on. Perfect studying habits and work some more on confidence in order to make the next examination experience even better than the last one.

Learn to avoid places where openings occurred for laziness, procrastination and day dreaming.

Use the time between this exam and the next one to better learn to relax, even learning to relax on cue, so that any anxiety can be controlled during the next exam. Learn how to relax the body. Slouch in your chair if that helps. Tighten and then relax all of the different muscle groups, one group at a time, beginning with the feet and then working all the way up to the neck and face. This will ultimately relax the muscles more than they were to begin with. Learn how to breathe deeply and comfortably, and focus on this breathing going in and out as a relaxing thought. With every exhale, repeat the word "relax."

As common as test anxiety is, it is very possible to overcome it. Make yourself one of the test-takers who overcome this frustrating hindrance.

# Additional Bonus Material

Due to our efforts to try to keep this book to a manageable length, we've created a link that will give you access to all of your additional bonus material.

Please visit http://www.mometrix.com/bonus948/iltssocscihist to access the information.